WORLD CUP CRICKET
1992

Patrick Smithers

Martin Blake

Greg Baum

Edited by Patrick Smith

The Five Mile Press

Acknowledgements

The Authors would like to thank the Editorial Manager of the *Age*, Peter McLaughlin, for his enthusiastic support; Patrick Keane and Sue Smith for their help in reading; and David Harrison for his advice in the presentation of scoreboards and statistics.

Statistics provided by Ross Dundas.

The Five Mile Press Pty Ltd
P.O. Box 327
Poole
Dorset BH15 2RG
First published 1992
Text copyright © David Syme & Co. Limited, Patrick Smith, Greg Baum, Martin Blake, Patrick Smithers
Design and layout copyright © The Five Mile Press Pty Ltd.
Editor: Patrick Smith
Pictorial Manager: John French
Photographers: Mark Baker, Bryan Charlton, Neil Eliot, Stuart Hannagan, Ray Kennedy, Palani Mohan, Ross Setford, William West
Design: SBR Productions
Production: Emma Borghesi

Printed and bound in Australia by Griffin Press Limited

CONTENTS

Programme

Saturday 22 February:	New Zealand **v** Australia in Auckland, New Zealand
	England **v** India in Perth, Australia (D/N)
Sunday 23 February:	West Indies **v** Pakistan in Melbourne, Australia
	Sri Lanka **v** Zimbabwe in New Plymouth, New Zealand
Tuesday 25 February:	New Zealand **v** Sri Lanka in Hamilton, New Zealand
Wednesday 26 February:	Australia **v** South Africa in Sydney, Australia (D/N)
Thursday 27 February:	Pakistan **v** Zimbabwe in Hobart, Australia
	England **v** West Indies in Melbourne, Australia (D/N)
Friday 28 February:	India **v** Sri Lanka in Mackay, Australia
Saturday 29 February:	West Indies **v** Zimbabwe in Brisbane, Australia
	New Zealand **v** South Africa in Auckland, New Zealand
Sunday 1 March:	Australia **v** India in Brisbane, Australia
	England **v** Pakistan in Adelaide, Australia
Monday 2 March:	Sri Lanka **v** South Africa in Wellington, New Zealand
Tuesday 3 March:	New Zealand **v** Zimbabwe in Napier, New Zealand
Wednesday 4 March:	Pakistan **v** India in Sydney, Australia (D/N)
Thursday 5 March:	Australia **v** England in Sydney, Australia (D/N)
	West Indies **v** South Africa in Christchurch, New Zealand
Saturday 7 March:	Australia **v** Sri Lanka in Adelaide, Australia
	India **v** Zimbabwe in Hamilton, New Zealand
Sunday 8 March:	Pakistan **v** South Africa in Brisbane, Australia
	New Zealand **v** West Indies in Auckland, New Zealand
Monday 9 March:	England **v** Sri Lanka in Ballarat, Australia
Tuesday 10 March:	Zimbabwe **v** South Africa in Canberra, Australia
	West Indies **v** India in Wellington, New Zealand
Wednesday 11 March:	Australia **v** Pakistan in Perth, Australia (D/N)
Thursday 12 March:	England **v** South Africa in Melbourne, Australia (D/N)
	New Zealand **v** India in Dunedin, New Zealand
Friday 13 March:	West Indies **v** Sri Lanka in Berri, Australia
Saturday 14 March:	Australia **v** Zimbabwe in Hobart, Australia
Sunday 15 March:	India **v** South Africa in Adelaide, Australia
	Pakistan **v** Sri Lanka in Perth, Australia
	New Zealand **v** England in Wellington, New Zealand
Wednesday 18 March:	Australia **v** West Indies in Melbourne, Australia (D/N)
	England **v** Zimbabwe in Albury, Australia
	New Zealand **v** Pakistan in Christchurch, New Zealand
Saturday 21 March:	First semi-final in Auckland, New Zealand
Sunday 22 March:	Second semi-final in Sydney, Australia (D/N)
	Reserve day
Monday 23 March:	Reserve day (D/N)
Wednesday 25 March:	Final in Melbourne, Australia (D/N)
Thursday 26 March:	Reserve day (D/N)
Friday 27 March:	Reserve day (D/N)

* D/N denotes day/night matches

Introduction

The HMAS Canberra sailed from Wooloomooloo Naval Dock, Port Jackson, on the morning of 19 February 1992 with one of the most precious human cargoes ever assembled.

On board the guided missile frigate were the elite cricketers of nine nations, perched on scaffolding for a photograph opportunity in front of Australia's most internationally recognisable landmarks, the Sydney Harbour Bridge and the Sydney Opera House.

When the 126 competing players gathered that evening at the absurdly priced $175-a-head black tie dinner to launch the 1992 World Cup, Malcolm Gray, the joint chairman of the organising committee, described it as the most extraordinary collection of cricket talent – 'with the possible exception of when Sir Donald Bradman dines alone.'

More than 200 years earlier, the First Fleet sailed into Port Jackson to mark the beginning of the white settlement of Australia. By the time of the 1992 World Cup, Australia was undergoing a surge of republican sentiment, with Prime Minister Paul Keating threatening to finally cut the umbilical cord with Britain.

The pace of change in the ancient game of cricket had not been nearly so sluggish. Only 17 years after the memorable first World Cup final at Lord's, the world one-day championship would be played in coloured clothes, with one white ball at each end and, in part, at night.

The idea of playing the tournament down under germinated not in Australia, but in New Zealand, in the mind of former Wellington cricketer Bob Vance. In June 1987, Vance, then the chairman of the NZ Cricket Council, put his idea to Australian officials at the annual International Cricket Council meeting in London.

The Australians needed convincing that the project would be financially viable, but their hesitation turned to enthusiasm five months later when Allan Border held the World Cup aloft in front of 85,000 cheering Indians at Eden Gardens in Calcutta.

India and Pakistan had confounded the killjoys and staged a highly successful World Cup. What better place for Australia to defend its title than in its own backyard? The formal bid was submitted one year after the re-birth of Australian cricket at Eden Gardens.

Remarkably, the list of competing nations was not finalised until four months before the opening match when, at an extraordinary meeting of the ICC in Sharjah, South Africa was given a wildcard to play in its first World Cup.

The invitation followed months of high-level political negotiations in which South Africa's participation was endorsed by the African National Congress leader, Nelson Mandela, the British Prime Minister, John Major, the then Australian Prime Minister, Bob Hawke, and the (initially reluctant) chairman of the ICC, Sir Colin Cowdrey.

That took the number of competing teams to nine, although South Africa was easily accommodated under the new round-robin format which had superseded the group system. Australia went in as raging favourites, supported by figures showing that it had won 75 per cent of one-day games since the 1987 World Cup final.

The other sides had, in order, won the following percentage of matches in that period: Pakistan 56, West Indies 55, England 51, India 44, New Zealand 36, South Africa 33 and Sri Lanka 24. Zimbabwe had not played in that time.

South Africa's late entry added a new dimension to the competition. Competing under the multi-racial banner of the United Cricket Board of South Africa, it would compete against the West Indies, Pakistan and Sri Lanka for the first time in officially sanctioned matches. Tickets for the return match against Australia were soon available only on the black market.

Perhaps not coincidentally, a referendum asking whites if they wanted President F. W. de Klerk to continue reforms towards a multi-racial government was timed to take place during the tournament. Advertising hordings urging a 'yes' vote were erected at some grounds – sporting contact with the outside world dangled like a carrot in front of swinging voters – and the South African team effectively became an ambassador for change in their homeland.

South Africa's involvement became controversial for cricketing as well as political reasons. There was a furore when three of the most accomplished players of an almost forgotten generation of South African cricketers – Clive Rice, Jimmy Cook and Peter Kirsten – were left out of the original squad. Petitions were gathered and Kirsten was eventually reinstated. Rice and Cook were not.

Kepler Wessels, a former Australian citizen and Test batsman, was named as the captain and returned in a capacity no one would have predicted in a pink fit when he left Australia in acrimonious circumstances in 1986, accused of helping recruit rebel players.

Perhaps the teams keenest to win the first World Cup staged in the southern hemisphere were England and Pakistan, the two strongest cricketing nations never to have worn the one-day crown.

England made the World Cup such a high priority on its 1992 southern tour that it did not pick a second specialist opening batsman for its three-Test series with New Zealand, preferring to cram its team with allrounders. It even gave 36-year-old pantomime king Ian Botham three weeks leeway in joining the party in New Zealand so that he could complete his commitments to a Bournemouth production of 'Jack and the Beanstalk'.

Micky Stewart and Graham Gooch had done something of a Bob Simpson/Allan Border with the English squad, weeding out those perceived as less than totally dedicated to the cause (Carrara-flying aces, David Gower and John Morris, were grounded) and placing the emphasis on fielding and physical fitness. Its 14-man squad included five men – Botham, Chris Lewis, Phil DeFreitas, Derek Pringle and Dermot Reeve – who could reasonably be classified as allrounders for the purposes of one-day cricket. England also had form on its side, beating the West Indies and New Zealand 3-0 in its previous two one-day series.

Pakistan had coveted the World Cup with a passion bordering on jealousy ever since it had to endure the celebrations across the border in India in 1983. Imran

Khan, at 39, said he had never been more motivated; a World Cup victory would help raise money for his hospital building project in Lahore – 'my main reason for staying in cricket'.

To that end, Pakistan was the only side to organise first-class fixtures in Australia as part of its preparation. It also adopted a revolving door policy with its squad; at one point, its numbers swelled to 17 as players appeared and disappeared overnight during its search for the right combination.

Pedigree fast bowler Waqar Younis, diagnosed as having two stress fractures in his lower back only days before the competition began, joined the traffic home in a massive blow to Pakistan's hopes. Imran hurt his bowling shoulder at a similar stage and carried the injury into the tournament.

The only consolation was that Javed Miandad was fit enough to fly out and join the team. Although early reports indicated a back injury would keep him out of his fifth World Cup, he and Imran were to become the only two players to have competed in every one. Viv Richards was also in contention for this honour, but the West Indies selectors ended his international career after the 1991 tour of England; having given the captaincy to Richie Richardson, they decided to make a clean break of the succession.

The selectors stuck by their decision even after Richardson returned to the Caribbean in January, having failed to qualify for the finals of the triangular series in Australia. Richardson returned a month later with a more experienced side, the international careers of Roger Harper, Winston Benjamin and Phil Simmons having been revived. Unfortunately, fast bowler Ian Bishop was not with the team; he, too, discovered in Australia that he had been touched by the curse of the stress fracture.

In a sense, no team had had a more thorough preparation than India, which had been in Australia more than three months by the time it played its first World Cup match. Many, including Mohammad Azharuddin, thought it was a little too thorough and that the Indians should have been allowed to return home for a break between commitments.

Having beaten the West Indies into the finals of the triangular tournament in Australia, the Indians were well placed to make an impact. They boasted in their number the world's most exciting cricketer, as well as the tournament's youngest player, 18-year-old Sachin Tendulkar. Tendulkar's Bombay schoolmate, Vinod Kambli, was summoned from India, re-uniting the pair that once put on a world-record partnership of 664 in an under-age match.

Australia, of course, came off a similarly taxing programme. The Australian Cricket Board persisted with the lucrative triangular one-day series (even though its significance was reduced to virtually nothing in a World Cup summer), rather than allowing the tournament favourites to devote all their one-day energies to defending the title.

New Zealand, despite being one of the hosts and playing all its qualifying matches on home soil, went into the tournament down on form and confidence and with little prospect of repeating its successes of 1975 and 1979 and making the semi-finals for the third time.

Martin Crowe had a knee injury – he rated himself as only 50 per cent fit on the day of the launch – and was feeling the heavy burden of New Zealand's sporting expectations following the defeat of the once-invincible All Blacks by Australia in the rugby union World Cup. The bland collection of cricketers under

Crowe's command hardly shaped as avengers of Kiwi pride.

As ever, the Sri Lankans arrived enthusiastic for international exposure, although they were a touch apprehensive about their schedule. By their own reckoning, they would cover about 24,000 kilometres in the tournament, taking in the scenery of the north and south islands of New Zealand and fixtures in far-flung corners of Australia from Mackay to Perth.

Zimbabwe, the only non-Test playing side, was competing following its victory in the 1990 ICC Trophy, played on coconut matting wickets in The Netherlands. Zimbabwe beat The Netherlands in the final (Kenya and Bangladesh were the unsuccessful semi-finalists) and, with its application for Test status on the books for the 1992 ICC meeting, needed at least a competent showing in the World Cup.

The Teams

Australia

ALLAN BORDER

Born: 27/7/55. Left-hand batsman, left-arm orthodox spin bowler. He has played more one-day internationals than any other player. A veteran, whose hitting in the middle-order is dangerous, and his throwing from the specialist mid-wicket position dynamic.

GEOFF MARSH

Born: 31/12/58. Right-hand opening batsman. Dogged veteran whose outstanding record in one-day internationals ensured that he was chosen for the World Cup despite indifferent form in the earlier matches of the summer.

DAVID BOON

Born: 29/12/60. Right-hand opening batsman. Marsh's friend and ally at the top of the order, gifted with more strokes but just as much fortitude. The Tasmanian is a fine player of fast bowling.

DEAN JONES

Born: 24/3/61. Right-hand batsman. Audacious strokeplayer who thrives on the intensity of limited-overs cricket. In recent years, he's been among the best in the world at this form of the game.

MARK WAUGH

Born: 2/6/65. Right-hand batsman, right-arm medium-pace bowler. A languid player who scores quickly without ever looking rushed. His medium-pacers have broken many a dangerous partnership, and his fielding, whether at slip or in the outfield, is superb.

TOM MOODY

Born: 2/10/65. Right-hand batsman, right-arm medium-pace bowler. Versatility earned him a berth for his second World Cup, with his handy bowling and powerful throwing from the outfield complementing his big hitting.

STEVE WAUGH

Born: 2/6/65. Right-hand batsman, right-arm medium-pace bowler. He always manages to contribute in some way. His late-innings hitting has won games for Australia, as has his clever bowling, with the patented slower ball. Like twin brother Mark, he fields brilliantly.

IAN HEALY

Born: 30/4/64. Wicketkeeper, right-hand batsman. Vastly improved player who struggled in his initial outings at international level. Handy gloveman and efficient hitter at the end of an innings. A fierce competitor.

PETER TAYLOR

Born: 22/8/56. Right-arm off-spin bowler. Left-hand batsman. Although he has struggled to make an impact at Test level, his record in one-day matches is excellent. Generally bowls 10 overs in the middle part of an innings, and fields well.

CRAIG MCDERMOTT

Born: 14/4/65. Right-arm fast bowler. Australia's premier bowler with a swag of wickets against India in the Test series to complete a remarkable 12 months in the game. Especially dangerous with the white ball now that he has mastered the fast outswinger.

BRUCE REID

Born: 14/3/63. Left-arm fast bowler. High quality paceman who was included in Australia's squad as a wildcard despite yet another injury, this time to the ribs, which restricted him to two Tests in the series against India.

MIKE WHITNEY

Born: 24/2/59. Left-arm fast bowler. Workhorse who performed with distinction during the triangular series in the lead-up to the World Cup. Used to merely push across the right-handers; these days he's able to bend one back as well.

MARK TAYLOR

Born: 27/10/64. Left-hand opening batsman. Tremendous accumulator of runs, even when his form is not necessarily good. Has not established himself in Australia's one-day side because of the pre-eminence of Marsh and Boon.

MERV HUGHES

Born: 23/11/61. Right-arm fast bowler. Not chosen for the one-day series against India and West Indies over the summer, but rarely left out of any Australian squad because of his inspirational qualities.

England

GRAHAM GOOCH

Born: 23/6/55. Right-hand opening bat, right-arm slow medium bowler. Leader and focus of England's gradual re-emergence. Strong of character and strokeplay, and has made even more runs as captain than ever before.

IAN BOTHAM

Born: 24/11/55. Right-hand bat, right-arm medium-fast bowler. An introduction seems unnecessary. All-time great, in performance, girth and command of public and media attention. Now primarily an opening bat.

NEIL FAIRBROTHER

Born: 9/9/63. Left-hand bat. Indomitable in county cricket, but in internationals has struggled to live up to his name, conferred by his parents in honour of the great Australian Harvey.

GLADSTONE SMALL

Born: 18/10/61. Right-arm medium fast bowler. Tight line-and-length bowler with durable character who came into this tournament still to live down a flurry of wides and no-balls in the 1987 final.

PHILLIP DEFREITAS

Born: 18/2/66. Right-arm fast-medium bowler, right-hand bat. International career has waxed and waned, but his type of cricket, especially his lusty late-order hitting, was thought to suit this tournament.

GRAEME HICK

Born: 23/5/66. Right-hand bat, right-arm off-spinner. Oppressed by crushing expectations when he became available for England, and floundered, but his sheer class should eventually win through.

RICHARD ILLINGWORTH

Born: 23/8/63. Left-arm orthodox spinner. Long seasoned and schooled in county cricket, he came into this tournament as understudy to Phil Tufnell in an English squad purpose-built for one-day cricket.

CHRIS LEWIS

Born: 14/2/68. Right-hand bat, right-arm fast-medium bowler. Of the DeFreitas line of cricketers, has the potential to wreak enormous havoc, and is ever-dangerous in the field.

PHIL TUFNELL

Born: 29/4/66. Left-arm orthodox bowler. Fiery Cockney whom England took to its heart even as Australia ridiculed him, the fuss obscuring a genuine talent. Declared by Botham, pre-tournament, to be England's trump.

ROBIN SMITH

Born 13/9/63. Right-hand bat. A thumping middle-order player who can intimidate cover fields when in form. Long experience of Australian conditions made him central to England's designs.

ALLAN LAMB

Born: 20/6/54. Right-hand bat. With Gooch and Botham, one of the elders of this party, but still one of the best one-day batsman in the world, with all the orthodox shots and a talent for improvisation.

DEREK PRINGLE

Born: 18/9/58. Right-hand bat, right-arm medium bowler. Tall and strong, has dwelled for a decade on the edge of the English team, but in the right circumstances is a foe to be treated with respect.

DERMOT REEVE

Born: 2/4/63. Right-hand bat, right-arm medium bowler. Essentially a seam bowler, England hoped his long and valiant county service would serve the very specific needs of this tournament.

ALEC STEWART

Born: 8/4/63. Wicketkeeper and right-hand bat. Son of England's former team manager, has outlived dark mutterings about nepotism to become an adaptable batsman whose sound keeping makes him ideal for the one-day game.

India

MOHAMMAD AZHARUDDIN
Born: 8/2/63. Right-hand batsman. A wristy, languid batsman who scores freely and quickly. He once struck a century from 62 balls – a world record – against New Zealand. He has captained since 1990, and is an immensely popular figure.

KRISHNAMACHARI SRIKKANTH
Born: 21/12/59. Right-hand opening batsman. A remarkable player who has scored more one-day international runs than any Indian, despite a suicidal manner to his play. A ferocious striker who also likes to run the ball through the gully.

AJAY JADEJA
Born: 1/2/71. Right-hand opening batsman, right-arm medium-pace bowler. Solid, top-order batsman who is a descendent of the famous Indian prince-cricketer, Ranjitsinhji. He was drafted into the squad just prior to the World Cup to bolster the batting.

SACHIN TENDULKAR
Born: 24/4/73. Right-hand batsman, right-arm medium-pace bowler. The 'wunderkind' of India, fresh from his superb summer against the Australians. With his brilliant batting, handy bowling and excellent fielding, he would appear to be ideally suited to the one-day game.

RAVI SHASTRI
Born: 27/5/62. Right-hand opening batsman, left-arm orthodox spin bowler. A highly valuable player over many years, in both forms of the game. He can be tied down while batting, but generally plays the anchor role. In form, his bowling is tight as well.

SANJAY MANJREKAR
Born: 12/7/65. Right-hand batsman. A stylist who is the son of former Indian captain Vijay Manjrekar. He is a superb technician with a century against the West Indies in the Caribbean to his credit.

VINOD KAMBLI
Born: 18/1/72. Left-hand batsman. A hustling, confident batsman, best-known for his 600-plus partnership with Tendulkar while at school – believed to be a record in any grade of cricket. He is destined to make a name for himself with his positive strokeplay.

PRAVEEN AMRE
Born: 14/8/68. Right-hand batsman. Another of the younger players introduced as India tries to rebuild, he showed himself to be a busy middle-order player during the World Series earlier in the summer.

KAPIL DEV
Born: 6/1/59. Right-arm fast-medium bowler, right-hand batsman. Still the premier cricketer in India's side, although age has taken the edge off his pace. He has superb command of swing, and strikes the ball tremendous distances with the bat.

KIRAN MORE
Born: 4/9/62. Wicketkeeper, right-hand batsman. A competitive player who has been India's wicketkeeper for several years. He beat off a late challenge by the veteran Syed Kirmani for India's tour of Australia. Has scored 181 in a first-class match.

MANOJ PRABHAKAR
Born: 15/4/63. Right-arm fast-medium bowler, right-hand batsman. A jack of all trades, he has opened both the batting and bowling for his country as well as fielded at first slip – an extremely rare combination. A fierce competitor.

SUBROTO BANERJEE
Born: 13/2/69. Right-arm fast-medium bowler, right-hand batsman. A graduate of Dennis Lillee's fast bowling school in Madras, he has a delightful outswinger that comes naturally. Impressed in the Sydney Test against Australia.

JAVAGAL SRINATH
Born: 31/8/68. Right-arm fast bowler, right-hand batsman. The quickest of India's young bowlers, he has a dipping inswinger and continues to work on a leg-cutter. With Kapil Dev as his inspiration, he has the talent to succeed the great man as his country's No. 1 paceman.

VENKATAPATHY RAJU
Born: 9/7/69. Left-arm orthodox spin bowler, right-hand batsman. An outstanding spin bowler in both forms of the game. Like the great Bishan Bedi, he can lull batsmen into a false sense of security with his inconsequential shuffle to the wicket, but is accurate and spins it sharply.

New Zealand

MARTIN CROWE

Born: 22/9/62. Right-hand batsman considered among the very best in the world. He has faultless technique and is unrelenting on balls on his pads, the signature of the very best. Has overcome constant knee problems, and is a calculating captain who sets a fine example. A brilliant fielder.

CHRIS CAIRNS

Born: 13/6/70. Son of Lance, right-arm opening bowler who tried very hard to be very quick before stress fractures of the back two years ago slowed him down. Has scored a first-class century and is a mighty hitter like his father.

MARK GREATBATCH

Born: 11/12/63. A left-hand high-order batsman whose greatest gifts are his grit and enormous power. Has failed to live up to the standard he set early in his international career, but is handy in the field.

ANDREW JONES

Born: 9/5/59. Was ridiculed early in his career for a quirky technique that saw him committed to the front foot. Has refined it slightly, but is still distinctly unorthodox. A clean striker of the ball and deadly on the drive.

DIPAK PATEL

Born: 25/10/58. Developed his off-spinners to become a legitimate international all-rounder. Classical right-hand bat with pretty timing but his modest output does not match his style.

GAVIN LARSEN

Born: 27/9/62. Key player typical of the New Zealand factory of all-rounders. Tight right-arm medium pacer bowler, competent hitter late in the innings, and has fine hands in the field. A fierce competitor.

IAN SMITH
Born: 28/2/57. New Zealand's most successful wicketkeeper is very safe if not always stylish. A belligerent late-order batsman who averages 17 runs in one-day cricket but can play the role of pinch hitter when pushed up the order. His aggressiveness and vocal support on the field are invaluable prods to his team.

KEN RUTHERFORD
Born:26/10/65. Recovered from a horrible debut when pounded by West Indian quick bowlers. A right-hand bat with a fine array of shots, nice timing, and is hard to quell when on the attack. Quick and alert in the field. A key player.

DANNY MORRISON
Born: 3/2/66. An enthusiast, he did his schooling under the great Sir Richard Hadlee. He bowls right arm and quite quickly. Will struggle to be a regular in the Kiwi line-up because his zest for the contest can often translate into inaccuracy.

WILLIE WATSON
Born: 31/8/65. Right-arm medium pace bowler who fits nicely into the bowling line-up. Will rarely tear the heart out of a batting line-up, but will never shy from the heat of battle. Has had a respectable strike rate since his debut in 1985-86.

CHRIS HARRIS
Born: 20/11/69. Another all-rounder. Right-arm and open chested, he delivers thoughtful inswingers of gentle medium pace. He'll supply good hitting power in the middle of the order and, being a left-hander, will cause bowlers an annoying change of line. Brilliant in the field.

ROD LATHAM
Born:12/6/61. A New Zealand version of Ian Botham in size and style. Can cause havoc as an opening bat with lusty hitting, and has a highest first-class score of 237 off 243 balls. His bowling is useful at best.

JOHN WRIGHT
Born 5/7/54. Veteran campaigner who has opened his country's batting for more than a dozen years. A left-hander with an upright stance, he's not a natural in the limited-over game. His captain will look to him to play the anchor role.

MURPHY SU'A
Born: 7/11/66. Left-arm new-ball bowler who made an instant mark in Test cricket when he claimed Allan Lamb on debut in Auckland. Lusty hitter down the list. A capable back-up to Cairns and Morrison.

Pakistan

IMRAN KHAN

Born: 25/11/52. Right-hand batsman, right-arm fast-medium bowler. A pre-eminent figure in the game over nearly 20 years who drew the various factions of Pakistani cricket together into a united force. A magnificent all-round player.

RAMEEZ RAJA

Born: 14/7/62. Right-hand opening batsman. Solid top-order batsman who likes to fill the role of the anchor man, in line with modern thinking on one-day cricket. A difficult man to dislodge.

AAMIR SOHAIL

Born: 14/9/66. Left-hand opening batsman, left-arm orthodox spin bowler. A newcomer who created an immediate impression with 91 against India in Sharjah, and who can bat down the order as well. Also used for a few overs of spin.

INZAMAM UL-HAQ

Born: 1/3/70. Right-hand batsman. Highly rated by Imran for his play against fast bowling, he hit two centuries in the pre-World Cup series against Sri Lanka. A tall and powerful hitter.

JAVED MIANDAD

Born: 12/6/57. Right-hand batsman. Played in all five World Cups, a tribute to his resilience, not to mention his considerable talent. A back injury hampered his preparation, but at his best he's in the top handful of one-day batsmen in the world.

SALIM MALIK

Born: 16/4/63. Right-hand batsman, right-arm medium-pace bowler. A brilliant exponent of the one-day game, with his flawless strokemaking and his handy seamers tossed in. Excellent off-side player who was a prolific scorer for Essex last season.

IJAZ AHMED

Born: 20/9/68. Right-hand batsman, left-arm medium-pace bowler. Outstanding shotmaker who impressed, despite his tender years, on Pakistan's previous tour of Australia in 1989-90. Also called upon for some bowling.

WASIM AKRAM

Born: 7/9/66. Left-arm fast bowler, left-hand batsman. Among the premier quick bowlers in the world, breath-takingly fast with a wicked inswinger. Also a fine middle-order batsman. A crucial figure in Pakistan's team.

MOIN KHAN

Born: 23/9/72. Wicketkeeper, right-hand batsman. A relative newcomer who replaced Salim Yousuf as gloveman, and had 14 matches under his belt prior to the World Cup. His best performance was four catches in a Sharjah match. Tidy rather than flamboyant.

AAQIB JAVED

Born: 5/8/72. Right-arm fast bowler. Another of Imran's project players, legend has it he played first-class cricket in Pakistan at 14. Last year he led his team to victory at Sharjah with a hat-trick against India. A talented bowler who has a tendency to be petulant.

MUSHTAQ AHMED

Born: 28/6/70. Right-arm leg-spin bowler. Hailed as the successor to Abdul Qadir, but has failed to meet expectations so far. Still young, he was included on the basis of Pakistan's recent tradition – not followed in many other parts — of using leg-spin in one-day cricket.

IQBAL SIKANDER

Born: 19/12/58. Right-arm leg-spinner. Veteran making his touring debut. Flat, accurate spinner who has been ignored by selectors in the past despite impressing observers in the English leagues.

WASIM HAIDER

Born: 3/6/66. Right-arm medium-pace bowler, right-hand batsman. Quasi-all-rounder who bowls handy seamers and bats reasonably well, too. Another of the new players called upon by Pakistan in its bid to rebuild the side.

ZAHID FAZAL

Born: 10/11/73. Right-hand opening batsman. First appeared in internationals in the 1990-91 season, but did not make an impact until hitting an unbeaten 98 against India at Sharjah in October, 1991. Heavy scorer in under-23 cricket.

South Africa

KEPLER WESSELS

Born: 14/9/57. Left-hand opening batsman. The only South African with Test experience, having made 1761 runs at 42 in his productive stint with Australia in the 1980s. His courage goes unquestioned, but he can be tied down by accurate bowling.

ALLAN DONALD

Born: 20/10/66. Right-arm fast bowler, right-hand batsman. The cutting edge of South Africa's attack, among the quickest bowlers in the game. Took 83 county wickets for Warwickshire last year, but can be expensive in one-day cricket.

TERTIUS BOSCH

Born: 14/3/66. Right-arm fast bowler, right-hand batsman. Genuinely quick bowler who has been rated in Donald's vicinity for speed. One of South Africa's best prospects.

WESSEL 'HANSIE' CRONJE

Born: 25/9/69. Right-hand batsman, right-arm medium-pace bowler. Tall middle-order player who led Orange Free State to its first night game win against Traansvaal with a century this summer. Good outfielder and handy bowler.

OMAR HENRY

Born: 23/1/52. Left-arm orthodox spin bowler, left-hand batsman. Another veteran, and as a so-called Cape Coloured, the only non-white player in South Africa's 14. He has extensive experience in Scotland as well as against touring 'rebel' teams.

ANDREW HUDSON

Born: 17/3/66. Right-hand opening batsman. Excellent top-order batsman who nevertheless struggled on the tour of India. Hit 673 runs in Currie Cup last season, confirming his status as one of his country's brightest prospects.

PETER KIRSTEN

Born: 14/5/55. Right-hand batsman, right-arm off-spin bowler. Another vastly experienced player, among the most prolific in South African cricket. Fine all-round batsman whose nagging off-spin is a bonus.

ADRIAN KUIPER

Born: 22/12/63. Right-hand batsman, right-arm medium-pace bowler. Powerful striker who battled in domestic cricket last season, averaging fewer than 20, but a key player for the World Cup. Played county cricket for Derbyshire.

BRIAN MCMILLAN

Born: 22/12/63. Right-arm fast-medium bowler, right-hand batsman. All-rounder whose international experience includes the tour of India and a stint in England with Warwickshire. Sharpish bowler who extracts some outswing and bounce.

JONATHON 'JONTY' RHODES

Born: 26/7/69. Right-hand batsman. Aggressive middle-order batsman who can improvise to score quickly, but best known for his superb fielding. Has been compared with the great Colin Bland. He hit a century on debut for Natal in 1988.

MEYRICK PRINGLE

Born: 22/6/66. Right-arm fast-bowler. Sharpish seam-up bowler who led the wicket-takers in South Africa's domestic competition last season. The outwinger is his stock ball.

DAVID RICHARDSON

Born: 16/9/59. Wicketkeeper, right-hand batsman. Tidy gloveman who beat off at least one serious challenge for the job on this tour. Also doubles as a batsman, having scored first-class centuries.

MARK RUSHMERE

Born: 7/1/63. Right-hand batsman. One of three potential openers in the touring party, but capable of batting at No. 3 as well. Tall, correct player who fits the opener's mould, although he has some shots in his repertoire.

RICHARD SNELL

Born: 12/9/68. Right-arm fast-medium bowler, right-hand batsman. Had a disappointing tour of India but is highly rated as a back-up for Donald. Keeps the seam upright and is accurate. Signed by Somerset for next English season.

Sri Lanka

ARAVINDA DE SILVA
Born: 17/10/65. Right-hand bat, right-arm off-spinner. His diminutive build belies one of the world's special batting talents, already well-known in Australia. Imran Khan once despaired of ever getting him out.

DON ANURASIRI
Born: 25/2/66. Left-arm orthodox spinner. Sparingly used before this tournament, but respected by his teammates for courage to flight the ball and his ability to spin it.

ASANKA GURUSINHA
Born: 16/9/66. Left-hand bat, right-arm slow-medium bowler. Regular No. 3 bat who does not enjoy the same international regard of others in his team, but plays a professional and polished brand of cricket.

SANATH JAYASURIYA
Born: 30/6/69. Left-hand batsman. Like de Silva, his seemingly frail body contains a truly precocious talent. Started his Test career with 66 against England and plundered more runs against Pakistan.

CHANDIKA HATHURUSINGHA
Born: 13/9/68. Right-hand batsman. Before this tournament, a big name only in length. His place in this party was earned by his aggression as an opener and occasional bowling.

ATHULA SAMARASEKERA
Born: 5/8/61. Right-hand bat, right-arm slow-medium pace. A tall and willowy opening bat, who likes to hit the ball hard from the front foot and, by Sri Lankan standards, is consistent.

ROSHAN MAHANAMA
Born 31/5/66. Right-hand bat. Technically the most correct of the Sri Lankans and generally opens in one-day games. Also an outstanding, athletic outfielder.

CHAMPAKA RAMANAYAKE
Born: 8/1/65. Right-arm fast-medium bowler. Big, strong and bowls at a lively pace. Since the retirement of Ravi Ratnayeke has shouldered an extra burden in the attack.

ARJUNA RANATUNGA
Born: 1/12/63. Left-hand bat, right-arm slow-medium bowler. Former captain, blessed with talent, an acute understanding of the game and, most importantly, an especially cool temperament in all situations.

RUMESH RATNAYAKE
Born: 2/1/64. Right-arm fast bowler. Replaced after the second game because of recurring problems with a shoulder injury.

PRAMODAYA WICKREMASINGHE
Born: 14/8/71. Right-arm fast-medium bowler. Announced himself to the world at large with five wickets against Pakistan shortly before this tournament. Await further announcements.

HASHAN TILLEKERATNE
Born: 14/7/67. Wicketkeeper and left-arm bat. Vibrant, courageous batsman, who adapts his game well to changing circumstances. Came late to wicketkeeping, but has excelled.

KAPILA WIJEGOONEWARDENE
Born: 23/11/64. Right-arm fast-medium bowler. Light on his feet, with a whippy action, he can generate real pace from time to time, but not yet consistently.

RUWAN KALPAGE
Born: 19/2/70. Promising off-spinner who was called up during Sri Lanka's tour of Pakistan. A brilliant fieldsman who will add much to Sri Lanka's work in the outfield. Capable down-the-list batsman.

West Indies

RICHIE RICHARDSON
Born: 12/1/62. Right-hand batsman. Class. Elan. With England's Gooch, one of the world's best batsmen, capable of demoralising an opponent in an hour. Succeeding Viv Richards is tough, but so is Richardson.

MALCOLM MARSHALL
Born: 18/4/58. Right-arm fast-medium bowler. Survived the recent purges and remains a truly great bowler because his effect has not diminished with his pace (or his hairline).

WINSTON BENJAMIN
Born: 31/12/64. Right-arm fast-medium bowler. Not as outrageously fast as so many of his countrymen, but bowls with cunning. Also bats usefully in the lower order.

CARL HOOPER.
Born: 15/12/66. Right-hand bat, right-arm off-spinner. An elegant batsman, his elders have less cause now to despair of his inconsistency. Tight bowler, in the frontline for this tournament.

GUS LOGIE
Born: 28/9/60. Right-hand batsman. Viv Richards said he would trust this courageous, compelling batsman alongside him in the trenches anywhere. Close to being the world's best fieldsman.

PATRICK PATTERSON
Born: 15/9/61. Right-arm fast bowler. In Ian Bishop's absence, the fastest and most furious of the Windies' attack, but whose style does not always work within the constraints of one-day cricket.

DAVID WILLIAMS

Born: 4/11/63. Wicketkeeper, right-hand bat. Diminutive, but only in stature. A silky smooth gloveman and seemingly the annointed successor to the great Jeff Dujon. Rod Marsh approves.

KEITH ARTHURTON

Born: 21/1/65. Left-hand batsman. Occasionally brutal striker of the ball, but consistency has been a failing. In the mould of the greats as a cover field.

ROGER HARPER

Born: 17/3/63. Right-arm bat, right-arm off-spinner. Resurrected from the scrapheap to form with Hooper an unusual double-spin Windies attack. The best fieldsman in the world.

CURTLY AMBROSE

Born: 21/9/63. Right-arm fast bowler. Succeeding Joel Garner and sometimes exceeding him. Has pace and bounce to spare, but nothing for the batsman. And he can bat.

ANDERSON CUMMINS

Born: 7/5/66. Right-arm fast bowler. The best of the next generation. Not terrifyingly fast, but moves the ball from wide on the crease and concedes every run grudgingly.

DESMOND HAYNES

Born: 15/2/56. Right-hand bat. The world's greatest one-day batsman – ever – with 16 centuries to his name before this tournament. Bitterness at losing succession to the captaincy has not dulled his appetite.

PHIL SIMMONS

Born: 18/4/63. Right-hand bat. Tall batsman, sometime opener, who thrives on attack, and is not afraid to hit a 6 in the first over if he thinks the ball merits it. Struggles for consistency.

BRIAN LARA

Born: 2/5/69. Left-hand bat. The latest and most attractive of an endless stream of precocious talents from the Caribbean. Plays with that indefinable charm peculiar to left-handers. In every sense, one to watch.

Zimbabwe

DAVID HOUGHTON

Born: 23/6/57. Right-hand batsman. The captain and premier batsman, he also played in the 1987 World Cup. Shortish, he nevertheless gives the ball a whack and uses his feet well to spinners.

KEVIN ARNOTT

Born: 8/3/61. Right-hand opening batsman. A solid player, more suited to first-class cricket but still capable at this level. He can also act as reserve wicket-keeper.

EDDO BRANDES

Born: 25/3/63. Right-arm fast-medium bowler, right-hand batsman. Zimbabwe's new-baller, he generates lively pace with his height and powerful build. A dangerous lower-order hitter as well.

MARK BURMESTER

Born: 24/1/68. Right-arm medium-pace bowler, right-hand batsman. He had not played a one-day international prior to the World Cup, but had moderate success against a touring Australian team in the lead-up.

IAIN BUTCHART

Born: 9/5/60. Right-hand batsman, right-arm medium-pace bowler. Like Burmester, he is a handy seamer who can hit at the end of an innings. A long-time member of Zimbabwe's national team.

ALISTAIR CAMPBELL

Born: 23/9/72. Left-hand batsman. A tall, strongly built player who spends the off-season in England. He likes to play shots, and will appreciate the experience of the World Cup.

KEVIN DUERS

Born: 30/6/60. Right-arm medium-pacer, right-hand batsman. A handy seamer who was called into the side after an injury to Kevin Flower. He had not played a one-day international before the World Cup.

ANDY FLOWER

Born: 20/12/62. Left-hand opening batsman and wicketkeeper. A gifted top-order batsman with the ability to improvise for one-day cricket, and an adequate gloveman.

WAYNE JAMES

Born: 27/8/65. Right-hand batsman. Debuted against New South Wales in 1987, although he had not competed in a limited-overs international until the World Cup.

MALCOLM JARVIS

Born: 6/12/55. Left-arm medium-pace bowler, right-hand batsman. A long-time opening bowler who looks innocuous enough, but swings the ball. Remains a key to the attack.

ANDY PYCROFT

Born: 6/6/56. Right-hand batsman. An experienced player who has been troubled by injury. He is a compact batsman who likes to nudge and push the ball around.

ALI SHAH

Born: 7/8/59. Right-arm medium-pace bowler, left-hand batsman. A fine all-rounder who does a bit of everything. He bowls in the middle of the opposition's innings, bats in the middle-order, and has performed in difficult times.

JOHN TRAICOS

Born: 17/5/47. Right-arm off-spin bowler, right-hand batsman. The old man of the World Cup at 44, this remarkable player has maintained excellent fitness so that he fields superbly in the gully. Played Test cricket for South Africa.

ANDY WALLER

Born: 25/9/59. Right-hand batsman. A big-hitter who loves nothing better than thrashing the bowling, but his lack of experience at international level has curtailed his results.

Match Locations

Note: Countries not drawn to scale

The Matches

Kiwis draw first blood .

22 February: New Zealand v Australia in Auckland

Stepping into the cacophony at Eden Park for the opening World Cup match between the tournament's joint hosts was like stepping into the bird enclosure at a zoo. As the Australians discovered, that can be a messy business.

Thirty-five thousand cheap party hooters – more than one per head – were shipped in from China and distributed free for the occasion. The people of Auckland blew with gusto as New Zealand, previously thought to be as capable of flight as the dodo, soared into the unexpected and descended on Australia from a great height.

The effect on the ears, if you closed your eyes, was that of a mass strangulation of ducks. The effect on the World Cup was to provide it with the spiciest opening imaginable.

Australia was the raging tournament favourite; New Zealand, consensus had it, a basket case.

The upset victory was designed and constructed by Martin Crowe, who dominated the match with his batting and unorthodox captaincy. He won an important toss and batted when the wicket was at its best, hit an exquisite unbeaten century to steer New Zealand to 6/248, and then defended the total with tactics that were radical for their ultra-defensiveness.

His bravest move was to open the bowling at the terrace end with the part-time off-spin of Dipak Patel, which sent a murmur through the crowd. He also adopted a revolving door policy with his anonymous band of medium-pacers, alternating them so often that he might as well have put stockings over their heads to prevent the batsmen from recognising them and getting into rhythm. Chris Harris, for example, bowled his 7.1 overs in four spells.

The strapping Chris Cairns bowled four expensive overs and was dispensed with on the grounds that his pace and waywardness gave the Australian batsmen something to work with. The policy of the rest seemed to be to land the ball as softly as a powder puff on a woman's cheek.

'They've done the dirty on us again,' Border said afterwards, albeit with a smile. The loss confirmed his worst fears that the opening match of Australia's World Cup defence was its most dangerous. 'As soon as Australia hit New Zealand soil they lift 50 per cent. I've seen it in rugby and I've seen it in cricket,' he said.

Australia did not adjust well to the conditions. On a wicket that had reasonable pace to start with but grew increasingly sluggish as the day progressed, it bowled too short, particularly to Crowe.

Crowe is one of the most classical and effective pullers in the game. Of his 11 boundaries, seven were the result of pull shots, some of them so savage that a fieldsman standing within five metres of the boundary had no hope of intercepting them.

Aside from three dropped catches – including a sitter by Tom Moody at first slip to reprieve Rod Latham – the luck seemed to run with the New Zealand batsmen. Perhaps a more logical explanation was that Australia had trouble with the strange angles and short boundaries created by Eden Park's bizarre shape. Border admitted afterwards that whenever he looked around the warped septagonal field his fielders seemed to be in the wrong place.

The essential difference between the sides was that while New Zealand, and Ken Rutherford in particular, batted cleverly around Martin Crowe, Australia's century-maker, David Boon, played the role of a lone and defiant standard-bearer for much of his innings.

Dean Jones was unlucky to be given run out by Pakistani umpire Khizar Hayat (just as New Zealand's Jones, Andrew, was unfortunate to be adjudged lbw by the same umpire earlier in the day). But after Dean Jones went, three Australian wickets fell in quick succession in a more culpable fashion.

Border presented his wicket to Patel, holing out to deep square leg from only his 11th delivery; Tom Moody thought he was back in Perth, completing his shot before the ball had arrived and popping up a diving return catch for Latham; and Mark Waugh persisted with his habit of playing across the line to be lbw to Gavin Larsen.

Australia's second best batsman on the day was Steve Waugh but, coming in at No. 7, he was invited to salvage the innings, not to shape it. Boon being a more conventional player, Australia's chances rested with Waugh's powerful forearms.

He struck gold once, putting Latham back over his head and into the sightscreen at the northern end for 6, but with five overs remaining and the scoreboard showing an asking rate that had crept above 10 per over – an event that was met with a chant of 'Kiwi, Kiwi' around the terraces – the odds were prohibitive.

The 46th over of the Australian innings, bowled by Larsen, was the decisive one. Boon, by this time hobbling on his dicky right knee, brought up his century from the first ball, giving Steve Waugh the strike.

Larsen then deceived Waugh with a shorter ball, the bowler diving away to his right to complete a brilliant return catch as Waugh's attempt to force the pace miscued. If that blow had not shattered Australia's hopes, they were blown out of Auckland Harbour when Boon was run out two balls later, by a direct side-on hit by Chris Harris running in from deep mid-wicket.

It was a fittingly spectacular end to the boldest of cricketing coups.

PLAYER PROFILE: *Martin Crowe*

As the crowd broke the barriers at Eden Park to celebrate New Zealand's 37-run win over Australia in the World Cup opener, it was impossible not to share in some of Martin Crowe's sense of delight.

Crowe is a complex man who has felt the burden of a nation's frustrated sporting expectations, particularly following the All Blacks' loss to arch-rival Australia in the rugby union World Cup.

If anyone suggested in an Auckland pub before the opening World Cup match that New Zealand's cricketers could avenge its rugby players, they would have been laughed out of the place.

Criticism, not all of it to do with cricket, reached its peak following a disastrous Test and one-day series against England. Crowe and his wife, Simone, told a New Zealand magazine shortly before the World Cup that they had had to endure rumours about their personal life and felt that 'the whole nation has turned against us.'

Crowe fashioned an eloquent and daring response in the opening match of the World Cup, hitting a compelling and unbeaten century and then using the part-time off-spinner Dipak Patel to open the bowling as part of a masterplan to frustrate the Australian batsmen.

'If we went out and played our normal pattern game we would have been wiped off the park as usual,' he said. 'I wanted to show the lads that I've got a bit of courage. That's what the team needed – someone to lead the way.'

No wonder, with his wife and parents watching from the grandstand, he described it as one of the greatest days of his life.

Leading from the front: The Australians paid for bowling too short at New Zealand captain Martin Crowe, a renowned horizontal-bat player, in Auckland. Here he pulls Peter Taylor during his unbeaten century.

Happy hunting ground: Gavin Larsen pegged down the Australian batting with his slow-mediums, and brilliantly caught and bowled the dangerous Steve Waugh to boot. Martin Crowe loves it.

22 February. New Zealand v Australia — Auckland.
Weather: overcast

NEW ZEALAND

	Runs	Balls	4s/6s
J WRIGHT b McDermott	0	1	-
R LATHAM c Healy b Moody	26	44	4/0
A JONES lbw b Reid	4	14	1/0
M CROWE not out	100	134	11/0
K RUTHERFORD run out	57	71	6/0
C HARRIS run out	14	15	2/0
I SMITH c Healy b McDermott	14	14	1/0
C CAIRNS not out	16	11	2/0
Sundries (6lb 7w 4nb)	17		
TOTAL for six wickets	248		

Fall: 2, 13, 53, 171, 191, 215.

	O	M	R	W	Eco	W	NB
C McDermott ...	10	1	43	2	4.3	2	-
B Reid	10	0	39	1	3.9	2	4
T Moody	9	0	37	1	4.1	-	-
S Waugh	10	0	60	0	6.0	2	-
P Taylor	7	0	36	0	5.1	-	-
M Waugh	4	0	27	0	6.7	1	-

Overs: 50.

AUSTRALIA

	Runs	Balls	4s/6s
D BOON run out	100	131	11/0
G MARSH c Latham b Larsen	19	56	2/0
D JONES run out	21	27	3/0
A BORDER c Cairns b Patel	3	11	0/0
T MOODY c and b Latham	7	11	-
M WAUGH lbw b Larsen	2	5	-
S WAUGH c and b Larsen	38	34	3/1
I HEALY not out	7	9	-
C MCDERMOTT run out	1	1	-
P TAYLOR c Rutherford b Watson	1	2	-
B REID c Jones b Harris	3	4	-
Sundries (6lb 2w 1nb)	9		
TOTAL	211		

Fall: 62, 92, 104, 120, 125, 199, 200, 205, 206, 211.

	O	M	R	W	Eco	W	NB
C Cairns	4	0	30	0	7.5	1	1
D Patel	10	1	36	1	3.6	1	-
W Watson	9	1	39	1	4.3	-	-
G Larsen	10	1	30	3	3.0	-	-
C Harris	7.1	0	35	1	4.9	-	-
R Latham	8	0	35	1	4.3	-	-

Overs: 48.1
Umpires: K Hayat, D Shepherd.
Crowd: approx. 27,000
Player of the match: Martin Crowe (NZ)
NEW ZEALAND WON BY 37 RUNS
* Economy rate is runs per six balls.

The Botham factor

22 February: England v India in Perth

England supporters claimed loudly and often that their team was the combination most likely to rip the World Cup away from defending champion Australia.

They had form on their side. England looked impressive and cohesive in winning the Test and one-day series against New Zealand enroute to Australia. And its captain, Graham Gooch, boasted a group of all-rounders essential for the limited-over format. It took just one match to appreciate the wisdom of supporters and Gooch alike.

Gooch's side won its opening game by nine runs, reaching 9/236 and then dismissing India for 227 in a day/night encounter at Perth's WACA Ground.

England batted first. Enter Ian Botham, who was given the task of opening the innings, clearly with instructions to smash at anything that moved off the straight and narrow.

He did his best for 21 balls and nine runs. It included a fierce drive over mid-off for four and ended with an edge to wicketkeeper Kiran More when he attempted to cut a ball that was much too close for comfort.

But, as is the way with Botham, he would bob up time and again during the game, changing the rhythm and direction of the encounter.

Robin Smith, whose international career had floundered slightly since his front-foot attacks against the 1989 Australians, replaced Botham and formed an alliance with skipper Gooch that was to set up the match for England.

The pair put together 110 runs in 21 overs even though Gooch was hampered by cramp in the calf muscle. He called for assistance. Enter Botham, the runner.

Gooch was out when he lofted Ravi Shastri to mid-off. Graeme Hick, continuing his wretched run with his adopted country, edged Subroto Banerjee to keeper Kiran More.

Smith fell for 91 when he cracked a cut to point where Mohammad Azharuddin held a brilliant low catch. He had batted with great power and authority, hitting two 6s over mid-wicket. 'I hope he's going to be a star of the tournament,' said Gooch. He certainly started that way.

The score was 5/198 and six overs remained. Given such a platform, the England hitters down the list could have done more than push the score to 236.

However Azharuddin was far from pleased with his bowlers, who delivered 13 wides, including six from the master Kapil Dev – and berated them after the game, demanding a more diligent approach at practice. 'Those wides don't count in the nets but they hurt in the matches,' said the skipper.

The Indians' early response to England's competitive total was emphatic, with Krish Srikkanth, as always, leading the way. England's opening bowlers Chris Lewis and Derek Pringle made it easy for him, though. More often than not they committed one-day howlers, bowling too short or too wide and giving Srikkanth enough space to wind up and whack.

He made 39 from 50 balls before he lofted Phil DeFreitas to Botham. Worse, skipper Azharuddin lasted just one ball, edging Dermott Reeve to More. Still, by 30 overs India had reached the relatively strong position of 2/126.

Enter Botham, the bowler. His medium-pace was both penetrating – claiming the wickets of Sachin Tendulkar and Vinod Kambli – and frugal, going for just 27 runs off his 10 overs. Azharuddin said the demise of Tendulkar was the turning point in the match, for the Indian tyro was 35 and warming to his task. But so was Botham, and Tendulkar fell to the perfect leg-cutter.

That should have cut the heart out of India, although Shastri (57) proved stubborn. However an unlikely late charge came from tail-enders Javagal Srinath and Banerjee.

With just seven balls and one wicket remaining, India needed 17, an unlikely target. But Banerjee remained cool, took aim at the last ball offered by Pringle, and sent it flying over the mid-wicket fence. The equation now read: 11 runs off six balls, one wicket standing.

Enter Botham, the fieldsman. With five balls remaining Srinath was caught short of his ground by a Botham return from extra cover and the Indian chase was over and short of its target.

Enter Botham, man of the match. It was a slightly controversial decision given Smith's earlier batting, but Botham's most simple of duties attracts the eye.

England had much to be pleased about. Their string of victories was growing daily and Allan Lamb was slowly overcoming his hamstring problem. The mood was so bright after the game that Gooch said England's bowling depth would become a decisive advantage in the World Cup. 'The flexibility of the attack is quite an advantage,' said Gooch. No one disagreed.

PLAYER PROFILE: Robin Smith

With each passing year the cricket world becomes increasingly smaller. Take, for example, the case of Robin Smith, Durban born, one-time Natal player, Hampshire professional and England batsman.

For Smith, going to Perth for England's opening round World Cup match against India was like a home-coming. For three straight southern hemisphere summers prior to his selection for England he tripped Down Under to smash run-making records in club cricket for South Perth.

Hence there were no fears for Smith in the bouncy WACA Ground wicket. Celebrating his return, he belted a superb 91 from 108 balls to set up England's win.

The powerfully built right-hander hit 10 of England's 13 boundaries and twice smote sixes to the square boundary at the longest part of the massive WACA Ground. Only a brilliant low catch backward of point by Indian skipper Mohammad Azharuddin halted his charge toward a century.

Smith arrived for the World Cup with plenty to prove to Australian cricket followers. The previous summer he had endured a disappointing Ashes series, having landed with a reputation as being among the top handful of batsmen in the world.

Not surprisingly, England captain Graham Gooch said after the Perth game he hoped Smith would be one of the players of the tournament. 'Robin has matured into a fine player even though he had a tough time in Australia with the bat last year,' said Gooch.

'He has since worked slavishly on his batting and I hope he is the star of this tournament because when he hits a ball it certainly stays hit.'

Power play: The ferocious-hitting Robin Smith pulled two sixes to the long boundaries at the WACA Ground. His 91 set up England's victory over India.

22 February. England v India — Perth.

Weather: fine

ENGLAND

	Runs	Balls	4s/6s
G GOOCH c Tendulkar b Shastri	51	89	1/0
I BOTHAM c More b Kapil Dev...................	9	21	1/0
R SMITH c Azharuddin b Prabhakar	91	108	8/2
G HICK c More b Banerjee	5	6	1/0
N FAIRBROTHER c Srikkanth b Srinath............	24	34	1/0
A STEWART b Prabhakar	13	15	1/0
C LEWIS c Banerjee b Kapil Dev	10	6	-
D PRINGLE c Srikkanth b Srinath	1	3	-
D REEVE not out	8	8	-
P DeFREITAS run out	1	5	-
P TUFNELL not out	3	5	-
Sundries (1b 6lb 13w)	20		
TOTAL for nine wickets	236		

Fall: 21, 131, 137, 197, 198, 214, 222, 223, 224.

	O	M	R	W	Eco	W	NB
Kapil Dev	10	0	38	2	3.8	6	-
M Prabhakar	10	3	34	2	3.4	-	-
J Srinath	10	1	47	2	4.7	5	-
S Banerjee	7	0	45	1	6.4	-	-
S Tendulkar	10	0	37	0	3.7	1	-
R Shastri	4	0	28	1	7.0	1	-

Overs: 50.

INDIA

	Runs	Balls	4s/6s
R SHASTRI run out	57	112	2/0
K SRIKKANTH c Botham b DeFreitas	39	50	7/0
M AZHARUDDIN c Stewart b Reeve	0	1	-
S TENDULKAR c Stewart b Botham	35	44	5/0
V KAMBLI c Hick b Botham	3	11	-
P AMRE run out	22	31	-
KAPIL DEV c DeFreitas b Reeve	17	18	2/0
S BANERJEE not out	25	16	1/1
K MORE run out	1	4	-
M PRABHAKAR b Reeve	0	2	-
J SRINATH run out	11	7	-
Sundries (9lb 7w 1nb)	17		
TOTAL	227		

Fall: 63, 63, 126, 140, 149, 187, 194, 200, 201, 227.

	O	M	R	W	Eco	W	NB
D Pringle	10	0	53	0	5.3	1	-
C Lewis	9.2	0	36	0	3.9	5	1
P DeFreitas.....	10	0	39	1	3.9	-	-
D Reeve	6	0	38	3	6.3	1	-
I Botham	10	0	27	2	2.7	-	-
P Tufnell	4	0	25	0	6.2	-	-

Overs: 49.2.

Umpires: P McConnell, J Buultjens

Crowd: 12,902

Player of the match: Ian Botham (England).

ENGLAND WON BY NINE RUNS

West Indies' early warning

23 February: West Indies v Pakistan in Melbourne

Only a handful more than 14,000 people shuffled into the cavernous Melbourne Cricket Ground for the first of five World Cup matches in the multicultural city, a mere trickle against the expected torrent of the final a month later.

In the shadows of the new Great Southern Stand, a complex that alone holds more people (48,000) than most of the world's cricket grounds, one group waved the green and white Pakistan flag and chanted for Javed Miandad as he carved out a brilliant short innings against his old rivals, the West Indies.

But those loyal supporters would have left the ground that evening with a more pessimistic outlook about Pakistan's chances. Conjuring a performance from their peerless 1984-85 vintage, the West Indians delivered the first significant warning of the World Cup with a crushing 10-wicket victory in a form of the game that, by design, is meant to produce close finishes.

Sent in to bat by Richie Richardson, the Pakistanis paced their innings well to reach 2/220, veteran opener Rameez Raja hitting an unbeaten century and Miandad infuriating the West Indian bowlers with a typically-cheeky 57 not out from just 61 balls.

But it never seemed to be enough runs once the West Indian openers Desmond Haynes and Brian Lara had seen off Wasim Akram's first spell with the new ball. With captain Imran Khan pulling out because of a shoulder strain, the acting skipper Miandad was left with a popgun attack including two international debutantes – medium-pacer Wasim Haider and 34-year-old leg-spinner Iqbal Sikander.

Pakistan had slipped from second to third-favourite in the betting immediately following the news a few days before the tournament that its 21-year-old fast-bowling prodigy, Waqar Younis, had stress fractures in the lower back and would return home. On this day, it became apparent why the bookies had reacted so strongly.

Haynes and Lara combined for a 175-run opening stand broken only when Akram's yorker dealt the younger West Indian a blow on the big toe of the right foot that sent him hobbling from the field. By then the result was beyond question anyway, with Lara having contributed a blistering 88 from just 101 balls, the innings that he had promised but failed to deliver in the World Series tournament against Australia and India earlier in the summer.

The Trinidadian, elevated to open for the first time ahead of full-time opener Phil Simmons, spanked anything short and garnered half his runs in fours. Said Richardson of the ploy: 'In one-day matches you have to be flexible. That way it's difficult for the other teams to plan against you.'

Barbadian Haynes, the consummate one-day opener, carried on to an unbeaten 93, and the West Indies reached their target with 3.1 overs to spare. The

Pakistanis did not help their cause by dropping two chances Haynes offered at 35 and 49, the first spilling from the gloves of wicketkeeper Moin Khan from the first ball delivered by left-arm spinner Aamir Sohail, and Sohail compounding the troubles by grassing a looping catch from his own bowling.

The final two runs required by the West Indians were provided by illegal bouncers from Aaqib Javed, an indiscretion that brought him a stinging rebuke from Miandad and one that encapsulated Pakistan's effort in the field.

'I thought 220 was a good score, but the wicket played very well and we had only two main bowlers,' said Miandad, who nonetheless expressed confidence that the Pakistanis would reach the semi-finals at least.

Richardson expressed delight that his reshaped team was entering a major series or tournament for the first time in perhaps 15 years unburdened by favouritism or unrealistic public expectations. 'The pressure's not on us. It's a wonderful opportunity to surprise a few people.'

But the man who replaced his fellow-Antiguan Viv Richards as captain was concerned about the standard of fielding. The West Indians conceded 81 in the final 10 overs of the Pakistan innings, largely because of Miandad's genius for improvisation. The Karachi batsman, who once was regarded as the best one-day batsman in the world, was in delightful touch despite the fact that his arrival in Australia was delayed by a back injury.

Rising 35, he retains the arrogance of youth. When Richardson dared to bring his fine-leg fielder inside the circle toward the end, Miandad walked across his stumps and tickled three deliveries from the West Indian pacemen down to the fence. 'Old man doing good,' he mused later, smiling as ever.

Signalling a healthy penchant for strategic change, the West Indians extracted 20 of their 50 overs with the ball from the off-spinners Carl Hooper and Roger Harper, leaving out pacemen Andy Cummins and Patrick Patterson. Given that their dominance of world cricket has been based around a quartet of outstanding fast bowlers, it was a significant change. 'I think you'll see a lot of Roger and Carl in the World Cup,' said Richardson.

PLAYER PROFILE: Brian Lara

As the West Indies cruised to a 10-wicket victory in their opening match of the World Cup, stand-in opener Brian Lara was being spirited away to a Melbourne hospital for a foot x-ray.

Fortunately for the brilliant young Trinidad left-hander, the results did not spoil one of his best days in an international career that promises to be long and fruitful. Medicos confirmed that the blow to the big toe on his right foot delivered by Pakistani paceman Wasim Akram had not broken a bone.

Lara's 88 retired hurt was his highest score in a one-day international. Punting on the 21-year-old's ability to strike the ball cleanly enough to clear the inner ring of fielders in the first 15 overs, the West Indians elevated him to the top order to join Desmond Haynes, and the move reaped immediate dividends.

The pair put on 175 for the first wicket, just seven short of the World Cup record for an opening stand, set by Alan Turner and Rick McCosker against Sri Lanka at The Oval in 1975.

Lara crashed 11 boundaries in the space of just 101 balls. Already a legend in cricket-loving Trinidad and Tobago, he had struggled to realise those expectations in the lead-up to the World Cup.

But with that flourishing backlift and sweet timing, he delivered a treat to those at the MCG for the game against Pakistan, and there was a feeling that perhaps, at last, Brian Lara had arrived as a big-time player.

Young talent time: Elevated to open the batting, Brian Lara swatted 88 in the West Indies' opener against Pakistan. Only an injury denied him a century.

Promises, promises: Gifted Brian Lara finally delivered the goods with his 88 retired hurt against Pakistan. Wicketkeeper Moin Khan can only admire this graceful cut.

Dynamic duo: Desmond Haynes and Brian Lara added 175 against Pakistan in their first outing together as openers. Had Lara not departed through injury, they might have broken the World Cup record of 182.

23 February. West Indies v Pakistan — Melbourne.
Weather: fine

PAKISTAN

	Runs	Balls	4s/6s
RAMEEZ RAJA not out	102	158	4/0
AAMIR SOHAIL c Logie b Benjamin.	23	44	3/0
INZAMAM-UL-HAQ c Hooper b Harper	27	39	-
JAVED MIANDAD not out	57	61	5/0
Sundries (1b 3lb 5w 2nb)	11		
TOTAL for two wickets	220		

Fall: 45, 97.

	O	M	R	W	Eco	W	NB
M Marshall	10	1	53	0	5.3	3	-
C Ambrose	10	0	40	0	4.0	1	2
W Benjamin.	10	0	49	1	4.9	1	-
C Hooper	10	0	41	0	4.1	1	-
R Harper	10	0	33	1	3.3	-	-

Overs: 50.

WEST INDIES

	Runs	Balls	4s/6s
D HAYNES not out	93	144	7/0
B LARA ret hurt	88	101	11/0
R RICHARDSON not out	20	40	1/0
Sundries (2b 8lb 7w 3nb)	20		
TOTAL for no wicket	221		

	O	M	R	W	Eco	W	NB
Wasim Akram . . .	10	0	37	0	3.7	7	-
Aaqib Javed	8.5	0	42	0	4.9	-	2
Wasim Haider . . .	8	0	42	0	5.2	-	1
Ijaz Ahmed	6	1	29	0	4.8	-	-
Iqbal Sikander. . . .	8	1	26	0	3.2	-	-
Aamir Sohail	6	0	35	0	5.8	-	-

Overs: 46.5
Umpires: S Randell, I Robinson
Crowd: 14,162
Player of the match: Brian Lara (West Indies)
WEST INDIES WON BY 10 WICKETs

The mice that roared

23 February: Sri Lanka **v** Zimbabwe in New Zealand

It shaped as the most low-key match of the World Cup. Tucked away in New Plymouth, New Zealand, with no television cover and just a tad of radio service back to Australia, the Sri Lanka v Zimbabwe match could safely have been billed as 'the clash of the also-rans'.

It ended as nothing of the sort. It was a celebration of everything supporters of limited-over cricket trumpet – dazzling shot-making, brilliant fielding and a heart-stopping finish.

The match started out ordinarily enough with Sri Lanka winning the toss and offering Zimbabwe first use of the benign pitch at pretty Pukekura Park.

But 50 overs, twenty-five 4s and five 6s later, the Zimbabweans had amassed a mammoth 7/312, a mixture of brutal hitting and shrewd stealing of singles. It easily surpassed their previous highest World Cup total of 240 registered against the hapless Australian team of the 1983 World Cup campaign.

Opener Andrew Flower blossomed as the innings developed. He batted through the 50 overs, collecting eight 4s and one 6 as well as the player of the match award for his unbeaten 115.

When Flower was joined by Andy Waller the Sri Lankans felt the full force of some frantic Zimbabwean hitting. The pair thrashed and crashed a fifth-wicket stand of 145 in less than 13 overs. Waller's contribution was a manic 83 off just 45 balls, one of his three mighty 6s landing in a duck pond next to the oval.

Sri Lanka's batsmen mounted a majestic and nerveless retaliation. The openers, Athula Samarasekera and Roshan Mahanama, sped Sri Lanka off the mark with an opening stand of 128 that was full of flair and wristy shots.

Old man cricket John Traicos tightened the match for Zimbabwe as his cunningly controlled off-spinners gave up just 33 runs in 10 overs. It was the 44-year-old's depth of experience that saw him give the Sri Lankans precious little room to swing their bats.

After Traicos got rid of Samarasekera, Aravinda de Silva and Asanka Gurusinha followed all too abruptly for the good of the Sri Lankan cause.

But once Traicos had finished his spell, the Zimbabwe bowlers were there for the plundering and Arjuna Ranatunga raced to 88 not out off 61 balls, hitting nine 4s and one six.

Ranatunga's vicious hitting reduced the winning equation to just three runs required from the last over. It was achieved with a minimum of fuss when Ranatunga thrashed a leg-side boundary.   Sri Lanka's unlikely victory was only their third in World Cup competition.   The match set several new standards for the competition:

● Sri Lanka's total of 7/313 was the highest second innings score.

● Waller's 50 off just 32 balls was the quickest ever.

● Waller and Flower's partnership of 145 is a record for the fifth wicket.

PLAYER PROFILE: Arjuna Ranatunga

Rightly or otherwise, Sri Lankan cricketers have reputations for hefty stature and powerful hitting. It is a trail blazed by men like Duleep Mendis, a diminutive tea company director from Colombo who entertained the masses with some electrifying innings during the 1975 World Cup in England, when Sri Lanka took its first tentative steps on the stage that is international cricket.

Arjuna Ranatunga, the former captain and left-hand batsman from the tropical teardrop, is of the same ilk. Ranatunga, 28, had come to Australia on the two-Test match tour of 1989-90 as his country's leader, only to become embroiled in the intricate political web of Sri Lankan cricket. A disagreement with a team manager on a tour of New Zealand soon afterwards saw him stripped of the captaincy and replaced by Aravinda de Silva.

But his pre-eminence as a left-handed batsman remained undiminished by the time he arrived for the World Cup. In the first game against Zimbabwe at New Plymouth's tiny ground, Ranatunga plundered a match-winning 88 not out, including nine 4s and a 6, from only 61 balls faced.

Set a mammoth 313 to win, the Sri Lankans achieved their target in the final over when Ranatunga thrashed Malcolm Jarvis to the leg-side boundary for four. It was only Sri Lanka's third victory in a World Cup match, and a famous one at that.

Athletic builds, you see, are not an essential in cricket, not even in the helter-skelter of one-day internationals. Just ask Merv Hughes, for one.

Unstoppable:
Sri Lanka's Arjuna Ranatunga, a left-hander of immense power and timing, scored 88 not out of 62 balls to help his teammates overhaul Zimbabwe's tough total of 312.

23 February. Sri Lanka v Zimbabwe — New Plymouth.
Weather: fine

ZIMBABWE

	Runs	Balls	4s/6s
A FLOWER not out ...'.	115	152	8/1
W JAMES c Tillekeratne b Wickeramasinghe	17	21	3/0
A PYCROFT c Ramanayake b Gurusinha	5	22	0/0
D HOUGHTON c Tillekeratne b Gurusinha	10	19	1/0
K ARNOTT c Tillekeratne b Wickeramasinghe	52	56	4/1
A WALLER not out	83	45	9/3
Sundries (2b 6lb 13w 9nb)	30		
TOTAL for four wickets	312		

Fall: 30, 57, 82, 167.

	O	M	R	W	Eco	W	NB
C Ramanayake ..	10	0	59	0	5.9	3	1
K Wijegunawardena	7	0	54	0	7.7	3	6
A Wickeramasinghe .	10	1	50	2	5.0	1	2
A Gurusinha ...	10	0	72	2	7.2	6	-
R Kalpage	10	0	51	0	5.1	-	-
S Jayasuriya	3	0	18	0	6.0	-	-

Overs: 50.

SRI LANKA

	Runs	Balls	4s/6s
R MAHANAMA c Arnott b Brandes	59	89	4/0
A SAMARASEKERA c Duers b Traicos	75	61	11/1
A DE SILVA c Houghton b Brandes	14	28	1/0
A GURUSINHA run out	5	6	-
A RANATUNGA not out	88	61	9/1
S JAYASURIYA c Flower b Houghton	32	23	2/2
H TILLEKERATNE b Jarvis	18	12	1/1
R KALPAGE c Duers b Brandes	11	14	1/0
C RAMANAYAKE not out	1	1	-
Sundries (5lb 5w)	10		
TOTAL for seven wickets	313		

Fall: 128, 144, 155, 167, 212, 273, 309.

	O	M	R	W	Eco	W	NB
M Jarvis	9.2	0	61	1	6.6	1	-
E Brandes	10	0	70	3	7.0	-	-
K Duers	10	0	72	0	7.2	-	-
I Butchart	8	0	53	0	6.6	3	-
J Traicos	10	1	33	1	3.3	1	-
D Houghton	2	0	19	1	9.5	-	-

Overs: 49.2

Umpires: P Reporter, S Woodward
Crowd: 3500
Player-of-the-match: Andy Flower (Zimbabwe).
SRI LANKA WON BY THREE WICKETS.

Flying run out: In this run out of Inzamam-Ul-Haq, South Africa's Jonty Rhodes was not prepared to chance a throw from side on so he launched himself at the stumps with the ball clasped in his hands; he spreadeagled the stumps; and when the dust settled, Inzamam was judged to be short of his ground.

Low-key Logie: The West Indian middle-order star Gus Logie had an ordinary World Cup by his standards but battered the South Africans for 61 off just 69 balls in Christchurch.

On the move: Dashing Sri Lankan left-hander Arjuna Ranatunga scored 88 not out in his country's thrilling victory over Zimbabwe.

Outsiders no more

25 February: New Zealand **v** Sri Lanka in Hamilton

New Zealand sustained the impetus gained from its first-up surprise victory over Australia by comfortably beating Sri Lanka at Hamilton. Once again making best use of familiar conditions, the Kiwis, 50-1 with some bookmakers before the World Cup, shaped as a candidate for the semi-finals with a six-wicket victory.

The Sri Lankans, still buoyant from their astonishing victory over Zimbabwe two days before, could not repeat the batting heroics of New Plymouth, where they gathered 313 on the table-top ground.

After New Zealand captain Martin Crowe invited them to bat first, they tallied 9/206. The Kiwis, spearheaded by John Wright, Andrew Jones and Ken Rutherford, achieved the target with 10 balls to spare.

Wright and the bulky Rod Latham laid the foundation with an opening stand of 77, the veteran Wright allaying fears that he had seriously damaged his left shoulder in a fall during the Sri Lankan innings. He was in sparkling touch, gathering his half-century in just 61 balls and taking seven boundaries off the wayward bowlers.

Not even the failure of the first-match century-maker Crowe (5) perturbed the home side, as Wright (57), Jones (49) and Rutherford (65 not out) carried the Kiwis home. It was Rutherford's second successive half-century in quick time and secured him the award for player of the match when he struck the winning runs.

The flashpoint of the match came when Arjuna Ranatunga at slip spilled a straight-forward catch offered by the in-form Rutherford before he had scored. Reprieved, the 26-year-old promptly won the match for New Zealand, his 65 taking just 71 balls to compile.

Once again Sri Lanka's bowling attack was decimated by the absence of its No.1 paceman, the headband-adorned Rumesh Ratnayake, who was suffering from a dislocated shoulder. Immediately after the match the World Cup Committee agreed to a Sri Lankan request for a replacement.

Captain Aravinda De Silva admitted after the match that he was in 'a desperate plight', with Ratnayake missing and opening batsman Athula Samarasekera troubled by a hamstring injury.

In Ratnayake's absence off-spinner Ruwan Kalpage was the pick of the bowlers, completing 10 overs for only 33 runs – 10 of those in his final over – as well as claiming two wickets.

Sri Lanka's innings was highlighted by Roshan Mahanama's gutsy 81, but cut short by the unfortunate run out of its premier player, De Silva, when he was poised on 31. Having reached a handy 4/172 at 42 overs, the Sri Lankan could not capitalise on the work of Mahanama, and lost 6/34.

The Kiwis brought back fast bowler Danny Morrison, but once again it was the medium-pacers who pegged back the batsmen. Willie Watson collected 3/37 and Chris Harris 3/43, including the wickets of Ranatunga and Mahanama with consecutive balls. Harris also played a hand in a run-out.

Gavin Larson's innocuous seamers, a critical factor in the Australian game, also troubled the Sri Lankans, who could only eke out 29 runs from his bowling.

PLAYER PROFILE: Ken Rutherford

In most parts of the cricket world other than New Zealand, Ken Rutherford is still remembered more for his failings as a teenager on debut against the West Indies than for any positive results.

Tossed headlong into the face of a firing squad of West Indian quick bowlers at just 19, he was spectacularly unsuccessful against the Caribbean team at its famous best.

The pity is that many fail to acknowledge Rutherford's fight back from those traumatic days, carving a niche for himself in the middle-order of New Zealand's batting, in one-day cricket especially.

Certainly no opponent would have been under-estimating the ability of the Otago 26-year-old after his first two outings of the 1992 World Cup. Against Australia in Auckland, his 57 came at nearly a run per ball and was timed to perfection for New Zealand's cause. Two days later at Hamilton, he took the long handle to Sri Lanka's unimpressive attack with an unbeaten 65 from only 71 balls.

Seizing upon the good fortune of a dropped chance before he had troubled the scorers, Rutherford made the winning hit with 10 balls to spare and was adjudged to be player of the match.

Where Sri Lanka had failed to build on a platform established by its top order, Rutherford and company spirited New Zealand to the top of the World Cup table with some sensible batting.

Capable Kiwi:
After an unhappy start to his Test career courtesy of the West Indian quicks, Ken Rutherford re-established himself in the New Zealand top-order as brave and punishing batsman.

25 February. New Zealand v Sri Lanka — Hamilton.
Weather: Overcast, humid.

SRI LANKA

	Runs	Balls	4s/6s
R MAHANAMA c and b Harris	81	132	6/0
A SAMARASEKERA c Wright b Watson	9	20	1/0
A GURUSINHA c Smith b Harris	9	33	1/0
A DE SILVA run out	31	45	2/0
A RANATUNGA c Rutherford b Harris	20	25	2/0
S JAYASURIYA run out	5	7	-
H TILLEKERATNE c Crowe b Watson	8	19	-
R KALPAGE c Larsen b Watson	11	17	-
C RAMANAYAKE run out	2	1	-
D ANURASIRI not out	2	2	-
P WICKERAMASINGHE not out	3	4	-
Sundries (1b, 15lb, 4w, 5nb)	25		
TOTAL (for nine wickets)	206		

Fall: 18, 50, 120, 172, 172, 181, 195, 199, 202.

	O	M	R	W	Eco*	W	NB
D Morrison	8	0	36	0	4.5	1	2
W Watson	10	0	37	3	3.7	1	2
G Larsen	10	1	29	0	2.9	1	-
C Harris	10	0	43	3	4.3	1	-
R Latham	3	0	13	0	4.3	-	-
D Patel	9	0	32	0	3.5	-	-

Batting time: 223 minutes. **Overs:** 50.

NEW ZEALAND

	Runs	Balls	4s/6s
J WRIGHT c and b Kalpage	57	76	9/0
R LATHAM b Kalpage	20	41	3/0
A JONES c Jayasuriya b Gurusinha	49	77	4/0
M CROWE c Ramanayake b Wickeramasinghe	5	23	-
K RUTHERFORD not out	65	71	6/1
C HARRIS not out	5	5	-
Sundries (3lb, 3w, 3nb)	9		
TOTAL (for four wickets)	210		

Fall: 77, 91, 105, 186.

	O	M	R	W	Eco	W	NB
C Ramanayake	9.2	0	46	0	5.0	2	2
P Wickeramasinghe	8	1	40	1	5.0	1	-
D Anurasiri	10	1	27	0	2.7		
R Kalpage	10	0	33	2	3.3	-	-
A Gurusinha	4	0	19	1	4.7	-	-
A Ranatunga	4	0	22	0	5.5	-	-
S Jayasuriya	2	0	14	0	7.0	-	-
A De Silva	1	0	6	0	6.0	-	1

Overs: 48.2.
Umpires: D Shepherd, P Reporter.
Crowd: 8500.
Player of the match: Ken Rutherford (NZ).
NEW ZEALAND WON BY SIX WICKETS.

The dream return

26 February: Australia **v** *South Africa in Sydney*

In a scene reminiscent of the sub-continent, scalpers outside the Sydney Cricket Ground charged as much as Australian $50 for a ticket to South Africa's maiden World Cup match, such was the level of interest.

The SCG was full to overflowing to mark the return of the republic, after a 28-year absence, and Kepler Wessels, after six, to top-level competition on Australian soil.

The goodwill towards the South Africans from the Sydney crowd was almost palpable. Until, that is, it became apparent midway through the evening that they were hellbent on abusing Australia's hospitality.

Australia worked frantically to get South Africa a wildcard into the tournament, but it had reason to regret that eagerness by the time South Africa had wiped the floor with the defending title-holder.

The sense of excitement amid a typically jingoistic crowd soon turned to awe and bewilderment as world cricket's newest member cruised to victory with the efficiency of a team that had spent the previous 22 years on top of the world, not in exile.

Wessels completed the nine-wicket win at 9.38 pm when he guided Bruce Reid for a single to third man. By the time the South African players emerged from their dressing room 10 minutes later and did a victory quarter-lap to the Bill O'Reilly Stand to acknowledge their small but boisterous band of supporters, the SCG was otherwise deserted.

Back home in South Africa, where it was lunch time, the celebrations were just beginning.

In a poignant symbol of the new South Africa, the African National Congress 'shadow' Minister for Sport, Steve Tshwete, who was imprisoned on Robben Island for 15 years by the racist white regime, embraced Wessels, the archetypal Afrikaaner.

Like Tshwete, Wessels too once strayed from the path white South Africa intended for him, although in a vastly different sense: He became an Australian citizen and played Test cricket for Australia.

He returned in triumph as captain of a brave, new South Africa. He marshalled a supremely disciplined effort in the field and then top-scored for his side as it made the runs with 13 balls to spare.

The Australians, many of whom were Wessels' former teammates, played right into his hands. By scoring 9/170 from 49 overs after electing to bat first, Australia allowed Wessels to reply at his personally preferred pace.

The first ball of the match, bowled by Allan Donald to Geoff Marsh, was very nearly one of cricket's priceless moments. Marsh sparred outside off-stump, the ball deviated substantially and the South Africans danced for joy as wicket-keeper Dave Richardson accepted the catch.

But New Zealand umpire Brian Aldridge kept his arms steadfastly by his side. If nothing else, that gesture made it plain that the time for sentiment had past.

Donald beat Boon once and Marsh once more before that first over was complete, and made both batsmen jump. But, while the speed of his bowling was never in doubt, he paid a price in terms of accuracy: his first four overs conceded 20 runs, including five wides.

Meyrick Pringle exhibited a similar lack of control at the other end as the Australian openers took the score to 42 at more than four per over. Then Boon was run out in the first of a series of Australian mishaps.

Adrian Kuiper, a swashbuckling fellow asked to pitch in with his part-time medium pacers, played a jovial executioner, felling Australia's captain and vice-captain with successive blows in the 21st over of the match.

Kuiper produced a leg-cutter to remove Marsh to a catch by Richardson at the wicket, and then claimed Allan Border with his next ball, bowling him through the gate with an inswinger for a first-ball duck. Two wickets in two balls.

Much of the damage had, in fact, been done at the other end, where Snell had just completed a miserly seven-over spell that conceded only 10 runs and regained the early lost ground.

Just as he promised, Donald returned to put his venom to more effective use. His final six overs cost 14 runs and claimed the wickets of Tom Moody, Ian Healy and Peter Taylor to put an end to any suggestion of an Australian fightback.

Wessels was never known in Australia for his free scoring in limited-over cricket and Andrew Hudson, his opening partner, arrived in the country with the dubious record of having made a duck in his only previous one-day international, the historic return match before almost 100,000 people in Calcutta the previous November.

Yet with fewer than four runs required per over it was simply a matter of not letting the occasion get to them. That was never an issue with Wessels, who played with all his usual determination for 81 not out. His only reprieve came at 23 when David Boon, filling in as wicketkeeper for Ian Healy, who tore a hamstring running between wickets, missed a diving catch to his left. Hudson, with 28, and Kirsten, 49 not out, made up the balance.

The Australian bowlers never really had a chance, although the dreadful standard of Australia's fielding, once its greatest strength, was a sign of a serious malaise in the home camp.

PLAYER PROFILE: *Kepler Wessels*

Six years after leaving Australia under a cloud of suspicion, a stony-faced, unsmiling Kepler Wessels walked through Customs at Perth international airport on 7 February 1992 to embark on the latest leg of his extraordinary career.

He was clutching a book entitled *White Ninja*. The martial overtones of the title were appropriate, given his passion for boxing and belief in the virtues of mental strength and self-discipline.

No one doubted his inner strength, but the question remained: could this introverted, 34-year-old cricketing wanderer mould a serious World Cup contender out of a group of South Africans with little or, in some cases, no international experience?

The answer was yes, or at least it was at the Sydney Cricket Ground on 26 February when South Africa resumed sporting contact with Australia after a 22-year stand-off.

Wessels led a highly-drilled side in the field, rotated his bowlers cleverly and then top scored with 81 not out as South Africa made a startling World Cup debut, defeating the defending champion by nine wickets.

The innings was typically dogged Wessels, although he did abandon his inhibitions at the end, carting Bruce Reid for three glorious boundaries. So, too, was the response, with Wessels barely raising a smile at his after-match press conference, despite the euphoric scenes in the South African dressing room.

For the man who has given his loyalty to, variously, World Series Cricket, the Australian Test team, the Australian rebels, South Africa against the English rebels and, finally, the official South African side, cricket has never been a light-hearted business.

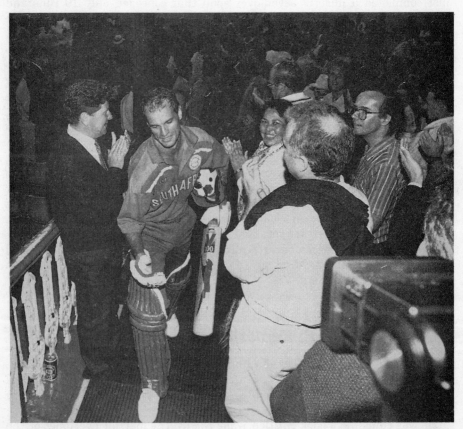

Emotional return: Former Australian opening batsman Kepler Wessels makes his way past supporters after scoring 81 not out in South Africa's historic victory over Australia, the early favourite to win the cup.

Historic toss: Allan Border tosses the coin before the start of the Australia-South Africa match at the Sydney Cricket Ground. Scalpers charged as much as $50 for a ticket.

26 February. Australia v South Africa — Sydney.
Weather: fine.

AUSTRALIA

	Runs	Balls	4s/6s
G MARSH c Richardson b Kuiper	25	72	1/0
D BOON run out	27	32	4/0
D JONES c Richardson b McMillan	24	51	1/0
A BORDER b Kuiper	0	1	-
T MOODY lbw b Donald	10	33	-
S WAUGH c Cronje b McMillan	27	51	1/0
I HEALY c McMillan b Donald	16	24	2/0
P TAYLOR b Donald	4	9	-
C McDERMOTT run out	6	12	-
M WHITNEY not out	9	15	1/0
B REID not out	5	10	-
Sundries (2lb 4nb 11w)	17		
TOTAL (for nine wickets)	170		

Fall: 42, 76, 76, 97, 108, 143, 146, 156, 161.

	O	M	R	W	Eco	W	NB
A Donald	10	0	34	3	3.4	5	-
M Pringle	10	0	52	0	5.2	1	2
R Snell	9	1	15	0	1.6	-	-
B McMillan	10	0	35	2	3.5	3	2
A Kuiper	5	0	15	2	3.0	1	-
H Cronje	5	1	17	0	3.4	1	-

Overs: 49.

SOUTH AFRICA

	Runs	Balls	4s/6s
K WESSELS not out	81	148	9/0
A HUDSON b Taylor	28	51	3/0
P KIRSTEN not out	49	90	1/0
Sundries (5lb 6w 2nb)	13		
TOTAL for one wicket for	171		

Fall: 74.

	O	M	R	W	Eco	W	NB
C McDermott ...	10	1	23	0	2.3	-	2
B Reid	8.5	0	41	0	4.8	4	-
M Whitney	6	0	26	0	4.3	-	-
S Waugh	4	1	16	0	4.0	1	-
P Taylor	10	1	32	1	3.2	1	-
A Border	4	0	13	0	3.25	-	-
T Moody	4	0	15	0	3.75	-	-

Overs: 46.5.

Umpires: B Aldridge, S Bucknor.

Crowd: 39,789

Player of the match: Kepler Wessels (S. Africa).

SOUTH AFRICA WON BY NINE WICKETS.

The new favourite

27 February: England v West Indies in Melbourne

Bookmakers in London had installed England as World Cup favourite – replacing the troubled Australians – by the time Graham Gooch's side strode on to the Melbourne Cricket Ground to meet the West Indies.

Many among the crowd of 18,521 would take some persuading that the widely-reported transformation of England's team was not a product of the English media's renowned imagination. After all, just 12 months earlier, Melbournians had seen an apparently spiritless bunch capitulate to Bruce Reid on its way to a 3-0 Ashes series defeat under the same captain.

But those Britons flying the Union Jack and the cross of St George on the first deck of the Great Southern Stand were not to be disappointed, as England justified the bookmakers' caution with an emphatic six-wicket triumph not long after the lights had warmed up.

As the last rites were delivered and Graeme Hick crafted one of his first innings of substance for his adopted country, the red, white and blue painted supporters repeatedly chanted 'Two-nil' in celebration of England's second straight victory.

Nobody who watched this performance could have doubted that Gooch had brought with him a well-drilled, flexible and almost mechanically efficient side in pursuit of England's first World Cup. Even more importantly, they were still riding on the momentum of a highly successful tour of New Zealand immediately before the tournament.

England's performance was so sharp as to ruin what had been forecast as a competitive match between last-start winners and cup contenders. After Gooch won the toss and opted to field first, his bowlers imposed such a straightjacket upon the West Indian strokeplayers that they collapsed in frustration for just 157.

In reply, half-centuries to Gooch and Hick saw England home with more than 10 overs to spare.

Gooch's decision to bowl first was based on an MCG match 12 months before in which the pitch provided some early life for the pace bowlers, and the equivalent of local knowledge proved to be decisive. The West Indians, who had found the wicket so much to their liking in the previous game that they had not lost a single wicket in compiling a target of 221, found themselves battling from the outset.

Derek Pringle and Chris Lewis were so miserly in their opening spells that Gooch was afforded the rare luxury of employing a bat-pad fielder for a period, Pringle managing three maidens in his first seven overs. Scarcely a single delivery drifted down the leg-side; indeed, only three wides and a no-ball were sent down for the innings.

Lewis landed two crucial blows when he removed Brian Lara (0), pushing tentatively at his second delivery to be caught behind, and Richie Richardson (5), desperately trying to withdraw his bat but edging a low catch to Ian Botham at slip. The West Indies never recovered.

Only the cheeky Keith Arthurton (54) and Desmond Haynes (38) bothered the scorers to any extent, Arthurton surviving chances at 13, with Botham spilling a sharp return catch, and at 45, when substitute fielder Gladstone Small messed up a skied drive to deep mid-off. The left-hander from the Leeward island of Nevis hoisted Phil Tufnell back over his head into the seats at the foot of the Members' Stand and reached his half-century by pulling Lewis over mid-wicket for another 6.

Haynes survived a shout for a catch at slip by Botham when he was only one – Botham apologised to the West Indian when he learned that replays showed that the ball had not carried – and was as diligent as ever in compiling 38 before he middled a pull from DeFreitas and was nicely caught at backward square by Neil Fairbrother.

Two run outs did not aid the West Indian cause, especially that of Gus Logie (20), who had swiped Botham over fine leg for 6 and promised a big innings before Fairbrother's direct hit sent him packing. Malcolm Marshall was stranded in mid-pitch after a mix-up with Arthurton.

Despite a brilliant spell by Winston Benjamin (2/22 from 10 overs), England was scarcely troubled, especially once Gooch and an oddly-restrained Botham added 50 for the first wicket.

Botham seemed to be taking too seriously this business of opening the batting; by the time he was beautifully caught by wicketkeeper David Williams for eight from 28 balls, Gooch had smote 35.

The captain was in ominously good nick, hitting 65 including seven boundaries before he was deceived by Carl Hooper and stumped by Williams. But even more encouraging for England was the effort of Hick, who accumulated 54 – just his second one-day international 50 – from 55 balls.

England, with its cluster of all-rounders and a pair of opening batsmen aged 36 and 38, had picked a specialist one-day side. And for the time, it looked the goods.

PLAYER PROFILE: Graham Gooch

Grown men have been known to shrivel up in corners at the thought of leading their countries at cricket, such is the pressure involved. No less a figure than Ian Botham, for one, went to jelly upon his elevation to England's leadership role in 1981, and had to be replaced almost as soon as he started.

But Graham Gooch, England's skipper for the 1992 World Cup, comes into another category. Taking the reins after England's 0-4 defeat at the hands of Allan Border's Australians in 1989, he master-minded an astonishing reversal of fortunes culminating in a captivating drawn series against the world champion West Indies at home in 1991.

Gooch, whose torture by Terry Alderman throughout that Ashes series raised doubts about his future, responded to the added responsibility by delving into a rich vein of form over two years. He averaged better than 100 in first-class cricket in the 1990 season, including one innings of 333 in a Test against India. Coming into the World Cup, he was averaging better than 70 in Tests since gaining the captaincy.

Yet for all that, the 38-year-old Essex captain had begun to talk of retirement from the game. Certainly he had no plans of returning to Australia after the World Cup. 'The next time I come here I expect it will be for Old England or something,' he said on the eve of England's match against the West Indies in Melbourne.

True to form, the captain stepped out the next day and top scored with 65 as England won comfortably.

Captain's knock: Graham Gooch cuts early in his innings against the West Indies. He was there for 101 balls and 65 runs.

Boundary bound: Promoted to open for the tournament, Ian Botham slashes a short ball for four in his short stay against the West Indies.

27 February. England v West Indies — Melbourne.
Weather: fine

WEST INDIES

	Runs	Balls	4s/6s
D HAYNES c Fairbrother b DeFreitas	38	68	5/0
B LARA c Stewart b Lewis	0	2	-
R RICHARDSON c Botham b Lewis	5	17	1/0
C HOOPER c Reeve b Botham	5	20	-
K ARTHURTON c Fairbrother b DeFreitas	54	101	2/2
G LOGIE run out	20	27	0/1
R HARPER c Hick b Reeve	3	14	-
M MARSHALL run out	3	8	-
D WILLIAMS c Pringle b DeFreitas	6	19	-
C AMBROSE c DeFreitas b Lewis	4	6	-
W BENJAMIN not out	11	16	1
Sundries (4lb 3w 1nb)	8		
TOTAL	157		

Fall: 0, 22, 36, 55, 91, 102, 116, 131, 145, 157.

	O	M	R	W	Eco	W	NB
D Pringle	7	3	16	0	2.2	-	-
C Lewis	8.2	1	30	3	3.6	-	1
P DeFreitas	9	2	34	3	3.7	2	-
I Botham	10	0	30	1	3.0	-	-
D Reeve	10	1	23	1	2.3	1	-
P Tufnell	5	0	20	0	4.0	-	-

Overs: 49.2.

ENGLAND

	Runs	Balls	4s/6s
G GOOCH st Williams b Hooper	65	101	7/0
I BOTHAM c Williams b Benjamin	8	28	1/0
R SMITH c Logie b Benjamin	8	28	-
G HICK c and b Harper	54	55	3/1
N FAIRBROTHER not out	13	28	1/0
A STEWART not out	0	1	-
Sundries (7lb 4w 1nb)	12		
TOTAL for four wickets for	160		

Fall: 50, 71, 126, 156.

	O	M	R	W	Eco	W	NB
C Ambrose	8	1	26	0	3.2	-	-
M Marshall	8	0	37	0	4.6	2	-
W Benjamin.....	9.5	2	22	2	2.3	2	1
C Hooper	10	1	38	1	3.8	-	-
R Harper	4	0	30	1	7.5	-	-

Overs: 39.5
Umpires: S Woodward, K Liebenberg
Crowd: 18,521
Player of the match: Chris Lewis (England)
ENGLAND WON BY SIX WICKETS.

Painful lesson for Zimbabwe

27 February: Pakistan **v** Zimbabwe in Hobart

The nuances of limited-over cricket are an acquired art. Much has changed from the early days of swipe and run. Each season sees the leading teams refining their game plan, tinkering with bowling line-ups and swapping batting roles.

England, Australia, the West Indies and Pakistan have been at it for 20 years. Spare a thought then for Zimbabwe whose exposure at international level has been, by any standards, minuscule.

In its first match of the competition it flogged Sri Lanka for more than 300 runs yet was too naive to protect such a total. And Sri Lanka is itself a minnow by any standard.

In its second match, against Pakistan at Hobart's Bellerive Oval, Zimbabwe's lack of sophistication was sadly exposed.

Pakistan made 4/254, thanks to the rare talent of Javed Miandad and the blossoming gifts of Aamir Sohail.

True, Sohail had handsome luck as he was dropped four times in his innings of 114 runs off 136 balls. The left-hander smacked twelve 4s in a telling partnership with Javed, who worked and thumped 89 runs off just 94 balls.

The pair were in tandem for 145 runs off 151 balls and toyed with Zimbabwe's bowlers who did not have the experience to handle such a confrontation.

Still, it was not an insurmountable challenge that faced the Zimbabwean batsmen if they adopted the same aggressive outlook of their first match. Their target was 5.08 an over, and the oval not that big that it did not reward the bold in full.

After 30 overs the score was a wretched 3/69 and Zimbabwe dead in the water. The pattern was set in the first 12 overs which hardly brought an attacking shot in front of the wicket.

The batsmen were immediately under extreme pressure from the masterful Wasim Akram who picked up his 150th wicket in international limited-over cricket.

Akram was forced to bear an enormous workload in the early part of the competition because the speedster, Waqar Younis, was injured (he was sent home to begin the long recuperation needed for stress fractures of the back), and his captain, Imran Khan, dared not bowl because of lingering shoulder soreness. But, as always, the big left-hander responded tellingly, and after he had bullied the early batsmen into submission, Imran used three spinners, Iqbal Sikander, Mushtaq Ahmed and Sohail, and the floating medium pace of Salim Malik to shut out Zimbabwe completely.

Zimbabwe's plan to be cautious early and emphatic later failed miserably as they obeyed the first part of their game plan slavishly and ignored totally the second.

Zimbabwe captain David Houghton was later at a loss to explain his batsmen's attitude. 'We've got to talk about that sort of thing in the dressing room. This is a huge step up for us. We went out trying to win the game, but for the first half of the overs we were just trying to survive.'

PLAYER PROFILE: *Javed Miandad*

Javed Miandad almost missed the 1992 World Cup, such was the pain he suffered from a recurring back injury during Pakistan's series against Sri Lanka in the lead-up. One of his nation's all-time great players, Javed was not among the first batch of Pakistanis to arrive in Australia under captain Imran Khan.

But upon arrival, he hit the tarmac with bat blazing. Unfazed by the shoulder injury to Imran which left him in charge of the side, Javed toyed with the West Indians in Melbourne and crushed the inexperienced Zimbabwe at Bellerive Oval in Hobart.

His 89 came from only 94 balls; his partnership with century-maker Aamir Sohail yielded 145 from 151 balls. Pakistan, desperately needing the victory, compiled a healthy 4/254 and duly cruised home with the two points.

At 34, Javed remains one of the world's premier exponents of one-day international cricket. His competitive urgency and his flair for the unorthodox make him a feared and respected opponent — even in Australia, where he invited trouble by tangling with a national deity, the great Dennis Lillee, during an ugly confrontation at Perth in 1981-82.

Many Australians blamed Javed for that incident, though Lillee plainly had a major part in it and was responsible for the most indictable action — that of delivering a kick in the direction of the Pakistani's leg.

But by 1992, much of this had been put in the past.

Pakistan's fighter:
Javed Miandad is one of the greatest one-day improvisers in the world and thrives in the heat of the battle.

27 February. Pakistan v Zimbabwe — Hobart.
Weather: fine.

PAKISTAN

	Runs	Balls	4s/6s
RAMEEZ RAJA c Flower b Jarvis	9	15	1/0
AAMIR SOHAIL c Pycroft b Butchart	114	136	12/0
INZAMAM UL-HAQ c Brandes b Butchart	14	43	-
JAVED MIANDAD lbw b Butchart	89	94	5/0
SALIM MALIK not out	14	12	-
WASIM AKRAM not out	1	1	-
Sundries (9lb 4nb)	13		
TOTAL wickets for	254		

Fall: 29, 63, 208, 253.

	O	M	R	W	Eco	W	NB
E Brandes	10	1	49	0	4.9	-	4
M Jarvis	10	1	52	1	5.2	-	-
A Shah	10	1	24	0	2.4	-	-
I Butchart	10	0	57	3	5.7	-	-
J Traicos	10	0	63	0	6.3	-	-

Overs: 50.

ZIMBABWE

	Runs	Balls	4s/6s
K ARNOTT c Akram b Sikander	7	63	-
A FLOWER c Ul-Haq b Akram	6	23	-
A PYCROFT b Akram	0	5	-
D HOUGHTON c Raja b Sohail	44	82	2
A SHAH b Sohail	33	59	2
A WALLER b Akram	44	36	3/0
I BUTCHART c Miandad b Javed	33	27	4/0
E BRANDES not out	2	3	-
J TRAICOS not out	8	7	1/0
Sundries (3b 15lb 6w)	24		
TOTAL for seven wickets for	201		

Fall: 14, 14, 33, 103, 108, 187, 190.

	O	M	R	W	Eco	W	NB
Wasim Akram ...	10	2	21	3	2.1	3	-
Aaqib Javed	10	1	49	1	4.9	1	-
Iqbal Sikander ..	10	1	35	1	3.5	1	-
Mushtaq Ahmed	10	1	34	0	3.4	-	-
Aamir Sohail	6	1	26	2	4.3	1	-
Salim Malik	4	0	18	0	4.5	1	-

Overs: 50
Umpires: S Randell, J Buultjens
Crowd: 1101
Player of the match: Aamir Sohail (Pakistan).

PAKISTAN WON BY 53 RUNS.

The first washout

28 February: India v Sri Lanka in Mackay

One of the great things about cricket's World Cup is that it takes the game to the rural areas. Wherever the Cup has been played – be it England (1975, 1979, 1983), India and Pakistan (1987), or Australia and New Zealand in 1992 – this has been the case.

Youngsters have the opportunity to get within touching distance of the men who come into their loungerooms through the medium of television each summer and shape their manner of play forever.

Sadly, though, a sojourn into Mackay, in tropical Queensland, was spoiled by rain when the match between Sri Lanka and India was abandoned.

Even with the weather threatening, a chirpy crowd of 3000 had moved into Harrup Park for the clash of teams from a world away. But by the end of the day they had seen only two balls of cricket, bowled by the Sri Lankan new-ball bowler Champaka Ramanayake to Indian opener Krishnamachari Srikkanth, and one run scored.

No sooner had these scarcely momentous events occurred than the rain – the first in Mackay for more than a month – intervened again in buckets. Umpires David Shepherd and Ian Robinson delivered the disappointing news that the match – already reduced to a 20-overs-a-side slog – would be abandoned.

There are few more forlorn sights in cricket than an unpopulated oval with the covers on the pitch. Pity the Mackay Cricket Club and local authorities, who had parted with hard-earned cash to install a new, temporary grandstand and perimeter fence for the occasion.

And pity the teams, who escaped with a point each when in truth they could have done with two. The Indians, especially, had previously lost to England and were cast into a desperate plight by this result.

PLAYER PROFILE: Kapil Dev

If it is possible to telegraph future tactics in the space of a game lasting a mere two deliveries, then India did so in the abandoned match against Sri Lanka at Mackay when it sent Kapil Dev out to open the batting.

Aside from being one of the greatest fast bowlers in the game's history, the former Indian captain is among the most powerful hitters. In 1983 at Tunbridge Wells in England, he played one of the most memorable single innings in cricket, a blistering, unbeaten 175 against Zimbabwe when India had slumped to four-for-not-many against cricket's minnows.

India, riding on the back of Kapil's all round feats and captaincy, went on to shock the West Indies in the final at Lord's and every member of that team instantly grabbed a place in the history books.

At Lord's in 1990, with India requiring 24 to save the follow-on and with a fully fledged No. 11 batsman in Narendra Hirwani at the other end, Kapil promptly slapped the English off-spinner Eddie Hemmings for four sixes in successive balls back down the ground. Such is his gift for spontaneous, match-turning efforts.

But what is most remarkable about Kapil Dev is his fast-medium bowling, especially given that he comes from a part of the world where fast bowlers are cannon fodder for good batsmen.

During the Perth Test against Australia this summer, he became only the second man, behind Sir Richard Hadlee, to pass 400 wickets in Test matches. Add 200-plus wickets in one-day international cricket, and Kapil emerges as a figure of true significance.

Power player: Kapil Dev proves to be one of the most ferocious hitters in the cup.

28 February. Sri Lanka v India — Mackay
Weather: Rain.

INDIA

	Runs	Balls	4s/6s
K SRIKKANTH not out	1	2	1/0-
K DEV not out	0	-	-
Sundries	0		
TOTAL for no wicket	1		

	O	M	R	W	Eco	W	NB
C Ramanayake	0.2	0	1	0	-	-	-

Overs: 0.2

Umpires: D Shepherd, I Robinson
Crowd: Approx 2500
Player of the match: Not awarded

NO RESULT

A frolic for the West Indies

29 February: West Indies **v** Zimbabwe in Brisbane

At stumps on the first day of the match between the West Indies and Zimbabwe at the Gabba, Zimbabwe was 7/189 in reply to the West Indies' 8/264.

Or at least that's the way Zimbabwe played it. The West Indies actually won by 75 runs, which was about as predictable as beer and singlets in Brisbane.

Rather than making what would certainly have been a suicidal dash for the runs, Zimbabwe was more intent on putting up a respectable show. Given the mis-match in talent and experience, they were perfectly reasonable tactics.

As David Houghton pointed out after the match, Zimbabwe's main problem is that its only one-day international experience comes around once every four years at the World Cup. The first part of the World Cup is part of a mountainous learning curve, and it is only later in the tournament that it can seriously contemplate trying to win a game or two.

The moment that best summed up the West Indies' approach to the match was when Richie Richardson caught Alistair Campbell right-handed in the covers to protect the fractured finger on his left hand. They were never required to extend themselves.

Curtly Ambrose and Desmond Haynes were rested, while Malcolm Marshall played as though his mind was more in tune with a distant beach somewhere in Barbados than the not-quite tense struggle being acted out in front of him at the Brisbane Cricket Ground.

Even the nature of the West Indies' batting was predictable. Brian Lara (72), Richie Richardson (56) and Carl Hooper (63) all produced gems, although they were spoilt by the lack of pressure and not one went on to really pummel the bowling on Australia's smallest Test ground.

Lara, with his extravagant backlift and natural flair, was the eye-catcher, scoring at better than a run a ball and producing some exquisite drives through the covers.

Keith Arthurton, the other dashing left-hander in the West Indian squad, contributed a rapid 26 towards the end, including two 6s and two 4s, although the Zimbabwean bowlers did well to restrict the West Indies to a sub-300 total given the launching pad they had built for themselves.

Most of the credit for that must go to medium pacer Ali Shah, the only bowler to concede fewer than 40, and the quicker Eddo Brandes, who was also comparatively cheap, conceding 45 runs, and took three wickets along the way.

Shah might have graduated from the Gavin Larsen school of innocuous wobblers, but showed that those tactics can occasionally be successful on Australian as well as New Zealand soil. He also showed his all-round abilities by top scoring with an unbeaten 60, making him the Zimbabwe success story for the match.

Shah and Houghton put on 69 for the fifth wicket, although at no stage did they make a genuine attempt to overhaul the West Indies' total. Zimbabwe's fate did not look promising from the moment Patrick Patterson bowled opener Andy Flower.

Winston Benjamin and Anderson Cummins then struck a pair of telling blows in the space of two overs. Benjamin hit Andy Pycroft under the left eye with a rising ball, forcing the No. 3 to receive treatment, and prompting his dismissal, caught behind, from the very next delivery.

In the next over, a lifter from Cummins hit opener Kevin Arnott on the middle finger of the right hand. Arnott retired hurt immediately with blood dripping from the wound and x-rays later revealed two cracks in the finger.

Richardson expressed concern at the lack of killer instinct shown by his side. 'We started relaxing a little bit, which I didn't approve of,' he said. 'I believe in beating somebody and grinding them into the ground.'

PLAYER PROFILE: *Winston Benjamin*

Winston Benjamin's presence in the West Indian squad for the World Cup was more than a mere matter of selection. It was a matter of life and death.

In the 1990-91 Red Stripe Cup series in the Caribbean, Benjamin was shot in the face while he and several Leeward Island teammates were horsing around with a gun. The bullet passed through his cheek and the wound was inconsequential, but it was only centimetres away from being far more serious.

Benjamin has always had a perilous existence in the West Indies squad, largely as a result of the over supply of fast bowlers from that part of the world. A magnificent athlete who bowls straight and fast, he would probably have been an automatic selection in all the other eight teams, even Pakistan after the loss of Waqar Younis.

Fellow Antiguan Richie Richardson recognised those talents in preparation for the World Cup and decided to give another chance to the man whose career began in 1986, but had spluttered along in fits and starts ever since.

Benjamin responded with some superb spells early in the tournament, his second World Cup, with Zimbabwe finding his line and pace a particular handful at the Gabba. He took three wickets and conceded only 27 from his 10 overs and struck Andy Pycroft a blow under the left eye that unsettled him sufficiently to prompt his wicket, caught behind by David Williams, to the next ball.

He could even afford the rare luxury of a few deliberate bumpers, conceding a no-ball each time, to make sure the Zimbabweans remained on the back foot, such was the dominance of the West Indies attack.

Happy return: Winston Benjamin, recalled to the West Indies squad to add experience, is congratulated by teammates after claiming another victim.

29 February. West Indies v Zimbabwe — Brisbane.
Weather: fine.

WEST INDIES

	Runs	Balls	4s/6s
P SIMMONS b Brandes	21	45	3/0
B LARA c Houghton b Shah	72	71	12/0
R RICHARDSON c Brandes b Jarvis	56	76	2/2
C HOOPER c Pycroft b Traicos	63	67	5/1
K ARTHURTON b Duers	26	18	2/2
G LOGIE run out	5	6	-
M MARSHALL c Houghton b Brandes	2	10	-
D WILLIAMS not out	8	6	1/0
W BENJAMIN b Brandes	1	4	-
Sundries (1b 6lb 1nb 2w)	10		
TOTAL eight wickets	264		

Fall: 78, 103, 220, 221, 239, 254, 255, 264.

	O	M	R	W	Eco	W	NB
E Brandes	10	1	45	3	4.5	2	1
M Jarvis	10	1	71	1	7.1	-	-
K Duers	10	0	52	1	5.2	-	-
A Shah	10	2	39	1	3.9	-	-
J Traicos	10	0	50	1	5.0	-	-

Overs: 50.

ZIMBABWE

	Runs	Balls	4s/6s
K ARNOTT retired hurt	16	36	1/0
A FLOWER b Patterson	6	20	-
A PYCROFT c Williams b Benjamin	10	24	-
D HOUGHTON c Patterson b Hooper	55	88	3/0
A WALLER c Simmons b Benjamin	0	9	-
A CAMPBELL c Richardson b Hooper	1	18	-
A SHAH not out	60	87	4/0
E BRANDES c and b Benjamin	6	9	-
J TRAICOS run out	8	19	-
M JARVIS not out	5	4	1/0
Sundries (9lb 8nb 5w)	22		
TOTAL for seven wickets	189		

Fall: 24, 43, 48, 63, 132, 161, 181.

	O	M	R	W	Eco	W	NB
P Patterson	10	0	25	1	2.5	1	-
M Marshall	6	0	23	0	3.8	-	2
W Benjamin.....	10	2	27	3	2.7	3	3
A Cummins	10	0	33	0	3.3	1	3
C Hooper	10	0	47	2	4.7	-	-
K Arthurton	4	0	25	0	6.3	-	-

Overs: 50
Umpires: K Liebenberg, S Woodward.
Crowd: 2190
Player of the match: Brian Lara (West Indies).
WEST INDIES WON BY 75 RUNS.

Great match, Greatbatch

29 February: New Zealand v South Africa in Auckland

A drug took hold of Mark Greatbatch at Eden Park, the same substance that has powered the whole New Zealand team on its overnight metamorphosis from wretches to riches in the World Cup, and officials are as powerless to act against it as the Kiwis' opponents. It is called adrenalin.

Batting as substitute for the injured John Wright, Greatbatch played an astounding innings of 68 from 60 balls (nine 4s, three 6s).

Greatbatch crowned his glory by belting Adrian Kuiper on to the roof of the North Stand. His strike rate was almost 107; his heart rate 'about 220', by his own estimation.

Greatbatch and Rod Latham, whose 60 (69 balls, seven 4s), was demure by comparison, shared an opening partnership of 114 in 18 overs to make a formality of New Zealand's quest for South Africa's too-modest 7/190. New Zealand duly won by seven wickets with 15.3 overs in hand, an inhospitable welcome for the first South African team here since 1964.

Greatbatch's previous five innings for New Zealand this summer had yielded 30 runs, New Zealand had suffered series defeats by England in Tests (2-0) and one-day matches (3-0) and the country was in despair.

But this victory was their third of the World Cup and thoughts of a semi-final berth – their first since 1979 – were not inappropriate.

New Zealand's tactics have been so unorthodox and successful that they may pass into the game's manuals as 'Crowe Theory'. Given an Eden Park pitch the South Africans considered to be no better than 'rolled mud', Crowe again opened with off-spinner Dipak Patel and otherwise attacked almost exclusively with slow-medium bowlers.

Willie Watson bowled the first over of the innings without a slip. Chris Cairns, the only fast-medium in the side, was the sixth and last bowler used, and the most expensive.

But theory is bunk unless it is expertly applied. Watson and Patel both bowled with discipline, withholding pace, mindful always of their fields and conceding not a single wide and only one no-ball. South Africa took 15 balls to make a run, 13 overs to hit a 4, lost two early wickets and never caught up, despite Peter Kirsten's industrious 90 and some lusty late hitting from Brian McMillan and Richard Snell.

The South African pacemen, in contrast, were astray in their line – McMillan bowled three wides in his first over – and seemed to come on to the bats of Greatbatch and Latham at an ideal pace for hitting. After 15 overs, the comparison read: South Africa 2/29, NZ 0/103. Thereby hangs the tale.

New Zealand is enjoying the luck that invariably accompanies boldness. Kuiper was run out in farcical circumstances. Kuiper gloved a hook at Cairns to wicketkeeper Ian Smith and made for the dressing room, not realising that square-leg umpire Piloo Reporter had called an over-the-shoulder no-ball. Cairns' hysterical shout to Smith alerted Kuiper, by now at the non-striker's end, and he tried in vain to scramble back to his crease.

The farce was that had he continued to walk, he would have been recalled, for you can be run out only while attempting a run, not because of a misapprehension.

Greatbatch and Latham hit the ball often just beyond the outstretched fingers of the South African fieldsmen, and Latham gained five runs from two separate overthrows.

Crowe's tactical pioneering is not confined to the field. With New Zealand comfortably in charge, he sent in wicketkeeper-slogger Smith at No. 4 to see what he could do about inflating the nett run-rate, cricket's equivalent of football's percentage column. Smith obliged by hitting his first three balls for 4s, and then charging probably his first-ever delivery from Allan Donald and clubbing it over mid-off for another boundary. White Lightning looked just white.

The Kiwis have been dubbed 'Young Guns' locally, which has become such a catchphrase in New Zealand that it is now written with proper noun capitals. It contrasts smugly with the popular image in New Zealand of an Australian team that is too set in its one-day ways, too predictable and too old to change.

New Zealanders display a curious ambivalence about Australia, acutely conscious at all times of its politics and culture, appreciative of the regional companionship and yet fiercely antagonistic when it comes to sport. The NZTV man was positively gloating when he noted: 'They said that one of the host nations would give this World Cup a shake and they were right,' he chortled. 'They just got the wrong team.'

PLAYER PROFILE: *Mark Greatbatch*

At the player-of-the-match press conference, Mark Greatbatch gazed at the assembled microphones and sighed: 'Haven't seen these for a while.'

Greatbatch had endured the most wretched summer imaginable, with just 30 runs from five previous innings for his country (two Test and three in one-day internationals). As he said himself, his last significant score was 'a few haircuts ago'.

But nor had Eden Park seen for a while anything like Greatbatch's great bash that day. Called into the New Zealand XI to replace injured opener, John Wright, Greatbatch assailed the South African attack to make 68 from nearly 60 balls, with nine 4s and three 6s, the last landing on the roof of a grandstand. Those three blows alone brought him as many runs as in his three previous one-day internationals that summer.

Greatbatch said he had not set out with the idea of batting this way, but had contrived to 'blank' from his mind the ghost of recent failures and just played shots as they occurred to him. His adrenalin, his stroke play and the crowd's din rose together in a crescendo until the whole of Eden Park was shrieking, Greatbatch included. Later, he admitted that it was all a blur in his mind.

His captain and friend, Martin Crowe, called it 'instinctive', 'unconscious' and 'fantastic', and compared it to similar runaway innings he had seen played by

Viv Richards and Ian Botham. South African captain, Kepler Wessels, said: 'When someone's batting like that in the first 10 overs, there's very, very little you can do."

Greatbatch even described the pitch, which everyone thought was tortoise-slow, as a 'belter', probably an indication that the fast men of the South African attack came on to him at an ideal hitting pace on this pitch.

To the end of the press conference, Greatbatch strove to maintain the I'm-just-happy-to-help-a-game-theme, but his eyes, still blazing, told another story.

Rare shot: Mark Greatbatch plays a defensive shot, something he seldom attempted when giving New Zealand its fast and furious starts.

**29 February. New Zealand v South Africa — Auckland.
Weather: fine.**

SOUTH AFRICA

	Runs	Balls	4s/6s
K WESSELS c Smith b Watson	3	18	-
A HUDSON b Patel	1	16	-
P KIRSTEN c Cairns b Watson	90	129	10/0
H CRONJE c Smith b Harris	7	22	-
D RICHARDSON c Larsen b Cairns	28	53	1/0
A KUIPER run out	2	2	-
J RHODES c Crowe b Cairns	6	15	-
B McMILLAN not out	33	40	1/0
R SNELL not out	11	8	1/0
Sundries (8lb 1nb)	9		
TOTAL for seven wickets	190		

Fall: 8, 10, 29, 108, 111, 121, 162

	O	M	R	W	Eco	W	NB
W Watson	10	2	30	2	3.0	-	-
D Patel	10	1	28	1	2.8	-	-
G Larsen	10	1	29	0	2.9	-	-
C Harris	10	2	33	1	3.3	-	-
R Latham	2	0	19	0	9.5	-	-
C Cairns	8	0	43	2	5.3	0	1

Overs: 50.

NEW ZEALAND

	Runs	Balls	4s/6s
M GREATBATCH b Kirsten	68	60	9/3
R LATHAM c Wessels b Snell	60	69	7/0
A JONES not out	34	63	4/0
I SMITH c Kirsten b Donald	19	8	4/0
M CROWE not out	3	9	-
Sundries (1b 5w 1nb)	7		
TOTAL for three wickets	191		

Fall: 114, 155, 179.

	O	M	R	W	Eco	W	NB
A Donald	10	0	38	1	3.8	1	1
B McMillan	5	1	23	0	4.6	3	-
R Snell	7	0	56	1	8.0	-	-
T Bosch	2.3	0	19	0	8.2	-	-
H Cronje	2	0	14	0	7.0	1	-
A Kuiper	1	0	18	0	18.0	-	-
P Kirsten	7	1	22	1	3.1	-	-

Overs: 34.3.
Umpires: K Hayat, P Reporter.
Crowd: Approx 32,000.
Player of the match: Mark Greatbatch (NZ).

NEW ZEALAND WON BY 7 WICKETS

Last-gasp victory

1 March: Australia **v** *India in Brisbane*

Australia conjured its first points in the 1992 World Cup in circumstances so bizarre they bordered on the unnatural.

One-day cricket prides itself on condensing the action for an instant society, but it took that quality to new extremes at the Gabba as Australia scrambled to a fortuitous, not to mention fortunate, victory over India.

There was more drama in the final delivery than some one-day internationals produce over 100 overs, or Test matches over five days for that matter.

India needed four runs, Australia one wicket. The bowler was Tom Moody, the result of what Allan Border conceded was a 'monumental cock-up' in his planning, the batsman was India's No. 9, Javagal Srinath.

Srinath swiped the ball in the direction of wide mid-on and Steve Waugh set off in pursuit from long-on. Border's first reaction was that the ball was going for 6. Moody suspected, correctly, that Srinath had not quite got on to it and waited for Waugh, one of Australia's finest, to take the catch.

Waugh made the ground easily, but dropped the catch. He did not drop his bundle, recovering to hurl the ball in from the deep as Srinath and Venkatapathy Raju set off madly for a third run, which would have made it a tie. The throw beat Raju home by a fraction. Australia by one run.

Just to add a final touch of unreality, the wicketkeeper, who moved so athletically to break the stumps in the final act of the match, was David Boon. No one would have been too surprised if it had turned out to be Father Christmas, such was the nature of the game.

No matter how they did it, the Australians had finally snatched a victory after two straight losses. India, which was also desperate for its first win, could only ponder its rotten luck.

For the second time in three days, Queensland's unsettled tropical weather had harmed India's prospects. The washout in Mackay deprived it of an opportunity to achieve full points against Sri Lanka and now, chasing Australia's 9/237, a brief rain interruption tilted the equation back in Australia's favour.

Three overs were lost but, because Australia's 'best' 47 overs were taken into account under World Cup rules, the target was reduced by only two runs. It was hardly equitable, but India chased bravely to the end.

Australia's innings revolved around one man, Dean Jones, with a polished 90. Mohammad Azharuddin provided a counter balance for India with a savage 93, smashing the damp white ball across the sluggish outfield for 10 boundaries, although his innings threatened much more.

So long as Azharuddin was at the crease India had a strong chance. In the end, the teams were separated by a touch of class from Allan Border, who pounced at mid-wicket and threw down the stumps from about 25 metres to remove his Indian counterpart.

It was one of four Indian run outs, including two in the eventful final over. Sanjay Manjrekar finally showed Australian crowds what he is capable of in one-day cricket with a quickfire 47, but he committed suicide by chancing Craig McDermott's arm.

Again it was Boon, standing in for injured wicketkeeper Ian Healy, who broke the stumps. Nicknamed 'Rod' for the day because of his resemblance to Rod Marsh, Boon did an admirable job behind the stumps. He was so proud of his work that, when New Zealand umpire Brian Aldridge erroneously called a bye, Boon gave him such a glare that Aldridge removed the blot from the scorebook after confirming with Kapil Dev that the ball had struck his pad.

Border meant to save Craig McDermott for the last over, but realised too late that his best bowler would not be allowed to bowl his full quota because of the reduction in the overs.

So it was left to the mild-mannered Moody to enter personally uncharted territory and ensure that India did not make the 13 runs needed. It looked as though Border's blunder would cost Australia dearly when Kiran More dispatched the first two balls, inviting full tosses on leg stump, behind square leg for 4.

More stepped across his stumps and tried the shot a third time, but he had stretched his luck too far and was bowled. Manoj Prabhakar rushed a single from the fourth ball and was run out from the fifth, again by Border, setting up the dramatic final ball.

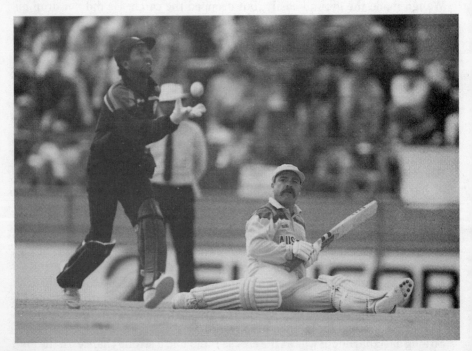

Down but not out: David Boon's technique leaves something to be desired but he remains not out after Kiran More gloves the ball which had struck the gritty Australian on the body.

PLAYER PROFILE: *Dean Jones*

Australia's World Cup defence was launched belatedly at the Gabba with one imperious swipe off Kapil Dev that sent the ball smashing into the leg-side boundary.

With that stroke, Dean Jones started the process of purging Australia of the defensive outlook that sunk its first two games without trace.

Jones's second scoring shot was a 6 over long-on that cleared the greyhound track that surrounds the Gabba. Ten runs from two hits. This was not so much the start of an innings as a statement of policy.

He reverted to type soon afterwards. Big hitting is only part of his game. Cheeky singles are his staple and, of his 90, exactly half were singles, including 22 in a row at one stage. He was back to his hustling best, producing his highest one-day score since smashing 145 against England on the same ground the previous summer.

Jones likes to control a match like a conductor controls an orchestra, and he had the Australian 12th men (Bruce Reid and Mark Waugh had to share the job, it was too much for one man) under as much pressure at the Indian fieldsmen as he called repeatedly for water and changes of gloves and headgear.

At one stage he reminded umpire Brian Aldridge to signal a no-ball after it slipped the New Zealander's mind. It would not have surprised if he offered Kapil Dev advice about his outswinger after hitting him for three 4s in one over.

Not a cricket follower in the world would have been surprised at the identity of the man who finally injected some attacking spirit into the Australian cause. Jones has a habit of shunning convention and doing things his own way. He is, after all, the author of that modestly titled treatise on the limited-over game, *One-day Magic*.

Fightback: Dean Jones signals the decision by struggling Australia to be bold from the start against India. His first two scoring shots were a four and a six.

1 March. Australia v India — Brisbane.
Weather: Warm, showers.

AUSTRALIA

	Runs	Balls	4s/6s
M TAYLOR c More b Dev	13	22	-
G MARSH b Dev	8	29	1/0
D BOON c Shastri b Raju	43	61	4/0
D JONES c and b Prabhakar	90	109	6/2
S WAUGH b Srinath	29	48	1/0
T MOODY b Prabhakar	25	23	3/0
A BORDER c Jadeja b Dev	10	10	-
C MCDERMOTT c Jadeja b Prabhakar	2	5	-
P TAYLOR run out	1	1	-
M HUGHES not out	0	4	-
Sundries (7lb 4nb 5w)	16		
TOTAL for nine wickets for	237		

Fall: 18, 31, 102, 156, 198, 230, 235, 236, 237

	O	M	R	W	Eco	W	NB
Kapil Dev	10	2	41	3	4.1	1	3
M Prabhakar	10	0	41	3	4.1	2	1
J Srinath	8	0	48	1	6.0	1	-
S Tendulkar	5	0	29	0	5.8	1	-
V Raju	10	0	37	1	3.7	-	-
A Jadeja	7	0	34	0	4.8	-	-

Overs: 50.

INDIA

	Runs	Balls	4s/6s
R SHASTRI c S Waugh b Moody	25	70	1/0
K SRIKKANTH b McDermott	0	11	-
M AZHARUDDIN run out	93	103	10/0
S TENDULKAR c S Waugh b Moody	11	19	1/0
K DEV lbw b S Waugh	21	21	3/0
S MANJREKAR run out	47	42	3/1
A JADEJA b Hughes	1	4	-
K MORE b Moody	14	8	2/0
J SRINATH not out	8	8	-
M PRABHAKAR run out	1	1	-
V RAJU run out	0	0	-
Sundries (8lb 5w)	13		
TOTAL	234		

Fall: 6, 53, 86, 128, 195, 199, 216, 231, 232, 234.

	O	M	R	W	Eco	W	NB
C McDermott	9	1	35	1	3.8	1	-
M Whitney	10	2	36	0	3.6	3	-
M Hughes	9	1	49	1	5.4	-	-
T Moody	9	0	56	3	6.2	-	-
S Waugh	10	0	50	1	50	1	-

Overs: 47
Umpires: B Aldridge, I Robinson.
Crowd: Crowd: 11,751.
Player of the match: Dean Jones (Australia).

AUSTRALIA WON BY ONE RUN

Rain thwarts England

1 March: England v Pakistan in Adelaide

'God Save The Queen' came blaring over the public address system at Adelaide Oval before play in the match between England and Pakistan, and, for a moment, one suspected this was some sort of South Australian apology for republican remarks uttered by Prime Minister Paul Keating, words that had sparked a storm in London.

But then the Pakistan anthem was played as well, and it emerged that this was just a little local ceremony to mark an important World Cup game – not a political broadcast.

Sadly it proved to be among the day's best entertainment, as the first rain in Adelaide for more than a month washed England's hopes of an early qualification for the semi-finals down the River Torrens. Having skittled Pakistan for its lowest score in a one-day international – a measly 74 on a seaming wicket – England's players were driven to distraction as rain reduced their reply to only eight overs in two separate attempts.

England had reached 1/24 when umpires Peter McConnell and Steve Bucknor abandoned the match at 5.23 pm, both sides departing with a single point and England feeling more than a trifle aggrieved.

Rain had been scarce in Adelaide over previous months but it had managed to spoil one other international sporting event, washing out the Australian Formula One Grand Prix in November. Locals who were forced to dig out brollies on the eve of this World Cup match reported that they could not recall any rain in the intervening period of nearly three months.

But rain it did, so much so that Adelaide Oval curator Les Burdett had the covers on the wicket throughout the day before the match and was denied the normal preparation time. If the weather came from Manchester in December, this pitch emanated from Headingley in April – a rarity for Adelaide, a minefield that gave even the most docile of England's medium-pacers ample lateral movement from the seam. With cloud hovering overhead as well to assist with swing, the conditions could scarcely have been more friendly to bowlers.

An hour after Gooch had won the toss and surprised nobody by inserting the Pakistanis, England had them reeling at 4/20. After a brief flurry by Salim Malik (17) it became 7/42, and Pakistan threatened to remove the World Cup record score of 45 by Canada in 1979, back in the days when non-Test nations competed.

Sensible batting by tail-enders Mushtaq Ahmed (17) and Wasim Haider (13) carried Pakistan to 74, replacing the 85 it scored against England at Old Trafford in 1978 as its lowest completed total in a one-day international.

Aside from Phil DeFreitas's seven wides, England's bowling and fielding was razor sharp again. Derek Pringle (3/8) and Ian Botham were the pick of the bunch, the latter proving all but unplayable in the conditions and conceding only 12 runs in 10 overs, as well as gathering the crucial wicket of Malik.

Pakistan was so quickly dispatched that England was batting before the lunch break, having time to gather 17 for the loss of Gooch's wicket, dubiously adjudged caught behind from Wasim Akram's bowling.

Then the rain came. By the time the umpires walked out for the recommencement of play at 5pm, the English supporters in the Sir Donald Bradman Stand had occupied themselves with several renditions of 'You'll Never Walk Alone', but hardly anyone else had bothered staying. And in any case, it rained again before Messrs McConnell and Bucknor had taken half a dozen steps on to the sodden ground, and they traipsed off.

Under Australia's unique rules for rain-reduced games, the target had been set at a further 47 runs from the 10 remaining overs when play finally resumed at 5.12 pm. Robin Smith and Botham managed seven more runs from the two overs bowled before the heavens opened again, and the umpires gave up in despair and drew stumps.

Gooch owned up to a belief that the regulations were 'strange', but added that the weather had made it irrelevant anyway. Cricket manager Micky Stewart also queried the validity of the regulations, which were introduced after a farcical one-day final between Australia and the West Indies at Sydney in 1988-89.

Under the previous system, and the English model, the average run-rate would have been applied to the team batting second. As such, England would only have been required to accumulate 24 runs in 16 overs if the same situation presented itself, plainly unfair. This illustrated that there appears to be no perfect system for rain-affected matches, a point echoed by Stewart.

Javed, who once again stood in as captain for the injured Imran Khan, lamented the absence of the usual Adelaide batting pitch. 'I don't think this was a wicket for one-day cricket,' he said. 'You want a wicket where you can score 230 or 240, not 60 or 70. This wicket was flying everywhere.'

PLAYER PROFILE: *Alec Stewart*

Alec Stewart is one of those cricketers who is too easily dismissed because he is low on style. He does not have the look of a top-class cricketer, but underestimate him at your peril.

The scepticism with which sections of the English public and press treat their nation's wicketkeeper-batsman is out of kilter with his productivity. When Stewart first broke into the English team, there were muffled cries about nepotism (his father, Micky, has been cricket manager since 1986), but he has risen above all that.

By the time Stewart arrived for England's World Cup campaign in 1992, he was entrenched in the side as No. 1 gloveman despite the presence of the brilliant, idiosyncratic Jack Russell at home, and he was a team leader. With Graham Gooch vacillating about his future, it was widely felt that Stewart would become captain of England for the tour of India later in the year.

Stewart's enthusiasm for the game knows no bounds. In the rain-marred game against Pakistan at Adelaide Oval, he clutched three superb catches, one coming off the rebound from Graeme Hick at slip. Then when the rain had stopped and a chance of a resumption emerged, he was out on the ground helping the ground staff remove the covers to speed up the process.

Sadly for England, which had bowled out Pakistan for just 74, the showers persisted and the game was declared a no-result.

Wicked keeper: England wicketkeeper Alec Stewart gave his bowlers marvellous support when they routed Pakistan on a seaming pitch in Adelaide. Ian Botham provides the back-up as Stewart takes a splendid diving catch off Phil De Freitas.

1 March. England v Pakistan — Adelaide.
Weather: humid, showery.

PAKISTAN

	Runs	Balls	4s/6s
RAMEEZ RAJA c Reeve b DeFreitas	1	10	-
AAMIR SOHAIL c and b Pringle	9	39	-
INZAMAM UL-HAQ c Stewart b DeFreitas	0	1	-
JAVED MIANDAD b Pringle	3	22	-
SALIM MALIK c Reeve b Botham	17	20	3/0
IJAZ AHMED c Stewart b Small	0	15	-
WASIM AKRAM b Botham	1	13	-
MOIN KHAN c Hick b Small	2	14	-
WASIM HAIDER c Stewart b Reeve	13	46	1/0
MUSHTAQ AHMED c Reeve b Pringle	17	42	1/0
AAQIB JAVED not out	1	21	-
Sundries (1lb 1nb 8w)	10		
TOTAL	74		

Fall: 5, 5, 14, 20, 32, 35, 42, 47, 62, 74

	O	M	R	W	Eco	W	NB
D Pringle	8.2	5	8	3	0.9	-	1
P DeFreitas	7	1	22	2	3.1	7	-
G Small	10	1	29	2	2.9	1	-
I Botham	10	4	12	2	1.2	-	
D Reeve	5	3	2	1	0.4	-	-

Overs: 40.2

ENGLAND

	Runs	Balls	4s/6s
G GOOCH c Moin b Akram	3	14	-
I BOTHAM not out	6	22	-
R SMITH not out	5	13	1/0
Sundries (1b 3lb 1nb 5w)	10		
TOTAL for one wicket	24		

Fall: 14.

	O	M	R	W	Eco	W	NB
Wasim Akram	3	0	7	1	2.3	3	1
Aaqib Javed	3	1	7	0	2.3	2	-
Wasim Haider	1	0	1	0	1.0	-	-
Ijaz Ahmed	1	0	5	0	5.0	-	-

Overs: 8
Umpires: P McConnell, S Bucknor.
Crowd: 7537
Player of the match: Not awarded

MATCH ABANDONED

Sri Lanka's memorable victory

2 March: Sri Lanka **v** *South Africa in Wellington*

In keeping with the theme of what was fast becoming the Upset World Cup, Sri Lanka defeated South Africa by three wickets at the Basin Reserve, reaching victory from the second last ball of a match of killing suspense. It was becoming apparent that it would be necessary to revise guidelines for what constituted an upset in this tournament.

Sri Lanka's two victories to that moment equalled its aggregate tally of wins in the four previous World Cups. Team management tried to keep a solemn face, but the supporters outside were singing themselves hoarse, something about 'semi finals'.

Sri Lanka had come far, in every sense, for its itinerary was the most arduous of any team in the World Cup – an estimated 25,000 kilometres of travel – and a series of injuries had reduced it to a bare 12 players this day.

In this first official match between these two most isolated of cricketing countries, South Africa was expected to win comfortably. In fact, South Africa was probably a better all-round cricket team, but Sri Lanka played smarter cricket on the day, the one day, which is what the World Cup was all about. That was captain Aravinda de Silva's motto.

The South African's problems were largely of their own making. Batting first, they were again confounded by a slow wicket, as they had been against New Zealand in Auckland two days before. 'This was an even slower wicket than Auckland,' remarked Kepler Wessels. 'I didn't think they would be as slow as they are. I thought they would be somewhere between Australian pitches and English pitches. We were caught out.'

The promotion of big-hitting Adrian Kuiper to address the problem was a limited success; he made 18 from 44 balls. Wessels himself idled from the front, managing merely three singles in the first 10 overs and eventually a scandalously slow 40 without a single boundary.

The other South Africans tried to catch up, but tried too hard and South Africa lost its last nine wickets for 81 in 85 balls. Champaka Ramanayake, who bowled his first seven overs for seven runs led a mean attack.

South Africa was also unfortunate to run into perhaps the best single exhibition of fielding by a Sri Lankan team ever. The waif-like Sanath Jayasuriya took two screamers at short cover, the second by flinging himself high to his left to catch Jonty Rhodes in one hand. Rhodes, who had been the most enterprising South African batsman, took a moment to applaud the catch, high praise indeed from a fellow jack-in-the-box.

Allan Donald's first two overs were a match in themselves, Donald v. Donald. They included six wides and an over-shoulder no-ball (which Chandika Hathurusinghe fenced overslip for four), but also two wickets, and when he dismissed de Silva with a murderous yorker soon after, he seemed to have repaid his profligacy.

But Roshan Mahanama shared partnerships of 52 with Hashan Tillekeratne and 67 with Arjuna Ranatunga, and although his dismissal for 68 in the 43rd over was inopportune, he had pointed the way to victory. Ranatunga played the coolest of innings, full of flicks and tickles, but always alert for any wide ball which might bring four. He remained 64 not out and was player-of-the-match.

Extras eventually grew to 25, giving Sri Lanka virtually three more crucial overs. Sri Lanka needed seven from the last over, and Ramanayake secured the victory when he slashed the second last ball behind point to the boundary. De Silva called it 'one of our great wins.'

PLAYER PROFILE: Roshan Mahanama

As the tournament entered its second week, the runs were flowing freely from all the expected sources. Already there had been five centuries and five other scores of 90 or more, and Messrs. Boon, Crowe, Miandad, Richardson, and Gooch had all embellished their handsome reputations. But the leading run-maker in the tournament was a big name only if you counted syllables.

Sri Lankan opener, the ever-smiling, ever-modest Roshan Mahanama had made consecutive scores of 59, 81, and now 68, this latest innings the rock upon which Sri Lanka founded its upset win over South Africa.

Mahanama, 25, lean, upright and steadfastly straight, stood in the middle of the storm whipped up by Allan Donald and, while it whisked away teammates Chandika Hathurusinghe, Asanka Gurusinha and captain Aravinda de Silva, he rode it until it was spent. Mahanama battled more than three hours and faced 121 balls for his 68, gathered mostly by running good balls away to gully for singles and by cutting fiercely at the occasional wide ball. His planning and his haste between wickets was a lesson to the South Africans.

Later in his innings, Mahanama betrayed signs of fatigue, which was understandable. Not only had he batted for at least a couple of hours in every match, he had also, with his teammates, faced up to the rigours of travel, for the Sri Lankans' itinerary was a whistle-stop tour of every outpost in the Antipodes.

Two days before this match, Sri Lanka had travelled for 14 hours to get from Mackay to Wellington. Later though, Mahanama was smiling broadly, for as player-of-the-match, Arguna Ranatunga, sagely observed: 'When you are on the winning side, travelling doesn't matter. When you are on the losing side, it hurts double.'

Mahanama also appeared to be hobbling, but de Silva said it was only that a stone had lodged in his boot. 'He thought it might be precious,' laughed de Silva. The stone was actually worthless, but the innings was a gem.

2 March. Sri Lanka v South Africa — Wellington.
Weather: fine.

SOUTH AFRICA

	Runs	Balls	4s/6s
K WESSELS c and b Ranatunga	40	94	-
A KUIPER b Anurasiri	18	44	3/0
P KIRSTEN c Hathurusinghe b Kalpage	47	82	5/1
J RHODES c Jayasuriya b Wickremasinghe	28	21	2/0
M RUSHMERE c Jayasuriya b Ranatunga	4	7	-
H CRONJE st Tillekeratne b Anurasiri	3	6	-
R SNELL b Anurasiri	9	5	-
B MCMILLAN not out	18	22	2/0
D RICHARDSON run out	0	-	-
O HENRY c Kalpage b Ramanayake	11	13	1/0
A DONALD run out	3	6	-
Sundries (9lb 4w 1nb)	14		
TOTAL	195		

Fall: 1, 114, 114, 128, 149, 153, 165, 165, 186, 195.

	O	M	R	W	Eco	W	NB
C Ramanayake ...	9	2	19	1	2.1	-	1
P Wickremasinghe	7	0	32	1	4.5	1	-
D Anurasiri	10	1	41	3	4.1	-	-
R Kalpage	10	0	38	1	3.8	-	-
A Gurusinha	8	0	30	0	3.7	2	-
A Ranatunga	6	0	26	2	4.3	1	-

Overs: 50.

SRI LANKA

	Runs	Balls	4s/6s
R MAHANAMA c Richardson b McMillan	68	121	6/0
C HATHURUSINGHE c Wessels b Donald	5	9	1/0
A GURUSINHA lbw b Donald	0	4	-
A DE SILVA b Donald	7	161/0	
H TILLEKERATNE c Rushmere b Henry	17	63	-
A RANATUNGA not out	64	73	6/0
S JAYASURIYA st Richardson b Kirsten	3	7	-
R KALPAGE run out	5	11	-
C RAMANAYAKE not out	4	2	-
Sundries (1b 7lb 13w 4nb)	25		
TOTAL for seven wickets	198		

Fall: 11, 12, 35, 87, 154, 168, 189.

	O	M	R	W	Eco	W	NB
B McMillan	10	2	34	1	3.4	-	3
A Donald	9.5	0	42	3	4.4	9	-
R Snell	10	1	33	0	3.3	2	-
O Henry	10	0	31	1	3.1	2	1
A Kuiper	5	0	25	0	5.0	-	-
P Kirsten	5	0	25	1	5.0	-	-

Overs: 49.5.
Umpires: K Hayat, S Woodward
Crowd: Approx 5500.
Player of the match: Arjuna Ranatunga (Sri Lanka)
SRI LANKA WON BY THREE WICKETS.

An earthquake called Crowe

3 March: New Zealand **v** Zimbabwe in Napier

An earth tremor shook Napier the night before this match, but it was a long way down the Richter scale from the violent quake produced by New Zealand captain Martin Crowe against Zimbabwe that overcast afternoon at McLean Park.

Crowe belted the quickest half century in World Cup history (31 balls) and his final 74 not out came from merely 44 balls. If rain had not intervened, he would surely have broken Mohammed Azharrudin's record for the fastest century in one-day internationals (62 balls).

Andrew Jones was only slightly less awesome in making 57 from 57 balls, and shared with Crowe a 129-run partnership in less than an hour. This was not wanton sadism on Crowe's part, nor was he showing off. He was driven by fear that his team's perfect record in the tournament would be lost in the lottery of having to bat first in a match constantly stopped for rain.

New Zealand was 2/52 from 11.2 overs, with Crowe and Jones both 15 not out, when rain interrupted for the second time. When play was able to resume one and a half hours later, the Kiwis' allocation had been reduced to 24 overs.

This was the Crowequake's epicentre. From the next 57 balls, Crowe and Jones slathered 110, Crowe making 59 from a scant 26 balls in a sustained barrage. It was not quite a frenzy, because Crowe is too smooth for such a coarse approach, and he said later that he was happy with the fact that he had control over almost every shot. It is best described as artful slogging, highlighted by sixes over square leg and cover point from a hapless Ali Shah.

It was not easy for Zimbabwe, for ground and ball were both treacherously slippery by now, and bowlers and fieldsmen capsized often. It would also have been difficult for New Zealand, tactically, except that Crowe and Jones had made tactics redundant. The Kiwis' innings had been progressively scaled down from 50 overs to 43, 35, 24 and finally halted after 20.5 overs when another drizzly shower arrived.

The cricket clerks reset Zimbabwe's target to 154 from 18 overs, but it was never in this hunt, especially after Danny Morrison bowled Andy Waller, Zimbabwe's best pure hitter, with an exquisite out swinging yorker in only the third over.

But rain had ruled this day and almost decided how it would finish. The drizzle began again during the 14th over, and if play had been halted before 15 overs were bowled, the match would have been a no-result. The Kiwis hustled and bustled, and when Alistiar Campbell skied a...err...rain-maker in the 15th over, Crowe said he seriously considered dropping it, rather than absorb time for a change of batsman. But he caught it anyway, and soon after the Kiwis had their fourth consecutive win.

The Zimbabwe captain Dave Houghton said this was 'a bit of an artificial result', but it would have been worse to have no result. Crowe said he was pleased at how his rejuvenated team had maintained concentration. 'We never turned off throughout the day', he said. That night, for the first time, Crowe allowed that he was thinking of the semi-finals.

Success Story: Zimbabwean Andrew Flower made an impact on the world stage with fluent batting and capable keeping.

PLAYER PROFILE: *Iain Butchart*

The publicists, with their customary casual regard for reality, had proclaimed Iain Butchart as Zimbabwe's Ian Botham, but on this day, he must have felt more like one of Botham's victims. It was not a day he will care to remember.

Butchart, a medium-pace seam bowler and lower-order clubber, was brought into the attack to try to staunch the flow of runs from the bats of Martin Crowe and Andrew Jones. Instead, he provided an entertaining diversion.

Before he had bowled two legal deliveries, he had twice been flat on his back. At his first attempt, his right foot slipped from beneath him on the wet turf and he crashed ignominiously. Butchart safely negotiated the next delivery, but then suffered another collapse.

'Butchart bowling with two slips,' mumbled an English journalist, as dry in his humour as it was wet outside. Butchart could not keep his feet, but he kept his sense of the ridiculous and was smiling broadly as he returned to his marker to try again. If he could have known what would befall him now, he might have stayed flat on his back.

Butchart was caught in the middle of the Crowe/Jones maelstrom, and his four overs cost 53 runs. He can claim that he broke the partnership, but as Jones was caught on the long-on boundary, from a shot which would have been six had not Andy Waller bravely intercepted, it was problematic what role the bowler played in the dismissal.

Batting at No. 4 to try to give impetus to Zimbabwe's impossible chase, Butchart made only three before he was out – caught at long-on, of course.

Butchered bowler:
Iain Butchart is one of Zimbabwe's capable all-rounders but, at times, found his medium pacers easy fodder for the world's best batsmen.

**3 March. New Zealand v Zimbabwe — Christchurch.
Weather: Rain.**

NEW ZEALAND

	Runs	Balls	4s/6s
M GREATBATCH b Duers	15	16	2/0
R LATHAM b Brandes	2	6	-
A JONES c Waller b Butchart	57	57	9/0
M CROWE not out	74	44	8/2
C CAIRNS not out	1	2	-
Sundries (6b 7lb)	13		
TOTAL for three wickets	162		

Fall: 9, 25, 154.

	O	M	R	W	Eco	W	NB
Brandes	5	1	28	1	5.6	-	-
K Duers	6	0	17	1	2.8	-	-
A Shah	4	0	34	0	8.5	-	-
I Butchart	4	0	53	1	13.2	-	-
M Burmester . . .	1.5	0	17	0	11.3	-	-

Overs: 20.5.

ZIMBABWE

	Runs	Balls	4s/6s
A FLOWER b Larsen	30	27	5/0
A WALLER b Morrison	11	11	1/1
D HOUGHTON b Larsen	10	14	2/0
I BUTCHART c Cairns b Larsen	3	7	-
E BRANDES b Harris	6	8	-
A PYCROFT not out	13	20	-
A CAMPBELL c Crowe b Harris	8	9	1/0
A SHAH b Harris	7	8	1/0
M BURMESTER not out	4	3	-
Sundries (9lb 3w 1nb)	13		
TOTAL for seven wickets for	105		

Fall: 21, 41, 63, 63, 75, 86, 97.

	O	M	R	W	Eco	W	NB
D Morrison	4	0	14	1	3.5	2	1
C Cairns	2	0	27	0	13.5	-	-
G Larsen	4	0	16	3	4.0	-	-
C Harris	4	0	15	3	3.7	1	-
R Latham	3	0	18	0	6.0	-	-
M Crowe	1	0	6	0	6.0	--	

Overs: 18
Umpires: J Buultjens, K Liebenberg.
Crowd: Approx 5000
Player of the match: Martin Crowe (New Zealand)

NEW ZEALAND WON BY 48 RUNS

India's historic win

4 March: Pakistan **v** India in Sydney

Having managed to avoid one another in the first four World Cups, India and Pakistan finally crossed paths at the Sydney Cricket Ground in the fifth.

The match did nothing to dispel the image of cricket between these two great sub-continental rivals as being a tense, testy affair only marginally less important than life and death itself.

The testiness was provided by Javed Miandad and Kiran More, who had a full-blown row that prompted the intervention of both umpires as well as a novel excuse for not laying a report – that the English-speaking umpires could not understand the finer points of the sledging. (The international panel of umpires will be an even more expensive proposition than first thought if umpires are to be tutored in everything from Afrikaans to Urdu).

The tension, despite India's relatively comfortable margin of victory in the end, survived until late into the night when Pakistan tripped over its own feet towards the end of its innings and was bowled out 43 runs short of India's 7/216.

From a position of relative strength at 3/127 in the 34th over, Pakistan lost its last seven wickets for 46. Manoj Prabhakar set up the win with three inspired spells of bowling, in which he took 2/22 and beat the outside edge more times than anyone cared to count.

The fireworks between Javed and More started when the Indian wicketkeeper appealed for a leg-side stumping off Tendulkar. As Tendulkar came in to bowl the next ball, Javed withdrew and complained to English umpire David Shepherd that More was making too much noise. Shepherd signalled to More to zip his mouth. Javed chuckled, More fumed and the pair exchanged words.

The mischievous Javed inflamed the situation after the next ball when More appealed for a run out. Mocking More's excited appeal, Javed did three acrobatic kangaroo hops, showing no sign of the back injury that threatened to keep him out of the World Cup. More words. Shepherd and Australian umpire Peter McConnell spoke to Javed and Mohammed Azharuddin at the end of the over in a plea for peace.

Azharuddin said after the match that the animosity between the pair had a long history. 'I don't blame Kiran,' he said. 'Javed's always been like that. I told Kiran to stay away from him.'

India created a stir of its own when, in the general trend of the tournament, it dropped vice-captain and opening batsman Ravi Shastri for slow, if not necessarily low, scoring.

Shastri's replacement, Ajay Jadeja, proved more than handy against Pakistan, with his lively footwork and running. Krish Srikkanth did a fair impersonation of Shastri from the other end with 5 from 40 balls, which only went to show that he is nothing if not unpredictable.

Once again, it was India's most reliable player, 18-year-old Sachin Tendulkar, who provided the innings with a solid core. Not only did he top score with an unbeaten 54, but his fine night continued with 10 steady overs and the wicket of Pakistan's most impressive batsman, Aamir Sohail, the match top-scorer with 62.

With Wasim Akram struggling to control the white ball, it was left to Aaqib Javed and Imran Khan (the latter bowling for the first time in the tournament and still feeling the effects of his injured shoulder) to maintain the pressure.

Azharuddin, who hit the ball beautifully for 32, and Vinod Kambli, with a precocious 24, were both out trying to force Mushtaq Ahmed. Kapil Dev had more luck with the leg-spinner, easing him over the extra cover fence for 6 during his 35-run assault-and-battery at the death.

For Pakistan, Sohail produced a fine collection of pulls and square drives, but once he was gone the rest collapsed in a heap around Javed, who ran between wickets with great industry but was prevented, mainly by Prabhakar, from scoring as freely as he would have liked for his 40. Extras were third top score.

Sensing a victory in front of hundreds of millions of television viewers back home across the Indian Ocean, the Indians players responded to each wicket as though it were a miracle, particularly the demise of the Big Three – Imran Khan, Wasim Akram and Javed – in the space of four overs.

Imran was run out after a misunderstanding with Javed; Akram stumped after charging an arm ball that Venkatapathy Raju cleverly pushed flat and wide of him; and Javed, who stepped away to force the pace, played on to a full pitcher from Javagal Srinath, prompting a special celebration.

Happily, the antagonism on the field did not extend beyond the fence. Sydney's Indian and Pakistani communities turned out in force, but they mingled happily and their flags flew side by side.

There was not a hint of the trouble that has clouded sporting relations between these nations on the subcontinent, where Pakistan cancelled its most recently planned tour of India following threats from Hindu extremists to disrupt the tour because of the Kashmir crisis.

The only politicisation of the event was done by a group of men from the International Sikh Youth Federation. Wearing the orange turbans of Khalistan, the homeland for which they are fighting the Indian government, they marched around the ground letting everyone know that they were barracking for Pakistan. Most people were too engrossed in the action to pay them any attention.

PLAYER PROFILE: *Manoj Prabhakar*

It was hardly surprising that Sachin Tendulkar, cricket's golden-haired boy, was preferred to Manoj Prabhakar by the player-of-the-match adjudicator. Hardly surprising, but hardly fair either.

Then again, one-day cricket is not in the habit of being fair to bowlers. Some believe that their role is reduced to little more than that of bowling machines.

The best bowlers manage occasionally to counter that theory, and Prabhakar was among their number against Pakistan with three of the best spells of the tournament. Tendulkar, as usual, was a fine allround contributor for India, but there was not much more that Prabhakar could have done than his 2/22 from 10 overs.

Unlike Tendulkar, of course, Prabhakar does not make the game look easy or graceful and he is not destined for greatness. Rather, he is a dogged, snarling cricketer without any pretensions to aesthetics. Above all, he is a competitor.

It was Prabhakar who, with India defending a total smaller than it would have liked, ensured that Pakistan was on the back foot from the start. His stock ball for the evening was the leg-cutter. It claimed the scalps of Zahid Fazal and Salim Malik and produced many dot balls besides, as a succession of batsmen failed to lay bat on ball.

His duel with Javed, a clash of two of the most forceful personalities in world cricket, was a treat, with Prabhakar winning comfortably on points.

It was a wide call from Australian umpire Peter McConnell that stirred an angry Prabhakar into action. He beat the bat with the next ball and claimed Zahid with the next. Malik fell in almost identical fashion, Prabhakar giving him a mouthful on his way back to the pavilion.

Hopping Mad: Pakistan's non-stop agitator Javed Miandad leaps in the air to mimic Indian wicketkeeper Kiran More, who seconds earlier made an excited appeal for a run out.

4 March. Pakistan v India at Sydney.
Weather: fine.

INDIA

	Runs	Balls	4s/6s
A JADEJA c Zahid b Haider	46	81	2/0
K SRIKKANTH c Moin b Aaqib	5	40	-
M AZHARUDDIN c Moin b Mushtaq	32	50	4/0
V KAMBLI c Haq b Mushtaq	24	42	-
S TENDULKAR not out	54	62	3/0
S MANJREKAR b Mushtaq	0	1	-
KAPIL DEV c Imran b Aaqib	35	26	2/1
K MORE run out	4	4	-
M PRABHAKAR not out	2	1	-
Sundries (3lb 9w 2nb)	14		
TOTAL for seven wickets	216		

Fall: 25, 86, 101, 147, 148, 208, 213.

	O	M	R	W	Eco	W	NB
Wasim Akram	10	0	45	0	4.5	5	2
Aaqib Javed	8	2	28	2	3.5	-	-
Imran Khan	8	0	25	0	3.1	1	-
Wasim Haider	10	1	36	1	3.6	1	-
Mustaq Ahmed	10	0	59	3	5.9	1	-
Aamir Sohail	3	0	20	0	6.6	1	-

Overs: 49

PAKISTAN

	Runs	Balls	4s/6s
AAMIR SOHAIL c Srikkanth b Tendulkar	62	103	6/0
INZAMAM-UL-HAQ lbw b Kapil Dev	2	7	-
ZAHID FAZAL c More b Prabhakar	2	10	-
JAVED MIANDAD b Srinath	40	113	2/0
SALIM MALIK c More b Prabhakar	12	9	2/0
IMRAN KHAN run out	0	5	-
WASIM AKRAM st More b Raju	4	8	-
WASIM HAIDER b Srinath	13	25	-
MOIN KHAN c Manjrekar b Kapil Dev	12	12	1/0
MUSHTAQ AHMED run out	3	4	-
AAQIB JAVED not out	1	13	-
Sundries (6lb 15w 1nb)	22		
TOTAL	173		

Fall: 8, 17, 105, 127, 130, 141, 141, 161, 166, 173.

	O	M	R	W	Eco	W	NB
Kapil Dev	10	0	30	2	3.0	5	1
M Prabhakar	10	1	22	2	2.2	4	-
J Srinath	8.1	0	37	2	4.5	1	-
Tendulkar	10	0	37	1	3.7	3	-
V Raju	10	1	41	1	4.1	-	-

Overs: 48.1
Umpires: D Shepherd, P McConnell
Crowd: 10,330
Player of the match: Sachin Tendulkar (India)

INDIA WON BY 43 RUNS

Mother country reigns supreme

5 March: Australia v England in Sydney

Australia versus England at the Sydney Cricket Ground was more than a game of cricket. It became a metaphor for the War of Independence that Australia never fought.

Prime Minister Paul Keating's pro-republican statements during the Queen's 1992 visit struck a chord in much of the community ('Poll Shock: Keating's Popular', read one newspaper headline) and a nerve among the thousands of English supporters in Australia for the World Cup.

They came to the Sydney Cricket Ground with their Union Jack waistcoats, Tottenham Hotspur scarves and soccer chants and took over the Doug Walters Stand, which must have made the laconic one choke on the fag that hangs permanently from the corner of his mouth.

When the Australian supporters waved their flags, the English taunted them with: 'Union Jack on the Aussie flag, do da, do da....'

The Australians only had to look at the top left-hand corner of their flag to see they had no retort. Certainly they could not point to the scoreboard which read, in BBC sporting service style, 'Beefy Botham 1, Australia nil'.

Having expressed his desire to beat Australia in front of '100,000 convicts' in the final, Botham had his way three weeks early in front of 38,951 at the SCG. 'I hope the Queen was watching,' he said afterwards.

Botham might be unconventional, but he is first and foremost an Englishman. He played as a self-appointed personal envoy to Her Majesty, sent down under to give the revolting colonials a hiding.

In that sort of mood, Botham does not just take part in a cricket match – he takes over. The other 21 players loitered around the wings as Botham strode to centre stage with career-best figures of 4/31, including seven balls of mayhem in which he took 4/0, and a crashing innings of 53 as an opening batsman.

In truth, England's comfortable seven-wicket victory was more of a team effort than it appeared. It was just that the other heroes – Derek Pringle, Phil DeFreitas, Chris Lewis and Graham Gooch – were happy to stand back and let the allrounder take the glory.

Indeed, there could have been no more emphatic statement to the Australian public that England was a rejuvenated force, following its abortive tour of the Antipodes the previous summer.

Fielding is often the best guide to such things, and England's was first rate. Snatches of brilliance in the field contributed directly to the removal of Australia's two most dangerous batsmen, Neil Fairbrother running out David Boon with a direct hit, and Lewis intercepting a bullet at point to send Dean Jones on his way.

Australians might have chuckled at a bowling attack featuring nothing quicker than fast-medium Lewis, but the Australian batsmen did not get the joke. Nor did they get a cracker to hit, with seamers Pringle, Lewis and DeFreitas contributing between them 29 disciplined overs at an average cost of two-and-a-half runs each.

The loss of Boon in the 10th over put Australia on the back foot from the start. His run-out, the result of backing up too far, was the third time in four World Cup innings that Australia's best batsman had been dismissed in that manner, which neatly encapsulated Australia's fortunes.

A week after coach Bob Simpson said that other teams had prospered by copying Australia's methods, the title-holders adopted a more humble approach and showed that they were prepared to learn, albeit belatedly, from others. Following the lead of England, the West Indies and New Zealand, they sent out one of their biggest hitters, Tom Moody, to open the innings.

Bob Simpson and Allan Border had decried the tactic in the preceding weeks, but it turned out to be the first thing that went right for Australia in the tournament, Moody top scoring with 51 before he was unluckily bowled by Phil Tufnell off his arm.

England had only 172 to make, and Botham did not muck around, launching into a thunderous off-drive off Bruce Reid in the fourth over to set the tone of the innings. Nor, for that matter, did Craig McDermott, who came out just as fired up as the English all-rounder and, by any conservative estimate, beat the outside edges of Graham Gooch's bat a dozen times.

But Gooch kept his head and, following Botham's lead, banged the loose balls for 4 on his way to 58. Pouncing on anything stray, Botham and Gooch hit 13 boundaries between them, more than the entire Australian team.

England got home with 9.1 overs to spare. Australia had been put firmly back in its place.

PLAYER PROFILE: Ian Botham

Ian Botham creaked his 36-year-old limbs to life and, just as he promised he would, gave Australia one more belting for the road.

Botham became a legend tormenting Australians and he could not have been more delighted to discover that, at a time in life when he was starting to think of more serious pursuits, such as pantomime acting, he still had the knack.

Purists will resist comparisons between his performance in coloured clothes in Sydney and his finest Aussie-bashing vintages – Trent Bridge '77, Headingly '81 and Melbourne '86-87, among others – but it was just as devastating a blow to the Australian ego.

True to his extraordinary life, when it came it came in a rush and in almost mythical proportions. He started in style, with Allan Border, the first wicket in a crazy spell of 4/0 from seven deliveries.

The ball that removed Border zapped back off the seam and penetrated the same gap South African Adrian Kuiper probed successfully the previous week. Border nodded in acknowledgement of a canny piece of cricket, although he would have been in a less accommodating mood minutes later when the dressing room had turned into a refuge for Botham victims, Australia having slumped from 4/145 to 8/155.

Botham took wickets with the first (Ian Healy caught at mid-wicket), third (Peter Taylor lbw) and fifth (Craig McDermott caught at mid-on) balls of his next over. The Australians seemed mesmerised more by the force of the Botham personality than by any wizardry in the bowling.

'They hit it to my fielders, which I thought was excellent,' was his neat summary. Less than an hour later, he was back at the crease delivering the Australian bowlers a hiding on his way to 53.

Australia was re-living its worst cricket nightmare, a nightmare called Botham.

Close call: Ian Botham turns to see the ball bounce just wide of the stumps.

Boon for batting: Australia's opener David Boon was his country's outstanding batsman. This shot brought him four runs on his way to an even 100 against the West Indians at the MCG. It was his second century of the competition.

Captivating Kapil: Indian allrounder Kapil Dev proved one of the hardest-hitting batsmen in the World Cup. More runs on this way with his lusty whack.

Airborne Brandes: Zimbabwean speedstar Eddo Brandes hurls himself into his work against England in Albury. He was rewarded with four wickets in his side's shock victory.

Unexpected resistance: Hansie Cronje sweeps the ball away to leg from out side off-stump in his timely innings of 24 runs. Alec Stewart is caught off guard.

for the moment: Graeme Hick made his finest
ribution for England against South Africa, this cut
g him on his way to 83.

Short, sweet: Allan Lamb thumps a short ball towards the boundary in his short but productive innings.

Veteran reflexes: Imran Khan moves quickly to his right to take a return in the tense semi-final in Auckland.

Weary warrior: Adrian Kuiper, who struck fear into the Englishmen with a rapid and telling 36 off 44 balls, is out, bowled after one attempted big hit too many.

Turning on the heat: After a laborious start Ken Rutherford raced to 50 with a combination of well-p cuts and well-timed drives.

5 March. Australia v England — Sydney.
Weather: fine.

AUSTRALIA

	Runs	Balls	4s/6s
T MOODY b Tufnell	51	91	3/0
M TAYLOR lbw b Pringle	0	11	-
D BOON run out	18	27	2/0
D JONES c Lewis b DeFreitas	22	50	2/0
S WAUGH run out	27	43	2/0
A BORDER b Botham	16	22	1/0
I HEALY c Fairbrother b Botham	9	7	0/1
P TAYLOR lbw b Botham	0	2	-
C MCDERMOTT c DeFreitas b Botham	0	2	-
M WHITNEY not out	8	27	1/0
B REID b Reeve	1	22	-
Sundries (2b 8lb 5w 4nb)	19		
TOTAL	171		

Fall: 5, 35, 106, 114, 145, 155, 155, 155, 164, 171.

	O	M	R	W	Eco	W	NB
D Pringle	9	1	24	1	2.6	1	3
C Lewis	10	2	28	0	2.8	2	-
P DeFreitas	10	3	23	1	2.3	1	-
I Botham	10	1	31	4	3.1	1	-
P Tufnell	9	0	52	1	5.7	-	1
D Reeve	1	0	3	1	3	-	-

Overs: 49

ENGLAND

	Runs	Balls	4s/6s
G GOOCH b S Waugh	58	115	7/0
I BOTHAM c Healy b Whitney	53	79	6/0
R SMITH not out	30	60	5/0
G HICK not out	7	5	1/0
Sundries (13lb 8w 4nb)	25		
TOTAL for two wickets for	173		

Fall: 107, 153.

	O	M	R	W	Eco	W	NB
C McDermott	10	1	29	0	2.9	3	1
B Reid	7.5	0	49	0	6.5	2	3
M Whitney	10	2	28	1	2.8	1	-
S Waugh	6	0	29	1	4.8	2	-
P Taylor	3	0	7	0	2.3	-	-
T Moody	4	0	18	0		-	-

Overs: 40.5
Umpires: K Hayat, S Bucknor
Crowd: 38,951
Player of the match: Ian Botham (England)
ENGLAND WON BY EIGHT WICKETS

Pringle, the unlikely hero

*5 March: West Indies **v** South Africa in Christchurch*

The cricket was as rich in quality as the day was in symbolism when South Africa and the West Indies met for the first time ever, on a grey, chilly day at Lancaster Park, Christchurch.

As the game began, the spare squad members from each side took their places in an enclosure next to the sight screen, side-by-side, and every now and then, intermingling. This would not have been so remarkable, for many players in these teams knew each other well from the English County circuit, except that here they were wearing their national colours, albeit the gaudy colours of the technicolourWorldCup.This sort of free association would have been unthinkable before South Africa was sent to exile, and simply impossible in the 21 intervening years to this day.

'You become proud of your country again,' remarked Dr Ali Bacher, South Africa's last Test captain, foremost administrator and leader of the crusade to liberate the Republic's cricketers. Bacher owned up to a feeling of future shock, for less than five months previously the West Indies had abstained from voting on a motion for South Africa's re-admission to the ICC. 'The West Indies led the charge against South Africa, and one can understand why, and that is why this day is so important,' he said.

For the players, though, there were no thoughts about the historic dimension of the day, for one-day cricket is so intense that it consumes all energies and sensibilities. The Lancaster Park pitch was hard and grassy, a veritable playground for perhaps the two finest seam attacks in the world. On both sides, there were deeds of courage, daring and, above all, class which suggested that although they had no common past and no heritage, they would share a great and glorious rivalry in the future.

South Africa's top-scorer, Peter Kirsten, strained a calf muscle mid-innings and made more than half of his 56 via a runner, a considerable feat of concentration and coordination by all three parties in a one-day game. With Kirsten, now the World Cup's leading run-maker, as their inspiration, the South Africans reached 8/200, a modest score but their first 200 of the tournament. Their technical skills were able to withstand the West Indies, but they were still apprehensive about the finer requirements of one-day cricket, such as running between wickets.

The West Indies caught well, Desmond Haynes and Brian Lara tracking three high balls down from the gloomy Christchurch sky and Lara diving practically from backward point to gully for another.

But their ground fielding was slovenly; with a run-out on, Curtly Ambrose missed the stumps from five metres away, directly in front. Disbelieving, he signalled 'wide'.

The pitch remained a lively thing in the afternoon, and all eyes were on Allan Donald, whose fame as White Lightning had preceded him here. But the flash came from the other end, where Meyrick Pringle produced the single most heroic effort of the match. In the space of 11 balls, he terminated Lara, Richie Richardson, Carl Hooper and Keith Arthurton in a magnificent display of swing and seam bowling. Donald, meanwhile, bowled tightly without wickets, the converse of his previous matches.

The evergreen Haynes survived this ambush, but when he was struck on his already sore right index finger a third time, he was compelled to retire hurt. A press box bulletin said he was bound for hospital for x-rays and unlikely to bat again. But as further calamity befell the West Indians, he chose instead to return to the crease to mount with Gus Logie one last death-or-glory campaign.

For a time, it seemed it might be glory, with Haynes somehow smiting fours to long-on and mid-wicket despite a deadened right hand. Meanwhile, Logie, who has not heard of a lost cause yet, had launched a counter-offensive, lashing Adrian Kuiper for four 4s in five balls to reach 50.

But they were powerless against the curse of the No. 1 Stand end, from where Kuiper had them both caught a few balls apart. The first eight wickets all fell at this end, and it was there, too, that Ambrose was run out, a decision which displeased him so much he momentarily brandished his bat in the general direction of umpire Brian Aldridge. The West Indies had now made their two lowest World Cup scores in this tournament, 136 here and 157 against England.

Both captains reported only harmony between their teams after play, each properly visiting the other's room with beer in hand. Kepler Wessels was less enamoured of what he thought was the antagonism of the South African press, implying that it had brow-beaten the selectors into picking the wrong team for previous matches. But to most, the lively public debate about selection and tactics was the surest sign that South Africa was alive and well and living in the real world again.

The last vestige of apartheid was in the press box, with the New Zealanders and South Africans in a superbox behind the bowlers arm and the rest of us in a kind Soweto at square leg.

PLAYER PROFILE: *Meyrick Pringle*

Meyrick Pringle's part in South Africa's re-emergence from the cricketing cold was causing complications in his life even as it was bringing him accolades. Pringle had not been widely expected to make the South African squad, his name was missing from most of the tournament's pre-publicity, and he himself made plans to marry at the end of March.

But he had burst to prominence by taking more wickets than anyone else in the 1991/92 South African domestic season, and suddenly he was in the cup squad. And with South Africa due to tour the West Indies in April, he was fast running out of available weekends for his wedding.

Pringle had started inauspiciously in the World Cup with 0/52 against Australia in Sydney and was promptly dropped. He sat out South Africa's games in Auckland and Wellington, on sluggish wickets which he admitted would not have suited his bowling.

But a seaming, bouncing Lancaster Park wicket was his type. In quick succession, he had Brian Lara caught at point, Richie Richardson lbw while driving imprudently, and Carl Hooper and Keith Arthurton, caught at first slip. From 11 balls, he had 4/0 and had effectively bowled the West Indians out of the match.

Pringle finished the day with figures of 4/11 (four scoring shots) from eight overs. 'I'll be in there for a while now,' he beamed.

Previously, Pringle had been chiefly renowned for mishaps. He had missed the plane to his first one-day international, a South African Invitation XI against Mike Gatting's touring rebel team two years ago. And a couple of days before this match, he lost a substantial sum of money down a hotel liftwell. Now, he had the last laugh.

Tough toiler: Meyrick Pringle is fast and honest and the big right-hander routed the West Indies top-order when he exploited a seaming pitch.

South African jig: Meyrick Pringle and his skipper Kepler Wessels high-five after the South African quick claims an early wicket.

**5 March. West Indies v South Africa — Christchurch.
Weather: cool.**

SOUTH AFRICA

	Runs	Balls	4s/6s
K WESSELS c Haynes b Marshall	1	9	-
A HUDSON c Lara b Cummins	22	60	3/0
P KIRSTEN c Williams b Marshall	56	91	2/0
M RUSHMERE st Williams b Hooper	10	24	-
A KUIPER b Ambrose	23	29	0/1
J RHODES c Williams b Cummins	22	27	-
B MCMILLAN c Lara b Benjamin	20	29	2/0
D RICHARDSON not out	20	26	1/0
R SNELL c Haynes b Ambrose	3	6	-
M PRINGLE not out	5	6	-
Sundries (8lb 3w 7nb)	18		
TOTAL for eight wickets	200		

Fall: 8, 52, 73, 118, 127, 159, 181, 187.

	O	M	R	W	Eco	W	NB
C Ambrose	10	1	34	2	3.4	-	3
M Marshall	10	1	26	2	2.6	-	-
C Hooper	10	0	45	-1	4.5	1	-
A Cummins	10	0	40	2	4.0	-	4
W Benjamin	10	0	47	1	4.7	2	-

Overs: 50

WEST INDIES

	Runs	Balls	4s/6s
D HAYNES c Richardson b Kuiper	30	83	3/0
B LARA c Rhodes b Pringle	9	13	2/0
R RICHARDSON lbw b Pringle	1	3	-
C HOOPER c Wessels b Pringle	0	4	-
K ARTHURTON c Wessels b Pringle	0	4	-
G LOGIE c Pringle b Kuiper	61	69	9/1
M MARSHALL c Rhodes b Snell	6	10	1/0
D WILLIAMS c Richardson b Snell	0	3	-
C AMBROSE run out	12	13	2/0
A CUMMINS c McMillan b Donald	6	17	-
W BENJAMIN not out	1	10	-
Sundries (9lb 1w)	10		
TOTAL	136		

Fall: 10, 19, 19, 19, 70, 70, 116, 117, 132, 136.

	O	M	R	W	Eco	W	NB
A Donald	6.4	2	13	1	2.0	1	-
M Pringle	8	4	11	4	1.3	-	-
R Snell	7	2	16	2	2.2	-	-
B McMillan	8	2	36	0	4.5	-	-
A Kuiper	9	0	51	2	5.6	-	-

Overs: 38.4
Umpires: B Aldridge, S Randell.
Player of the match: Meyrick Pringle (South Africa).

SOUTH AFRICA WON BY 64 RUNS.

Australia's form reversal

7 March: Australia **v** Sri Lanka in Adelaide

In a match that confirmed the validity of the official 1992 World Cup cliche – that any side is capable of beating any other side on any given day – downtrodden Australia upset finals' aspirant Sri Lanka in their match at the Adelaide Oval.

Sri Lankan captain Aravinda de Silva was kind enough to resist saying, before the match, something like: 'Of course, we're not going in over-confident. Even Australia or Zimbabwe can cause an upset in one-day cricket.'

An exaggeration, of course, but the fact remained that if Sri Lanka had won, it would have been on the verge of a semi-final berth. A win for Australia would simply have put it on a long and treacherous road out of the wilderness.

In the end, much to the relief of officials still trying to sell tickets for the final, the old, pre-World Cup order was restored for a day. For the first time in five World Cup matches, Australia was indisputably the better side.

Somehow, the setting was right for an Australian recovery, no matter how modest. Playing in brilliant sunshine on everybody's favourite wicket against one of the friendliest attacks in the competition, Australia cruised home with seven wickets and six overs to spare.

It was not always like that. Australia was chasing 190, but its form had been so shoddy that the normally sedate Adelaide crowd grew restless only nine overs into the innings.

Geoff Marsh, returning to the side after two games on the sidelines for slow scoring, was dragging his feet on two. 'Boring' and 'Get on with it' went up the cry from the outer. The Australian vice-captain, whose omission from the Test side at the same ground six weeks earlier caused an angry response from his chief ally, Allan Border, was again at the crossroads.

Marsh hit nine from the next over, bowled by Champaka Ramanayake and, while he still looked streaky, his luck had turned. He produced a punching cover drive for 4 from Ramanayake's next over and followed it by going down on one knee to spinner Don Anurasiri and depositing him over square leg in front of the Victor Richardson Gates for 6. The confidence came flooding back.

There was no such hesitation from the batsmen down the order, Mark Waugh and Dean Jones both launching into massive 6s that cleared the fence on Adelaide's long straight boundary. Jones's hit off the hapless Ramanayake was a rare shot that actually cleared the first set of seats and almost landed under the shade of the Moreton Bay fig trees.

Marsh and Tom Moody made 120 for the first wicket, which basically put an end to the matter. Sri Lanka simply did not make enough runs for its modest attack to defend, although Pramodaya Wickremasinghe deserved to be mentioned in dispatches for a supremely disciplined effort with the ball.

Sri Lanka's problems started in the opening minutes of the match when Roshan Mahanama, one of the form batsmen of the tournament, was run out in a mix-up with Athula Samarasekera. That set a trend with four Sri Lankan run outs in all and the brilliant Mark Waugh involved in three of them.

Sri Lanka's best chances of setting a reasonable target rested with de Silva, who chipped the ball around with great industry for 62, but skied Craig McDermott to the leg-side boundary just when his side needed him to lift the tempo.

His innings featured one amazing reverse sweep off Allan Border after dancing down the wicket to his opposite number. Border threw his head back and laughed at the audacity of his opposite number. De Silva's innings also included 20 successive singles and, with Sri Lanka managing only eight 4s on a ground with such short boundaries, a total of 9/189 was unlikely to be enough.

Australia was even allowed to get away with opening the bowling with Steve Waugh, an experiment that failed with Waugh conceding 15 runs from his first wayward three-over spell. He was replaced by Michael Whitney, who hurried on to the bat and denied the batsmen any latitude as well as maintaining the pressure that Craig McDermott was exerting, as usual, from the other end.

Border was at last presented with a set of circumstances in which he was confident enough to bowl Peter Taylor, who was kept in cotton wool for all but three overs in the previous two matches. In fact, Taylor extracted enough turn to give Border the confidence to bowl himself for 10 overs, a rare thing indeed.

The Sri Lankan innings included a moment of controversy when Zimbabwean umpire Ian Robinson gave Sanath Jayasuria not out after he clipped a half-volley from Steve Waugh to Mark Waugh at mid-wicket. The Waugh twins did not even bother appealing, although Steve pointed Jayasuria angrily in the direction of the dressing room as soon as he realised that the left-hander was going to stand his ground.

Border descended from cover and, standing in the middle of the wicket, demonstrated his version of the shot for the benefit of Robinson. Robinson then demonstrated his version for Border, which was hardly necessary as he and not Border was the umpire, although for a moment the lines were a little blurred.

PLAYER PROFILE: Michael Whitney

Michael Whitney, the sweathog of Australian cricket, never used to enjoy one-day cricket. For the man who cut his teeth on the principle of a fair reward for a 23-over day, aggression and risk taking was an extension of his personality.

Whitney's perception of limited-over cricket was not improved by an unfortunate encounter with Ian Botham in Perth during the 1986-87 season. The harder Botham hit him, the harder and faster Whitney tried to bowl.

The transition from Whitney the raging bull to Whitney the calculating one-day bowler, a man worthy of selection in Australia's World Cup squad, occurred in the West Indies in 1991.

Whitney was genuinely shocked to be included in Australia's one-day side in the Caribbean, but quickly realised that a solid performance could be a passport to extending an international career that had always dangled from the thinnest of threads.

'I thought then and there: "You've got to come to terms with it" ' he said. 'I never used to like it and didn't enjoy playing it. I always thought it was the "pyjama game". It wasn't a true reflection of you as a bowler – your innermost self.'

Whitney knuckled down, shortened his run-up, concentrated more on deceiving batsmen with his inswinger than knocking their blocks off, and turned himself into one of Australia's leading one-day bowlers.

Against Sri Lanka, Whitney stood back as Steve Waugh took the new ball with Craig McDermott. Waugh lasted three expensive overs before Border called on Whitney to stem the flow of runs, which he did with successive maidens.

Whitney finished with 1/26 from his 10 overs and even took time out to entertain the outer by dancing a little jig on the fence. The man who never used to like one-day cricket enjoyed every moment of it.

Run stopper: Michael Whitney's left-arm fast mediums applied the brakes several times for Australia and he moved ahead of Merv Hughes and Bruce Reid in the bowling pecking order.

7 March. Australia v Sri Lanka — Adelaide.
Weather: fine.

SRI LANKA

	Runs	Balls	4s/6s
R MAHANAMA run out	7	10	1/0
A SAMARASEKERA c Healy b Taylor	34	63	3/0
A GURUSINHA lbw b Whitney	5	23	1/0
A DE SILVA c Moody b McDermott	62	83	2/0
A RANATUNGA c Jones b Taylor	23	52	-
S JAYASURIYA lbw b Border	15	29	1/0
H TILLEKERATNE run out	5	13	-
R KALPAGE run out	14	15	-
C RAMANAYAKE run out	5	10	-
D ANURASIRI not out	4	4	-
Sundries (3b 6lb 1nb 5w)	15		
TOTAL for nine wickets	189		

Fall: 8, 28, 72, 123, 151, 163, 166, 182, 189.

	O	M	R	W	Eco	W	NB
C McDermott ...	10	0	28	1	2.8	1	-
S Waugh	7	0	34	0	4.8	4	1
M Whitney	10	3	26	1	2.6	-	-
T Moody	3	0	18	0	6.0	-	-
P Taylor	10	0	34	2	3.4	-	-
A Border	10	0	40	1	4.1	-	-

Overs: 50

AUSTRALIA

	Runs	Balls	4s/6s
T MOODY c Mahanama b Wickremasinghe	57	86	4/0
G MARSH c Anurasiri b Kalpage	60	113	3/1
M WAUGH c Mahanama b Wickremasinghe	26	26	0/2
D BOON not out	27	37	1/0
D JONES not out	12	8	0/1
Sundries (2lb 3nb 3w)	8		
TOTAL for three wickets	190		

Fall: 120, 130, 165.

	O	M	R	W	Eco	W	NB
P Wickremasinghe	10	3	29	2	2.9	1	1
C Ramanayake ..	9	1	44	0	4.8	2	2
D Anurasiri	10	0	43	0	4.3	-	-
A Gurusinha	6	0	20	0	3.3	-	-
R Kalpage	8	0	41	1	5.1	-	-
A Ranatunga	1	0	11	0	11	-	-

Overs: 44
Umpires: P Reporter, I Robinson
Crowd: 11,663
Player of the match: Tom Moody (Australia)

AUSTRALIA WON BY 7 WICKETS.

Rain foils Zimbabwe

7 March: India **v** *Zimbabwe in Hamilton*

Rain is the natural enemy of cricket, and was fast becoming the bane of this tournament, for no one had yet devised a fair method of determining the winner of a rain-interrupted match.

India and Zimbabwe both had already been victims of bad weather and bad rules. India's match against Sri Lanka in Mackay was washed out, and Zimbabwe lost a rain-shortened match to New Zealand at Napier earlier that week.

What there was of this day (about three-and-a-half hours) belonged eventually to India. It made 7/203 from 32 overs and Zimbabwe was 1/104 from 19.1 overs when the rain became intolerable. But was the margin (a) 99 runs (the actual difference in scores), (b) 55 runs (the margin corrected against India' best 19 overs), or (c) three runs (the margin corrected against India's progress at 19 overs)? In this last scenario, Zimbabwe had lost two less wickets and in the view of some was not behind at all. Official answer: b.

Zimbabwe was privately aggrieved, and with some reason, for injustice had not only been done but had been seen to be done. Zimbabwe captain, Dave Houghton, had calculated that his team could beat Sri Lanka, New Zealand and India in the World Cup. Now, he had lost all three, failing to defend 312 against Sri Lanka and failing to reach artificial targets against the other teams. Sometimes, cricket is a computer game.

India, at least, deserved this perverse justice after two narrow losses and the washout. It always had the talent to impose itself on this tournament; now it had points and form, too. Sachin Tendulkar, 18, went pinging in the rain for 81 from 77 balls with eight 4s and a 6, his highest score in one-day internationals. Tendulkar is a master, both in the sense of 'commanding' and 'younger than a mister'. Krish Srikkanth (32, 32 balls) and Sanjay Manjrekar (34, 34 balls) also relieved a little of the gloom.

For Zimbabwe, vintage off-spinner John Traicos, took 3/35, wet ball notwithstanding, which were also his best one-day international figures. Traicos is 44, and his brief Test career with South Africa finished three years before Tendulkar was born. Here they showed each other respect; such is the fraternity of cricket.

Left-hander Andy Flower (43 not out, 57 balls), Zimbabwe's revelation in this tournament, and Ali Shah (31, 51 balls) propelled their team into a sound position. Quite reasonably, Zimbabwe had been pacing itself towards 32 overs. In anticipation of rain, it could have taken more risks and lost more wickets for more runs. But if the rain then failed to arrive, it would have been in an impossible position. The rain came anyway.

India's initial concern was to bowl 15 overs in a hurry, the minimum needed to guarantee a result. Its haste was unseemly and the game by now was barely recognisable as cricket. From the amount of slip-sliding this day, and the unsatisfactory method of arriving at a winner, this might as well have been figure skating.

PLAYER PROFILE: John Traicos

The new-era South Africans were far away, but the India v Zimbabwe match in Hamilton was something of a modest triumph for the only remaining active cricketer to have played a Test match for South Africa.

Off-spinner John Traicos, in his 16th one-day international for Zimbabwe, took 3/35, his best figures. At 44, Traicos was the oldest player in the World Cup. Before independence in 1980, Zimbabwe, nee Rhodesia, played in the Currie Cup, South Africa's domestic competition. In 1970, Traicos was picked for three Tests against Bill Lawry's touring Australians, in what turned out to be South Africa's last series for 22 years.

'I was as successful as I could ask for, really,' he said. 'I enjoyed it. I didn't do too much bowling...the seamers (Peter Pollock, Eddie Barlow, Mike Procter and Trevor Goddard) did most of the bowling, but I thoroughly enjoyed it.'

After independence, Traicos appeared for Zimbabwe, though his international career was necessarily restricted. He has played against the B teams of every Test nation, and in three World Cups.

Traicos said the standard of Zimbabwean cricket was as good now as 1980, though it had been even stronger in the intervening years when Graeme Hick, Kevin Curren and Peter Rawlston, were emerging. As to whether Zimbabwe was good enough for Test cricket, he said it was a 'chicken and egg situation', with Zimbabwe needing the hard edge of Test competition to improve. He feared South Africa's return to Test cricket would tempt young Zimbabweans to desert their homeland and weaken the standard.

There had been rumours that Zimbabwe would rejoin the South African domestic competition. 'I understand that there have been discussions along those lines,' he said. 'What will eventuate probably depends on how Zimbabwe's Test status application goes.

'With our own set-up, we would struggle to have a really meaningful first-class competition. It would certainly be better to play against the provinces, but how you would structure that with South Africa's Test status is the difficulty.'

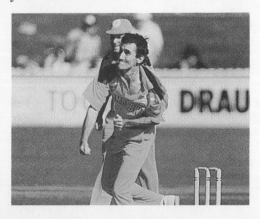

Timeless Traicos:
The oldest man in the competition at 44, John Traicos played three Tests for South Africa and now lends his experience and off-spinners to Zimbabwe's cause.

7 March. India v Zimbabwe — Hamilton.
Weather: cold, showers.

INDIA

	Runs	Balls	4s/6s
K SRIKKANTH b Burmester	32	32	5/0
KAPIL DEV lbw b Brandes	10	14	0/1
M AZHARUDDIN c Flower b Burmester	12	15	2/0
S TENDULKAR c Campbell b Burmester	81	77	8/1
S MANJREKAR c Duers b Traicos	34	34	2/0
V KAMBLI b Traicos	1	2	-
A JADEJA c Shah b Traicos	6	6	-
K MORE not out	15	8	0/1
J SRINATH not out	6	4	1/0
Sundries (3lb 3w)	6		
TOTAL for seven wickets	203		

Fall: 23, 43, 69, 168, 170, 182, 184.

	O	M	R	W	Eco	W	NB
E Brandes	7	0	43	1	6.1	-	-
K Duers	7	0	48	0	6.9	-	-
M Burmester	6	0	36	3	6.0	3	-
A Shah	6	1	38	0	6.3	-	-
J Traicos	6	0	35	3	5.9	-	-

Overs: 32.

ZIMBABWE

	Runs	Balls	4s/6s
A SHAH b Tendulkar	31	51	3/0
A FLOWER not out	43	57	3/0
A WALLER not out	13	7	2/0
Sundries (1b 11lb 5w)	17		
TOTAL for one wicket	104		

Fall: 79.

	O	M	R	W	Eco	W	NB
Kapil Dev	4	0	6	0	1.5	2	-
M Prabhakar	3	0	14	0	4.6	1	-
J Srinath	4	0	20	0	5.0	1	-
S Tendulkar	6	0	35	1	5.8	1	-
V Raju	2.1	0	17	0	7.4	-	-

Overs: 19.1
Umpires: J Buultjens, S Randell.
Crowd: Approx 2000
Player of the match: Sachin Tendulkar (India).

INDIA WON BY 55 RUNS

South Africa
eyes the semis

8 March: Pakistan v South Africa in Brisbane

South Africa announced its challenge for the semi-finals with a 20-run victory over Pakistan at the Gabba ground, at the same time all but condemning Pakistan to a premature flight back to Karachi.

The republic's third victory, aided by a rain interruption and highlighted by two inspired pieces of fielding by the hyperactive Jonty Rhodes, pole-vaulted it to third place on the table in its first World Cup.

The pivotal point of the match came in the 31st over of Pakistan's reply to South Africa's 7/211. Rain had halted Pakistan's effort at 2/74 after 21.3 overs, and, by the time umpires Steve Bucknor and Brian Aldridge sanctioned a resumption, the innings had been shortened to 36 overs. Under the controversial rain rules in operation for the tournament, the target had been recast at 194. That is, the Pakistanis required a further 120 in just 14.3 overs – a hefty asking rate of more than eight runs per over.

Captain Imran Khan and tyro Inzamam Ul-Haq were making a spirited chase when Rhodes intervened in the 31st over. The tall, powerful Inzamam, who had spanked 48 from only 45 balls, set off for a quick single only to be sent back by Imran. Rhodes, approaching from point, ran him out by centimetres with a touchdown dive that sent all three stumps flying as he declined the option of a side-on throw.

Both camps agreed later that the match hinged on this incident. Pakistan promptly lost 6/36 as the chase became too much. Imran (34) expired in the same over with a top-edged swipe, and another three wickets tumbled in the 34th, Rhodes completing his day with a brilliant, back-peddling catch from Ijaz Ahmed's skier to deep point.

The Pakistanis, reasonably placed before the rain came, thus suffered an injustice to balance their good fortune in escaping with a point from the match against England in Adelaide, where they were skittled for 74 only to be saved by rain.

Kepler Wessels acknowledged that the side batting second was disadvantaged by the rain rules. 'I think they need a balance,' he said. 'In the past it was too much the other way. They should be looking at something in between the two.'

Pakistan's cricket manager Intikhab Alam was frank: 'I think it's a bad rule. I don't want to make excuses, but...'

Rhodes' two match-winning efforts in the field contrasted with the flow of a match in which neither side impressed greatly. South Africa's 211 scarcely seemed enough on the small Gabba ground, and could have been considerably fewer had it not been for some deplorable Pakistan outfielding. Intikhab thought his side should have restricted South Africa to around 180; Wessels agreed that his side's batting was a worry, although the prolific Peter Kirsten was absent because of a calf muscle injury.

South Africa's bowling was wayward from the time Allan Donald conceded six wides, including one 4, in his opening over. One spectator carried a sign reading 'Duck, here comes Donald', but it scarcely seemed appropriate on this day. All up, the republic handed Pakistan 18 in wides and no-balls, and three catches were spilled as well.

The South African innings was built around opener Andrew Hudson's fine 54. Hudson spanked an out-of-sorts Wasim Akram for two boundaries through point in the first over and was in command until he chipped Imran to mid-wicket. In fact, the innings stalled between the 30th and 40th overs, and only some intelligent hitting from Wessel 'Hansie' Kronje (47 not out, 53 balls) and Brian McMillan (33) took South Africa past 200, that pair gathering a healthy 68 from the final 10 overs.

In the circumstances, Pakistan's batting was commendable. It had lost Rameez Raja (shoulder) and Javed Miandad (stomach infection) before the game, and Imran had just 12 fit players at his disposal. Only Pakistan, with its penchant for defying western cricket logic, could go into a one-day match at seamer-friendly Brisbane with two leg-spinners (although in fairness, it must be said that Iqbal Sikander and Mushtaq Ahmed both extracted some turn and bowled well).

Encapsulating its efforts was the bizarre incident which put paceman Aaqib Javed in hospital for an hour. Bowling the 49th over of South Africa's innings, Aaqib had David Richardson caught at long-off by Ijaz only to watch the batsmen scamper two runs as the fielder failed to hear Aldridge's call of no-ball. When the throw finally came in to wicketkeeper Moin Khan, he tossed an underarm throw in the direction of Aaqib, who was returning to his mark, and hit the bowler flush on the face as he turned.

X-rays cleared Aaqib of any fracture, but the incident could only have heightened Pakistan's suspicion that, from the time its hired gun Waqar Younis broke down before the tournament, it had been cursed.

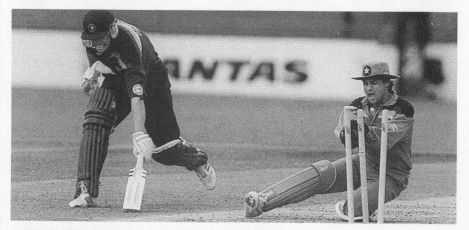

Close call: South Africa's Hansie Cronje struggles to make his ground as Pakistan's Moin Khan breaks the wicket.

PLAYER PROFILE: *Jonty Rhodes*

Who is the best fielder in world cricket? Roger Harper, with his telescopic arms and radar throws? Gus Logie, with his lightning-quick reflexes? Or Mark Waugh, with his soft hands for cradling hot slips catches?

Hold the presses. Another candidate has raised his hand. Introducing Jonathon 'Jonty' Rhodes, 22-year-old South African batsman and livewire outfielder.

Rhodes is the republic's answer to Australian Greg Matthews, or going back further, England's Derek Randall. He is never still on a cricket field. He trots between overs, collecting bowlers' hats and delivering to umpires, clapping and encouraging his teammates. But it is not just show; his catching and throwing is dynamic, as Pakistan learned at the Gabba.

Rhodes' run-out of Inzamam-Ul-Haq turned a game South Africa's way, not to mention thrilling the 8000 people at the ground. Declining the option of a side-on throw, he hurtled through the air to break the stumps with his right hand, leaving Inzamam centimetres short of his ground.

Rhodes admitted that, for an instant, he had been concerned about injury from Channel Nine's innovative stump-camera, a device implanted in the middle peg. But he spreadeagled them anyway. 'I haven't hit the wickets too often in the last few days so I thought the best bet was to get there as quickly as possible.'

Soon afterwards, he delivered another telling blow by running back 25 metres at point to hold a difficult catch to remove Ijaz Ahmed. Imagination not being one of the qualities immediately obvious in player-of-the-match judges, Rhodes was overlooked in favour of batsman Andrew Hudson. But no one was left in any doubt who had won this match for South Africa.

Jaunty Jonty: South African Jonty Rhodes, who earned high praise for his effervescent fielding, sweeps for runs.

8 March. Pakistan v South Africa — Brisbane.
Weather: showers.

SOUTH AFRICA

	Runs	Balls	4s/6s
A HUDSON c Ijaz b Imran	54	81	8/0
K WESSELS c Moin b Aaqib	7	26	-
M RUSHMERE c Sohail b Mushtaq	35	70	2/0
A KUIPER c Moin b Imran	5	12	-
J RHODES lbw b Sikander	5	17	-
H CRONJE not out	47	53	4/0
B MCMILLAN b Akram	33	44	1/0
D RICHARDSON b Akram	5	10	-
R SNELL not out	1	1	-
Sundries (8lb 9w 2nb)	19		
TOTAL for seven wickets	211		

Fall: 31, 98, 110, 111, 127, 198, 207.

	O	M	R	W	Eco	W	NB
Wasim Akram	10	0	42	2	4.2	7	2
Aaqib Javed	7	1	36	1	5.1	2	-
Imran Khan	10	0	34	2	3.4	-	-
Iqbal Sikander	8	0	30	1	3.7	-	-
Ijaz Ahmed	7	0	26	0	3.7	-	-
Mushtaq Ahmed	8	1	35	1	4.3	-	-

Overs: 50.

PAKISTAN

	Runs	Balls	4s/6s
AAMIR SOHAIL b Snell	23	53	2/0
ZAHID FAZAL c Richardson b McMillan	11	46	1/0
INZAMAM-UL HAQ run out	48	45	5/0
IMRAN KHAN c Richardson b McMillan	34	53	5/0
SALIM MALIK c Donald b Kuiper	12	11	-
WASIM AKRAM b Kuiper	9	8	1/0
IJAZ AHMED c Rhodes b Kuiper	6	3	1/0
MUSHTAQ AHMED run out	4	4	-
MOIN KHAN not out	5	5	-
IQBAL SIKANDER not out	1	3	-
Sundries (2lb 17w 1nb)	20		
TOTAL for eight wickets	173		

Fall: 50, 50, 135, 136, 156, 157, 163, 171.

	O	M	R	W	Eco	W	NB
A Donald	7	1	31	0	4.4	7	-
M Pringle	7	0	31	0	4.4	3	1
R Snell	8	2	26	1	3.2	1	-
B McMillan	7	0	34	2	4.8	4	-
A Kuiper	6	0	40	3	6.6	2	-
H Cronje	1	0	9	0	9.0	-	-

Overs: 36.
Umpires: B Aldridge, S Bucknor.
Crowd: 8108.
Player of match: Andrew Hudson (S Africa)
SOUTH AFRICA WON BY 21 RUNS.

Don't laugh, this is serious

8 March: New Zealand v West Indies in Auckland

If New Zealand were not so utterly serious about it, and successful, and by now wildly popular, one might have started to suspect it was taking a rise out of the World Cup and out of the whole concept of limited-overs cricket.

What else was a sober, serious student of cricket supposed to believe when, for the third match in a row at Eden Park, New Zealand used sometime off-spinner Dipak Patel as a successful opening bowler? Or when Mark Greatbatch opened the batting and made another half-century swinging like a baseball slugger? – except no baseballer ever charged a fast-ball pitcher like Greatbatch charged Curtly Ambrose. Or when New Zealand captain Martin Crowe set two short mid-wicket fieldsmen almost within fingertip distance of each other, like a lost slips cordon? And what to think when all this novelty cricket not only amused, but worked, with New Zealand beating the West Indies by five wickets with nine balls remaining, to be unbeaten thus far in the tournament?

This was all Crowe's doing, and yet it was he who also provided a touchstone of sanity in this Mad Hatter's tea party in the Garden of Eden. For all its gimmickry, New Zealand was starting to falter a little at 4/135 in pursuit of the West Indies 7/203 when Crowe exerted his final, and finalising influence on this match.

He made 81 not out from 81 balls, with twelve 4s, the last a straight drive for the winning runs. Crowe's genius is that no matter how pressing the demand for runs, or how tight the supply of wickets, he always bats like a batsman. It was like going to an exhibition and happening upon a classic. First there was madness with method, now there was method with result.

On a new, but equally slow, Eden Park wicket, New Zealand again tickled the West Indies to death with a feather. Patel's 10 overs yielded 19 runs and the wicket of the impatient Carl Hooper, caught by Greatbatch, who watched and waited for 10 long seconds (as timed by television) for the ball to travel via the stratosphere and ionosphere to long-on. Thereafter, he was Greatcatch, and later Greatbash.

Gavin Larsen's first over cost 14, as did Rod Latham's, and Willie Watson gave up 27 in his last two overs, more than a quarter of the West Indies score yielded in just four overs. This demonstrated just what fine judgement, discipline and especially nerve it took to play this game of Kiwi cricket, and how narrow was its margin for error. In other words, how serious was this game. Larsen recovered manfully to take 2/27 from his other nine overs. Suddenly, bland was beautiful.

Brian Lara made his third half-century of the tournament, itself worth the cost of a ticket; Keith Arthurton made 40; and wicketkeeper David Williams made a breezy 32 not out at the finish. But the West Indies could not reach terms with the slow wicket, and stopped at 7/203.

It took New Zealand a while to warm up to its batting. The venerable John Wright had been available again after injury, but the selectors had swallowed hard and kept faith with Greatbatch. Neither he nor Latham managed to lay bat on ball until the 18th delivery of the innings, which Greatbatch sliced over gully for a boundary.

Greatbatch had a foot in the door, but instead of opening it, he kicked it down. He made 50 with these scoring shots: 4, 4, 4, 4, 6, 1, 6, 1, 6, 1, 4, 1, 1, 4, 1, 2. He wasn't fussy about his sixes, hitting Ambrose, Marshall and Cummins for one each, to three of Eden Park's four corners.

As if that was not provocative enough, he played and missed two dozen times at Ambrose and Marshall. Unrepentant, he then walked down to Ambrose, swung and missed. Ambrose was beside himself with rage, and both of him advanced the length of the pitch to warn Greatbatch of the folly of messing with 'Big Ambi' from any closer than 22 yards. In one-day cricket, of course, Ambrose could be short only with words.

The crowd thought this was their cue, and began a fusilade of bottles and other debris at third-man fieldsman Winston Benjamin. The umpires stopped the game and summoned match referee Peter McDermott, who had extra police sent to the offending quarter. The West Indies emerged from a huddle and promptly had Latham caught behind. But this was the storm before the calm.

Crowe's imperious manner at the crease masked some alarm in the Kiwi camp, for wickets fell at awkward moments and its later order batsmen had had few opportunities even to bat in this tournament, let alone find form. Patel at No. 7, for instance, was having his first innings. If Patel had been given out when plainly run out by Desmond Haynes, or the West Indies had not botched another run-out chance two balls later, this story might have had a different ending.

But Crowe supervised his team back through the looking glass. He now had 263 runs for the tournament (for once out) and had won three player-of-the-match awards in five games. 'Regardless of how many great players you have, it's what you do out there that matters,' said West Indies captain Richie Richardson. It stood then as an apt epitaph to New Zealand's efforts in this World Cup.

PLAYER PROFILE: *Dipak Patel*

Of Dipak Patel's many adventures in a cricket career spanning three decades and three corners of the world, this World Cup was becoming the greatest.

New Zealand's carefully planned trap for visiting teams on Eden Park's soporific pitch was Patel's off-spin, but it took courage and nerve on the part of Patel himself to spring it. If he failed, New Zealand would have had to revert to an orthodox approach and, possibly, failure.

This day against the West Indies, Patel bowled his 10 overs for a mere 19 runs, and in his last over picked up the wicket of Carl Hooper. True to theory, the infamously impatient Hooper lashed Patel high to long-on, where Mark Greatbatch clasped the catch.

In all three of New Zealand's games at Eden Park, Patel had opened the bowling, and still had not conceded 40 runs in an innings, the bowler's break-even mark in one-day cricket. Yet in Test cricket, he was primarily a batsman; his Test bowling average was more than 100. Before this tournament, his one-day international bowling average was more than 50.

Patel, 33, was born in Nairobi, played for a long time on the English county circuit and then, in pursuit of his long-held dream of playing Test cricket, moved to New Zealand. He realised that dream, but was inconsistent in the game's highest theatre. He suffered, too, from frequent comparisons with New Zealand's former Test off-spinner, the aggressive and poplular John Bracewell.

Now, though, Patel was creating for himself a permanent place in the folklore of the game.

Opening off-spin: A frustrated New Zealander Dipak Patel after beating the bat without result. The Kiwis surprised by using Patel's off-spinners to open their attack.

8 March. New Zealand v West Indies — Auckland.
Weather: overcast.

WEST INDIES

	Runs	Balls	4s/6s
D HAYNES c and b Harris	22	61	0/1
B LARA c Rutherford b Larsen	52	81	7/0
R RICHARDSON c Smith b Watson	29	54	1/0
C HOOPER c Greatbatch b Patel	2	9	-
K ARTHURTON b Morrison	40	54	3/0
G LOGIE b Harris	3	4	-
M MARSHALL b Larsen	5	14	-
D WILLIAMS not out	32	24	5/0
W BENJAMIN not out	2	1	-
Sundries (8lb 7w 1nb)	16		
TOTAL for seven wickets	203		

Fall: 65, 95, 100, 136, 142, 156, 201.

	O	M	R	W	Eco	W	NB
D Morrison	9	1	33	1	3.7	2	1
D Patel	10	2	19	1	1.9	1	-
W Watson	10	2	56	1	5.6	-	-
G Larsen	10	0	41	2	4.1	-	-
C Harris	10	2	32	2	3.2	-	-
R Latham	1	0	14	0	14	4	-

Overs: 50

NEW ZEALAND

	Runs	Balls	4s/6s
M GREATBATCH c Haynes b Benjamin	63	77	7/3
R LATHAM c Williams b Cummins	14	27	1/0
A JONES c Williams b Benjamin	10	35	-
M CROWE not out	81	81	12/0
K RUTHERFORD c Williams b Ambrose	8	32	1/0
C HARRIS c Williams b Cummins	7	23	-
D PATEL not out	10	23	-
Sundries (7lb 5w 1nb)	13		
TOTAL for five wickets	206		

Fall: 67, 97, 100, 135, 174.

	O	M	R	W	Eco	W	NB
C Ambrose	10	1	41	1	4.1	3	-
M Marshall	9	1	35	0	3.8	1	1
A Cummins	10	0	53	2	5.3	1	-
W Benjamin	9.3	3	34	2	3.5	-	-
C Hooper	10	0	36	0	3.6	-	-

Overs: 48.3
Umpires: K Liebenberg, P McConnell
Crowd: Approx 29,000
Player of the match: Martin Crowe (New Zealand)

NEW ZEALAND WON BY FIVE WICKETS

Sri Lankan invasion fails

9 March: England v Sri Lanka in Ballarat

Australia's Sri Lankan community headed to Ballarat for its engagement with England in a much-publicised invasion of planes, trains, cars and buses. More than 5000 turned the Ballarat Oval into a 'home game' for their team that, for the most part, had played creditably throughout the tournament.

Unfortunately for the Sri Lankans, 11 Englishmen turned up as well. That was sufficient to give the Sri Lankans an awful pounding and comprehensively knock them out of reckoning in the dash for the semi-finals.

The Sri Lankan community, more than slightly miffed that the match was not considered for the Melbourne Cricket Ground and its grand new stand, took over ticket sales for the match. On that score the match was an overwhelming success; on the scoreboard it was not.

The Sri Lankans had shown throughout the competition to be batsmen of flair and spontaneity, but suffered from a lack of depth and venom in the bowling.

England did not escape unharmed. Captain Graham Gooch tore the hamstring in his left leg while fielding when the Sri Lankan innings was but four overs old and was immediately ruled out of England's next game, the important encounter against South Africa.

The win against Sri Lanka had all but secured England a spot in the semi-finals, and a win against South Africa would cement it.

'I've never had many injuries, but I seem to be catching a few over the last couple of years,' noted an observant Gooch. England's other premier batsman Allan Lamb was yet to play in the competition because of recurring hamstring problems.

England batted (thumped?) first, and swiftly set the Sri Lankans a target of 281 for victory. The final five overs gave up an extraordinary 73 runs as England ravaged the inconsequential attack.

Ian Botham, relishing his role as opener, set a torrid pace as he took an immediate liking to the short and wayward offerings of the whippy Pramodaya Wickremasinghe.

Botham struck five boundaries and two 6s on the way to 47. Had a hard chance been accepted at backward square by Asanka Gurusinha, Botham's batterings would have been curtailed at five.

Graeme Hick as always promised much, but provided just brief evidence of the form that had him rated as the best batsman in the world two years previously. He made a pleasant 41 off 62 balls and left with England 4/164 in the 39th over. Thereafter, the devastation of the Sri Lankan bowlers was comprehensive as left-hander Neil Fairbrother and vice-captain and keeper Alec Stewart struck hard and often. Their partnership lasted just nine overs but reaped 104 runs.

Stewart's 50, scored from just 32 deliveries, was one ball slower than the fastest scored in a World Cup, set by Martin Crowe earlier in this competition.

Chris Lewis was at the wicket for just six balls but was 20 not out when the umpires ruled enough is enough. Lewis continued to haunt the Sri Lankans, later with the ball, and took four wickets from eight overs as Sri Lanka fell 73 runs short.

Resistance was stout from Arjuna Ranatunga, but his teammates were overwhelmed by England's fleet of professional seamers.

Hick-up: Graeme Hick misses with a sweep shot. Keeper Hashan Tillekeratne makes good position.

PLAYER PROFILE: Chris Lewis

In the 1990s, the fountain of English cricket talent is situated not only among the boys watching from the terraces at Lord's or Old Trafford, but on the beaches of the West Indies.

Chris Lewis, a native of Georgetown, Guyana, is but one of those who have given a multi-national look to England's teams. Like so many of the West Indian cricketers who have taken up residence in England, he is a fast bowler, the geniuine article, too, and a good enough batsman to be called an allrounder.

Lewis moved to London at the age of 10, and went to the same high school (Willesden) as his future England teammate Phil DeFreitas, who had come from Dominica in the Caribbean.

Upon his first-class debut for Leicestershire he was adopted as a project player by the county's coach, Ken Higgs, the former England new-ball bowler. Higgs knew his stuff. Lewis joined England's touring team in the Caribbean in 1990, although he did not play a Test, that honour eluding him until later in the same year against New Zealand. Such is Lewis' respect for Higgs that when the latter joined Nottinghamshire, he signed with that county for 1992.

Lewis is an exceptional talent, and his first Test wicket was that of the Kiwi skipper Martin Crowe. But he is also something of an enigma, often falling victim to injury and illness. He was sent home from England's tour of Australia in 1990-91 because of stress fractures of the back, and he has also missed matches because of chronic migraine headaches.

Still, there were no doubts about his fitness or form in the World Cup game against Sri Lanka at Ballarat. He smashed an unbeaten 20 from just six balls at the end of England's innings, then ripped apart Sri Lanka's batting with 4/30 from eight overs.

Allround star:
One of England's great strengths was its number of talented allrounders. Chris Lewis was damaging with the new ball, and was a ferocious hitter late in the order.

9 March. England v Sri Lanka — Ballarat.
Weather: fine.

ENGLAND

	Runs	Balls	4s/6s
G GOOCH b Labrooy	8	28	1/0
I BOTHAM b Anurasiri	47	63	5/2
R SMITH run out	19	39	2/0
G HICK b Ramanayake	41	62	3/0
N FAIRBROTHER c Ramanayake b Gurusinha	63	70	2/2
A STEWART c Jayasuriya b Gurusinha	59	36	7/1
C LEWIS not out	20	6	1/2
D PRINGLE not out	0	-	-
Sundries (1b 9lb 9w 4nb)	23		
TOTAL for six wickets	280		

Fall: 44, 80, 105, 164, 244, 268.

	O	M	R	W	Eco	W	NB
P Wickremasinghe	9	0	54	0	6.0	3	-
C Ramanayake	10	1	42	1	4.2	3	4
G Labrooy	10	1	68	1	6.8	2	-
D Anurasiri	10	1	27	1	2.7	-	-
A Gurusinha	10	0	67	2	6.7	1	-
S Jayasuriya	1	0	12	0	12.0	-	-

Overs: 50

SRI LANKA

	Runs	Balls	4s/6s
R MAHANAMA c Botham b Lewis	9	19	1/0
A SAMARASEKERA c Illingworth b Lewis	23	29	4/0
A GURUSINHA c and b Lewis	7	9	-
A DE SILVA c Fairbrother b Lewis	7	10	-
A RANATUNGA c Stewart b Botham	36	51	6/0
H TILLEKERATNE run out	4	30	-
S JAYASURIYA c DeFreitas b Illingworth	19	16	2/0
G LABROOY c Smith b Illingworth	19	33	1/0
C RAMANAYAKE c and b Reeve	12	38	-
D ANURASIRI lbw b Reeve	11	19	-
P WICKREMASINGHE not out	6	16	-
Sundries (7lb 8w 6nb)	21		
TOTAL	174		

Fall: 33, 46, 56, 60, 91, 119, 123, 156, 158, 174.

	O	M	R	W	Eco	W	NB
D Pringle	7	1	27	0	3.8	1	3
C Lewis	8	0	30	4	3.7	2	2
P DeFreitas	5	1	31	0	6.2	3	1
I Botham	10	0	33	1	3.3	1	-
R Illingworth	10	0	32	2	3.2	-	-
D Reeve	4	0	14	2	3.5	1	-

Overs: 44
Umpires: K Hayat, P Reporter
Crowd: Approx 13,000
Player of the match: Chris Lewis (England)
ENGLAND WON BY 106 RUNS.

South Africa edges closer

10 March: Zimbabwe **v** *South Africa in Canberra*

When neighbours meet a long way from home, they exchange greetings, right? Certainly, the cricketers of South Africa and Zimbabwe were on good terms when they gathered in a bar at the Capital Parkroyal Hotel on the eve of their encounter at Canberra's delightful Manuka Oval.

But in the case of the South Africans, that was as far as the neighbourly niceties extended. Next day, they systematically crushed Zimbabwe, maintaining their push toward the semi-finals.

Sent in to bat on a slowish wicket, Zimbabwe's batting was disappointingly brittle, and it managed only 163. South Africa reached its target with 4.5 overs and seven wickets in hand, moving to third place on the table with eight points, and a breath away from qualification for the semi-finals in its first World Cup.

David Houghton, the Zimbabwe captain, was so impressed that he offered the view afterward that the South Africans would reach the final. 'If their bowlers get it in the right place, no one's going to get past 180 against them,' said Houghton, who, it must be said, is a candid man, untouched by the cynicism of the professionals he competes with.

On the day before this match he had contended that New Zealand was a pretender to the title, and that England was all but a certainty. Asked whether he thought the South Africans might have been advised to knock off the runs more quickly, given the possible implications of run-rates, he said: 'Actually, I was wishing we'd played the West Indies. They'd have done it in 25 overs and we'd have been home early.'

Plainly struggling to maintain morale after a string of five straight defeats, the Zimbabwe batsmen self-destructed after reaching a comfortable 2/72. The back-breakers were the losses of Houghton and Andy Waller in the 25th and 27th overs, both delivered by off-spinner Peter Kirsten. Both chipped catches to Hansie Cronje at deep mid-wicket and both were culpable. There was no rush at the time, and they must have known that Cronje was lurking on the boundary.

Zimbabwe never recovered, despite some wayward South African bowling (17 runs were conceded in wides and no-balls, and 28 of the total were in sundries). Apart from tail-ender Eddo Brandes, who smashed Kirsten over the mid-wicket fence, no one passed 20. Another blow was the temporary loss of talented opener Andy Flower, who had to retire hurt after being struck on the glove by Allan Donald when he was on six. Flower returned later to reach 19, but his inability to complete his customary wicketkeeping duties during the South African innings meant that Houghton, who had not donned the gloves for more than three years, had to fill in.

The South Africans would have liked to complete their chase sooner, although captain Kepler Wessels, who gathered 70 himself, said later they had aimed to finish it in around 45 overs. 'We wanted to make sure we won first,' he said. 'Run-rate won't matter if we can win another game.'

Kirsten's unbeaten and unfussed 62 saw South Africa home, and nicely complemented his efforts with the ball. Not bad for someone who was not expected to play, having missed the previous game because of a calf injury. 'If you don't play it works against you psychologically,' he said later. 'When the going's good, you have to hang in there.'

Opening star: Andrew Hudson defends against Zimbabwe. The right-hander combined with his captain Kepler Wessels to make a formidable opening pair.

PLAYER PROFILE: *Peter Kirsten*

Peter Kirsten had to wait until he was 36 before he could display his considerable talent to the followers of international cricket. Apartheid, and the world's response in the form of sporting isolation, saw to that.

But no sooner had he made his 'official' debut, against India on the subcontinent in November, than he was cast aside. Or so it seemed. South Africa named a squad of 20 'possibles' for the World Cup, and Kirsten's name was not on the list. Nor was Jimmy Cook, the republic's outstanding opening batsman, nor Clive Rice, its premier allrounder for more than a decade.

As a public tumult resulted, Kirsten, a former national captain and a fixture in South African sides for rebel Test matches throughout the 1980s, quietly set about convincing the selectors of their folly.

He reeled off such a string of big scores in domestic cricket that he more than requested selection for the trip to Australia and New Zealand; he demanded it. The rich vein of form continued in the antipodes, and his 62 not out against Zimbabwe at Manuka Oval in Canberra made him the tournament's top run-scorer at the time, with 304 at the remarkable average of 101.33.

Kirsten also bowls tidy off-spin, and his 3/31 on this day sealed the player of the match award.

The selection controversy is behind him. Asked about it at Canberra, he joked: 'They got my age wrong. No, that's passed and we're only interested in the next day. I'm just pleased to be here.'

Wise choice: Peter Kirsten, initially left out of the South African World Cup team, cuts against Zimbabwe.

10 March. Zimbabwe v South Africa — Canberra
Weather: fine.

ZIMBABWE

	Runs	Balls	4s/6s
W JAMES lbw b Pringle	5	12	1/0
A FLOWER c Richardson b Cronje	19	44	-
A PYCROFT c Wessels b McMillan	19	47	-
D HOUGHTON c Cronje b Kirsten	15	53	-
A WALLER c Cronje b Kirsten	15	28	-
A SHAH c Wessels b Kirsten	3	4	-
E BRANDES c Richardson b McMillan	20	28	1/1
M BURMESTER c Kuiper b Cronje	1	10	-
J TRAICOS not out	16	40	-
M JARVIS c and b McMillan	17	21	1/1
K DUERS b Donald	5	10	-
Sundries (10lb 13w 5nb)	28		
TOTAL	163		

Fall: 7, 51, 68, 80, 80, 115, 117, 123, 151, 163.

	O	M	R	W	Eco	W	NB
A Donald	9.3	1	26	1	2.7	1	2
M Pringle	9	0	25	1	2.7	6	3
R Snell	10	3	24	0	2.4	-	-
B McMillan	10	1	30	3	3.0	6	-
H Cronje	5	0	17	2	3.4	-	-
P Kirsten	5	0	31	3	6.2	-	-

Overs: 48.3

SOUTH AFRICA

	Runs	Balls	4s/6s
K WESSELS b Shah	70	137	6/0
A HUDSON b Jarvis	13	22	1/0
P KIRSTEN not out	62	103	3/0
A KUIPER c Burmester b Brandes	7	9	-
J RHODES not out	3	3	-
Sundries (4lb 2w 3nb)	9		
TOTAL for three wickets	164		

Fall. 27, 139, 151.

	O	M	R	W	Eco	W	NB
E Brandes	9.1	0	39	1	4.2	1	1
M Jarvis	9	2	23	1	2.5	-	2
M Burmester	5	0	20	0	4.0	1	-
A Shah	8	2	33	1	4.1	-	-
K Duers	8	1	19	0	2.3	-	-
J Traicos	6	0	26	0	4.3	-	-

Overs: 45.1
Umpires: S Bucknor, D Shepherd.
Crowd: Approx 2500
Player of the match: Peter Kirsten (South Africa)

SOUTH AFRICA WON BY SEVEN WICKETS.

Windies beat the weather

12 March: West Indies **v** India in Wellington

A difficult and unpredictable adversary awaited the West Indies this wintry afternoon at the Basin Reserve. Sometimes charging, sometimes feinting, sometimes moving in disguise, it almost deceived the West Indies into defeat. India, on the other hand, was surprisingly meek.

The weather was the problem. The West Indies ruled in almost every province of this match in their most convincing display since the first round. Yet for about half an hour in late afternoon, with some rain having fallen and more threatening, the West Indies stood in grave danger of untoward defeat. It was only when the more gloomy elements went off to play elsewhere that the West Indies could claim their rightful two points.

The West Indies left out Malcolm Marshall, officially because of a chronic ankle injury, more probably because he had become increasingly agitated by the hobbles one-day cricket placed on bowlers. Also, he had announced in a London newspaper that he was retiring after the World Cup. He was replaced this day by Phil Simmons.

India began classically, losing only one wicket in the first half of the innings, and at 3/166 in the 43rd over, appeared to have the basis of a score of more than 220. Krish Srikkanth had played with unusual restraint for 40 and captain Mohammed Azharuddin with his usual lordly aplomb for 61; one almost expected a train of courtiers to accompany him to and from the crease.

But after he was caught at deep extra cover, the rest of India sunk without trace, with no one below Sanjay Manjrekar at No. 5 reaching double figures. The beneficiary of India's charity was Anderson Cummins, who took four wickets in his last 22 balls and was player-of-the-match. But the best bowling came from Curtly Ambrose, who was called back mid-innings to deal with Sachin Tendulkar and duly fulfilled his contract with a beautiful leg-cutter.

Over lunch, the rainclouds thickened and darkened, and the respective team managers sent frantically to the scorers' box for photocopies of the books. Calculations duly made, the West Indies struck out boldly for their first objective, 103 runs in 15 overs, at which point a match would become an entity. Brian Lara, already the West Indies' success story of this tournament, was again in blistering form, swishing Manoj Prabhakar over square leg for 6 in his first over. Desmond Haynes attacked, too, and when he was out in the seventh over, Simmons opened his scoring by swinging Kapil Dev over mid-wicket for 6. Prabhakar, 3/0/32/0, was retired, and after 11 overs, the West Indies were 1/81.

Then, to the chagrin of the West Indians, the umpires stopped the game because of rain. Richardson thought it was more mist than rain. 'I wasn't getting wet,' he said later as he admitted his anxiety. When play was resumed 20

minutes later, the target had been modified to 195 from 46 overs, but with an eye
cocked to the still heavy skies, the Windies continued to blaze in anticipation of
a much shorter game. But Lara (41), Simmons (22), Richardson (3) and Gus Logie
(7) fell in 33 balls, the run rate dropped and if the rain had returned then, the
West Indies would have lost under the specious rain rule.

Fortunately, justice prevailed. The skies lightened and brightened and Keith
Arthurton and Carl Hooper, judging the danger to have passed, settled down to
bat the West Indies to victory at the comfortable clip of just more than three an
over. The need for risk was now obviated. Arthurton was sufficiently unpanicked
not to bother with a boundary until he had faced 77 balls, and he remained 58
not out. Hooper, who had previously reached double figures only against
Zimbabwe, at last showed the discernment which was needed to harness his
immense talent, and remained 34 not out. Their partnership grew apace to 83
and the West Indies won with 5.3 overs remaining. Sunshine now bathed the
Basin Reserve.

The rain rule remained a blight on the tournament. Its chief drawback was
that it constantly moved the goalposts for any team whose innings was interrupted by rain. It seemed impossible to have an equal match between teams
which did not bat for an equal number of overs. Richardson said he was always
confident of the West Indies batting this day, but not of the weather. 'I don't know
who made the rules, but to me it's a little bit unfair,' he said. 'Against New
Zealand (three days previously) they were in control for most of the match, but
had it rained when we were in the field, at any stage, we would have won. I think
that would have been unfair. I'm not sure if that rule is all that fair.'

PLAYER PROFILE: Anderson Cummins

West Indians are never quite so happy as when they are arguing, though these
disagreements are generally amiable, punctuated with 'high fives' and peals of
laughter.

One such argument broke out in the bar of a Wellington hotel on the night of
the Windies' victory over India between two of the West Indies' few supporters
on this tour. One maintained that the West Indies was lacking batsmen, the
other said it was bowlers. That, he said, was why he was rejoicing in the
performance of Anderson Cummins.

Cummins, 25, had been the leading wicket-taker in the West Indies the
previous season, emerging at the front of the Caribbean's endless queue of fast
bowlers. Tall, lean and possessing a flowing action in the style of all the West
Indian greats, he had already made a good impression during the World Series
in Australia.

He had been overlooked for the first two matches of the World Cup as the West
Indies resurrected Roger Harper for an ultimately failed experiment with double
spin. But with Malcolm Marshall literally carrying the drinks this day, Cummins
had become the third seamer in the side.

Maintaining tight control over his length and direction, Cummins compelled
mis-hits from Mohammed Azharuddin, Kapil Dev, Kiran More and Manoj
Prabhakar, all in his last 22 balls. His 4/33 was his second best one-day
international return. In more than 160 internationals, Marshall had never
taken more than four wickets in one innings.

Still, the man in the bar was not impressed. 'There's four more as good as him in Barbados alone,' he exclaimed, upon which the argument dissolved into fits of laughter. High fives and rum all round for the West Indian pair; a stiff, contemplative scotch for everyone else.

Sting in the tail: West Indian Anderson Cummins cuts short the Indian innings with four wickets in 22 balls.

**10 March. West Indies v India — Wellington.
Weather: cool, windy.**

INDIA

	Runs	Balls	4s/6s
A JADEJA c Benjamin b Simmons	27	61	2/0
K SRIKKANTH c Logie b Hooper	40	70	2/0
M AZHARUDDIN c Ambrose b Cummins	61	85	4/0
S TENDULKAR c Williams b Ambrose	4	11	-
S MANJREKAR run out	27	39	-
KAPIL DEV c Haynes b Cummins	3	5	-
P AMRE c Hooper b Ambrose	4	8	-
K MORE c Hooper b Cummins	5	5	1/0
M PRABHAKAR c Richardson b Cummins	8	10	1/0
J SRINATH not out	5	11	1/0
V RAJU run out	1	1	-
Sundries (6lb 5w 1nb)	12		
TOTAL	197		

Fall: 56, 102, 115, 166, 171, 172, 180, 186, 193, 197.

	O	M	R	W	Eco	W	NB
C Ambrose	10	1	24	2	2.4	-	-
W Benjamin	9.4	0	35	0	3.6	4	-
A Cummins	10	0	33	4	3.3	-	-
P Simmons	9	0	48	1	5.3	1	1
C Hooper	10	0	46	1	4.6	-	-
K Arthurton	1	0	5	0	5.0	-	-

Overs: 49.4

WEST INDIES

	Runs	Balls	4s/6s
D HAYNES c Manjrekar b Kapil	16	16	3/0
B LARA c Manjrekar b Srinath	41	37	6/1
P SIMMONS c Tendulkar b Prabhakar	22	20	2/1
R RICHARDSON c Srikkanth b Srinath	3	8	-
K ARTHURTON not out	58	99	3/0
G LOGIE c More b Raju	7	10	1/0
C HOOPER not out	34	57	3/0
Sundries (8lb 2w 4nb)	14		
TOTAL for five wickets	195		

Fall: 57, 81, 88, 98, 112.

	O	M	R	W	Eco	W	NB
Kapil Dev	8	0	45	1	5.6	-	-
M Prabhakar	9	0	55	1	6.1	1	1
V Raju	10	2	32	1	3.2	1	-
J Srinath	9	2	23	2	2.5	-	3
S Tendulkar	3	0	20	0	6.6	-	-
K Srikkanth	1	0	7	0	7.0	-	-
A Jadeja	0.3	0	5	0	10.0	-	-

Overs: 40.3
Umpires: S Randell, S Woodward
Crowd: Approx 5000
Player of the match: Anderson Cummins (West Indies)
WEST INDIES WON BY FIVE WICKETS

Tempers flare, Australia fails

11 March: Australia **v** Pakistan in Perth

The scrap between Australia and Pakistan – and that is about the only way to describe it – started on Wednesday afternoon, but the fallout did not settle until 12.30 the following morning when the fines were read out by a weary official at the members' bar.

Michael Whitney, Moin Khan and Aamir Sohail were each relieved of $250 for their parts in a game that was marked by a series of disputes, culminating in a clash between Whitney and Moin that turned physical.

These two pre-tournament fancies arrived in Perth nestled together near the bottom of the table, with only Zimbabwe to look down on. Their frustration was obvious as they squabbled like a couple of irritable children, the umpires repeatedly having to step in and replace spat dummies.

Moin, the Pakistan wicketkeeper, was annoyed when an appeal for caught behind was turned down in the second last over, even though by then Pakistan's victory was a formality. He spoke to Whitney and gestured accusingly at him; Whitney responded by lashing out angrily with his right arm, brushing Moin's glove away.

Non-striker Bruce Reid and Indian umpire Piloos Reporter moved in to separate Whitney from an expanding group of Pakistani players. South African umpire Karl Liebenberg spoke to Imran Khan, who defused the volatile situation by ordering his players back to their positions with a few words in Urdu.

Fortunately, the cricket was every bit as dramatic as the extra-curricular stuff. Pakistan played superbly for all but the final six overs of its innings to win the battle of the under-achievers by 48 runs.

Pakistan was sparked to life by a series of outstanding individual performances, none better than those from two precocious young men competing for alphabetical pre-eminence in the Pakistani side – Aamir Sohail and Aaqib Javed.

The senior professionals, Imran Khan and Javed Miandad, also made brave and telling contributions, despite being in varying degrees of discomfort.

Perhaps the main difference between the sides was attitude. Defending a total of 9/220, Pakistan came out and played in the uninhibited manner Australia promised itself it would, but somehow lacked the conviction to carry through.

Wasim Akram and Aaqib Javed followed Imran's instructions to attack and forget about their troubles (Akram in particular) controlling the white ball. They bowled 10 wides between them, but unsettled Australia's top-order in the process.

Aaqib was the pick of the bowlers. Of his three wickets, two were caught in slips, Tom Moody at first and David Boon at third. And any team that picks up the opposition's best player at third slip in one-day cricket, as Pakistan did with Boon, deserves its success.

Pakistan was also rewarded for having 10 overs worth of faith in a leg-spinner, another rarity in this form of the game. Mushtaq Ahmed varied his flight cleverly and threw in the odd wrong'un, claiming the key wickets of Dean Jones (caught at long off in the decisive dismissal of the night), Mark Waugh and Allan Border at a crucial stage of the Australian innings.

Then there was Imran, at his wily best despite a nagging shoulder injury that required a painkiller before the match and a cortisone injection afterwards. Imran did not try anything fancy, merely directing his body-seeking inswingers just short-of-a-length and cramping the batsmen for room.

He removed Geoff Marsh with precisely this method, ending an unfortunate evening for the Australian vice-captain, who was jeered by his home crowd during his laboured innings of 39 (91 balls). Marsh kept his sense of humour throughout, clenching his fists in an ironic salute when he French cut the only boundary of his innings.

Pakistan again turned to Sohail, who is yet to play a Test match but destined for those honours, for the bulk of its runs. The left-handed opener fashioned 76, pulling anything short (and even a few that weren't) until the shot finally brought about his downfall.

Sohail had a mixed evening, winning the $500 player-of-the-match award, but losing half the money in a fine for disputing a turned down appeal against David Boon for caught behind. The other booking was Moin, again, for unsportsmanlike behaviour following Steve Waugh's dismissal, although he was cleared on the grounds of mistaken identity.

The batting support came from Javed, who had been suffering from a severe stomach infection for more than a week, and doubled up in discomfort several times during his innings. He started with a nostalgic square drive, but relied on clever deflections after that.

Apart from Craig McDermott, the one constant in a faltering side, Australia's bowlers contrived to lack both vigour and control. Border twice queried Liebenberg for no-ball calls against Steve Waugh, whose first five overs cost 21. (Mind you, he was better value than Mark, whose one over cost 13). Displaying the qualities that earned him the 'Iceman' tag during the 1987 World Cup, Steve returned to take 3/15 in the second half of his stint as Pakistan failed to capitalise on its good start.

Both sides finished with death or glory dashes for runs, which proved more suicidal than sensible. Pakistan, after electing to bat on a hard, bouncy WACA ground wicket, lost its last 6 wickets for 27. Australia was a more terminal case, losing its last eight wickets for 56. Border failed for the fifth time in five World Cup innings as his side sunk to its nadir.

PLAYER PROFILE: Aaqib Javed

The yellow bible (aka Wisden) quotes Aaqib Javed's date of birth as 5 August 1972.

That means that he was 16 when he made his one-day international debut in Australia in 1988, and that he was still in his teens – 19 1/2 in fact – when he returned to Australia for the third time for the World Cup.

Despite that sort of experience, and the wispy moustache, Aaqib was still very much the baby-faced assassin of the Pakistani side. He warmed up for the World Cup in Sharjah, where he took 7/37 in the final against India, including a hat-trick of lbws.

Aaqib has had a surprisingly sparse Test career, but for a variety of reasons was suddenly elevated to a position of primary responsibility in the Pakistan attack during the World Cup.

Waqar Younis, the express bowler, went home before the competition started with stress fractures; Imran Khan, the veteran, was plagued by a shoulder injury; and Wasim Akram, the fiery swing merchant, was moving the white ball around too much for his own good.

Relishing a rare opportunity to bowl on the world's bounciest wicket, Aaqib responded superbly against Australia in Perth. Charging in with a full head of steam, he nevertheless resisted the temptation many visiting bowlers fall for – of pitching too short – and tormented the Australian batsmen with his fast outswingers and leg cutters.

Required for only eight overs because of Australia's collapse, he took 3/21, including the wickets of Tom Moody and David Boon, the first two to fall. Moody was neatly taken by Salim Malik at first slip and Boon by Mushtaq Ahmed at third slip in a devastating opening spell of 6-1-11-2.

Both deliveries were worthy of removing top-class players at Test level, where perhaps Aaqib will next make his mark.

Successful stand-in: Aaqib Javed joined Wasim Akram in the new-ball duties after Waqar Younis was sent home with stress fractures of the back.

11 March. Australia v Pakistan at Perth.
Weather: fine.

PAKISTAN

	Runs	Balls	4s/6s
AAMIR SOHAIL c Healy b Moody	76	106	8/0
RAMEEZ RAJA c Border b Whitney	34	61	4/4
SALIM MALIK b Moody	0	6	-
JAVED MIANDAD c Healy b S Waugh	46	75	3/0
IMRAN KHAN c Moody b S Waugh	13	22	0/1
INZAMAM-UL-HAQ run out	16	16	-
IJAZ AHMED run out	0	2	-
WASIM AKRAM c M Waugh b S Waugh	0	1	-
MOIN KHAN c Healy b McDermott	5	8	-
MUSHTAQ AHMED not out	3	5	-
Sundries (9lb 16w 2nb)	27		
TOTAL for nine wickets	220		

Fall: 78, 80, 157, 193, 194, 205, 205, 214, 220.

	O	M	R	W	Eco	W	NB
C McDermott ...	10	0	33	1	3.3	3	-
B Reid	9	0	37	0	4.1	4	2
S Waugh	10	0	36	3	3.6	6	-
M Whitney	10	1	50	1	5.0	2	-
T Moody	10	0	42	2	4.2	1	-
M Waugh........	1	0	13	0	13.0	-	-

Overs: 50

AUSTRALIA

	Runs	Balls	4s/6s
T MOODY c Malik b Aaqib	4	18	-
G MARSH c Moin b Imran	39	91	1/0
D BOON c Mushtaq b Aaqib	5	15	1/0
D JONES c Aaqib b Mushtaq	47	79	2/0
M WAUGH c Ijaz b Mushtaq	30	42	2/0
A BORDER c Ijaz b Mushtaq	1	4	-
S WAUGH c Moin b Imran	5	6	1/0
I HEALY c Ijaz b Aaqib	8	15	-
C McDERMOTT lbw b Akram	0	2	-
M WHITNEY b Akram	5	9	-
B REID not out	0	-	-
Sundries (7lb 14w 7nb)	28		
TOTAL	172		

Fall: 13, 31, 116, 122, 123, 130, 156, 162, 167, 172.

	O	M	R	W	Eco	W	NB
Wasim Akram ...	7.2	0	28	2	3.8	4	3
Aaqib Javed	8	1	21	3	2.6	6	1
Imran Khan	10	1	32	2	3.2	-	-
Ijaz Ahmed	10	0	43	0	4.3	4	3
Mushtaq Ahmed .	10	0	41	3	4.1	-	-

Overs: 45.2. Umpires: P Reporter, K Liebenberg.
Crowd: Approx 22,500. **Player of the match:** Aamir Sohail (Pakistan)

PAKISTAN WON BY 48 RUNS.

Stewart leads from the front

12 March: England v South Africa in Melbourne

England's match against South Africa at the Melbourne Cricket Ground put the No Gooch-No England theory to the test, when the English captain made himself unavailable through injury. Unfortunately for South Africa, which required just one more victory to reach the semi-finals, the theory went the way of the Flat Earth Society.

This meeting of founder nations of the International Cricket Council was their first sanctioned rendezvous in 27 years, since South Africa toured England in 1965 under Peter van der Merwe, coincidentally the republic's present chairman of selectors.

Befitting such an historic occasion, the teams played a marvellous match – one of the World Cup's best. Sent in by England's stand-in captain Alec Stewart, South Africa batted soundly to reach 4/236. England reached 0/62 in 12 overs, but its task was made more difficult by a 43-minute rain interruption, after which the target was reset at 226 from 41 overs. Suddenly, the asking rate was 164 from the last 29 overs, at a rate of nearly a run per ball, and England promptly lost three wickets for a single run in the space of two overs.

But blazing hands from Stewart, Neil Fairbrother and Chris Lewis saw England home with one ball to spare, and later Gooch joined the growing line of critics of the World Cup rain rules. 'It's just not a fair system,' he said. 'But you can't change it midway through a tournament.'

England's win was made all the more remarkable considering the absence of the hamstrung Gooch and Allan Lamb, not to mention the fact that bowlers Phil DeFreitas and Dermot Reeve had to leave the field with leg ailments, and all-rounder Lewis could not bowl because of a side strain.

Little wonder Gooch, was in rare form at the press conference, England having clinched a semi-final berth along with New Zealand. Someone pointed out that it was England's 11th straight one-day international since the last defeat. 'Let's hope we can make it 14,' said Gooch, then realising his mistake, '... or it's 15, isn't it?'

Upon reflection the South Africans would acknowledge that they did not make enough of the 151-run opening stand between Kepler Wessels and Andrew Hudson. Hudson, a handsome striker, laced his 79 with sparkling drives and cuts, and his onslaught on Gladstone Small saw the paceman permanently banished to the outfield after only two overs.

Wessels eschewed unnecessary risk and played intelligently, taking 92 balls to reach his half-century, then striking at run-a-ball pace until he holed out at 85. But once that pair departed South Africa could not push on, paying dearly for the loss of the prolific Peter Kirsten (11), who chipped a catch to Robin Smith in the outfield.

England was so short of able bodies that it had to draft Essex batsman Paul Pritchard (in Australia to play Sydney grade cricket) as a substitute fielder. Off-spinner Graeme Hick, who would not have figured in Stewart's pre-match bowling plans, had to complete 8.2 overs when Reeve slipped and fell heavily during his third over.

The South African bowlers had been troubled by inaccuracy in previous games, but right from the time Allan Donald began his furious opening spell, they were on song during this game. As ever, the fielding was outstanding. England simply batted too well.

Stewart led superbly, making light of his heavy-duty workload (Gooch had directed him to open the innings in his absence, as well as taking the captaincy, not to mention the wicketkeeping duties). He was perilously close to lbw at 45, shouldering arms to Brian McMillan, but otherwise he assumed complete command, thrashing seven boundaries in his 77 from 88 balls. Only a dynamic piece of fielding by Jonty Rhodes, making a diving save at backward point and cleverly throwing to the non-striker's end, brought Stewart undone after he had completed his highest score in a one-day international.

The flying start provided by the acting skipper along with Ian Botham (22) proved critical, given the rain interruption. Upon the resumption, Robin Smith marred his first game against his native land with a second-ball duck, and Hick failed again.

Fairbrother and Lewis borrowed from their acting captain's tactics and confident demeanour. Fairbrother played a couple of murderous short-arm jabs past point on his way to an unbeaten 75, while Lewis vindicated his selection as a batsman only with 33 from just 22 balls, including four picket-rattling 4s and one astonishing on-drive.

Even so, England had to get 134 from the last 20 overs, and 67 from the last 10. The target was only two when Richard Snell began the last over. Fairbrother was unable to score from the first two deliveries, then took a single from the third, and 25,000 hearts fluttered together when Derek Pringle was superbly caught at short mid-wicket by Adrian Kuiper from the fourth. DeFreitas pushed the second-last ball past cover to clinch England's fifth win of the tournament, leaving South Africa the task of beating India in Adelaide to reach the semi-finals.

PLAYER PROFILE: Neil Fairbrother

Lancastrian left-hander Neil Fairbrother probably was destined to play for England from the time of his birth. After all, his parents had decreed on the birth certificate that he be known as Neil Harvey Fairbrother, honouring one of the greatest of all lefties, the Australian Neil Harvey, scorer of 21 Test centuries.

But that is not to say cricket honours came easily for N.H. Fairbrother. Although he made his debut for England at Test level in 1987, his Test match caps had been well-spaced by the time he arrived in Australia for the World Cup at 28.

At first-class level, and in one-day cricket, though, there was another story. In 1990, Fairbrother accumulated more than 1500 runs at county level, averaging

85.   His 366 for Lancashire against Surrey at The Oval was the second-highest in first-class cricket by an Englishman, surpassed only by the 424 by another Lancastrian, Archie McLaren, nearly a century earlier at Taunton.

In limited-overs cricket he was one of the secrets to Lancashire's domination of the abridged game in England. A brilliant fielder and punishing batsman, he was considered to be one of the specialists in England's side for the World Cup.

And so it proved at the Melbourne Cricket Ground against South Africa, when his unbeaten 75 from only 83 balls spirited England to a memorable victory that sealed its place in the semi-finals. Fairbrother had a century against the West Indies at one-day international level to his credit, but captain Graham Gooch could not recall his man playing better for England.

'No, I've not seen him play better in a tight pressure situation,' said Gooch. 'Neil knows what his job is, and that's to bat in the middle-order and win matches. He's doing a fine job of it.'

One-day specialist: Neil Fairbrother swings the ball to leg in his fast and furious match-winning innings against South Africa.

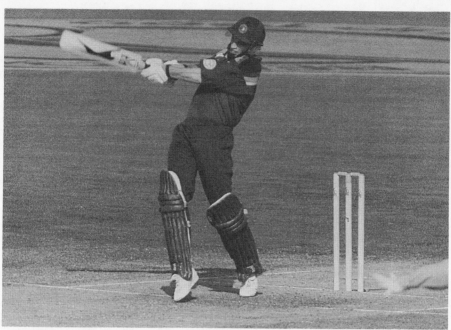

Swinging skipper: After a slow and cautious start Kepler Wessels thumps a short delivery to leg late in the South African innings.

This could be out: Ian Botham has his middle stump shattered as England restarts its run chase in the rain-reduced game against South Africa.

**12 March. England v South Africa — Melbourne.
Weather: warm, showers.**

SOUTH AFRICA

	Runs	Balls	4s/6s
K WESSELS c Smith b Hick	85	126	6/0
A HUDSON c and b Hick	79	115	7/0
P KIRSTEN c Smith b DeFreitas	11	12	0/1
J RHODES run out	18	23	-
A KUIPER not out	15	12	1/0
H CRONJE not out	13	15	-
Sundries (4b 4lb 4w 3nb)	15		
TOTAL for four wickets for	236		

Fall: 151, 170, 201, 205.

	O	M	R	W	Eco	W	NB
D Pringle	9	2	34	0	3.7	2	3
P DeFreitas	10	1	41	1	4.1	1	-
I Botham	8	0	37	0	4.6	-	-
G Small	2	0	14	0	7.0	1	-
R Illingworth	10	0	43	0	4.3	-	-
D Reeve	2.4	0	15	0	5.7	-	-
G Hick	8.2	0	44	2	5.3	--	

Overs: 50.

ENGLAND

	Runs	Balls	4s/6s
A STEWART run out	77	88	7/0
I BOTHAM b McMillan	22	30	1/0
R SMITH c Richardson b McMillan	0	2	-
G HICK c Richardson b Snell	1	4	-
N FAIRBROTHER not out	75	83	6/0
D REEVE c McMillan b Snell....................	10	15	-
C LEWIS run out	33	22	4/0
D PRINGLE c Kuiper b Snell	1	3	-
P DEFREITAS not out	1	1	-
Sundries (3lb 1w 2nb)	6		
TOTAL for seven wickets	226		

Fall: 62, 62, 64, 132, 166, 216, 225.

	O	M	R	W	Eco	W	NB
A Donald	9	1	43	0	4.7	-	1
M Pringle	8	0	44	0	5.5	1	1
R Snell	7.5	0	42	3	5.3	-	-
B McMillan	8	1	39	2	4.8	-	-
A Kuiper	4	0	32	0	8.0	-	-
H Cronje	3	0	14	0	4.6	-	-
P Kirsten	1	0	9	0	9.0	-	-

Overs: 40.5
Umpires: B Aldridge, J Buultjens
Crowd: 25,248
Player of the match: Alec Stewart (England)

ENGLAND WON BY THREE WICKETS

Kiwis burn in the cold

12 March: New Zealand **v** India in Dunedin

The winds of change were fairly howling at Carisbrook, cricket's southernmost outpost in the reproduction Scottish city of Dunedin. Gusting at up to 120 kmh, express from the South Pole, they knocked a panel out of a sightscreen and threatened to carry away a beer tent. Snow glistened on the peaks of the nearby Southern Alps and the forecast maximum of 14° Celsius proved wildly optimistic. New Zealand's captain, Martin Crowe, said he had never before felt so cold on a cricket ground.

Or so warm. Austere Carisbrook was becoming special in the hearts of New Zealanders. It was here on 12 February, as Crowe tried desperately to turn around a ruinous summer, that he hit upon the theory with which the Kiwis were ambushing all comers in this World Cup. With England about to win another one-day international, Crowe threw the ball to ultra-slow medium Rod Latham, who promptly had Ian Botham caught and finished with three wickets. New Zealand still lost, but by a margin narrow enough to represent a victory.

Slow bowlers for slow wickets; from desperation, inspiration, from inspiration, sensation. It was thus that off-spinner Dipak Patel had become New Zealand's regular opening bowler; and slow-medium Chris Harris, who rarely bowls for his provincial team, Canterbury, was now the tournament's leading wicket-taker.

It had become New Zealand's joke on the cricket world. At Wellington, as the Indians boarded their plane to Dunedin, the pilot welcomed them, promised them clear weather and spectacular views, then added: '...and remember, the Carisbrook wicket is low and slow.'

Later, and again virtually by accident, Mark Greatbatch became a loose cannon of an opening batsman. These three men were New Zealand's shock troops, and again its best players as India succumbed on this day.

There was another significant development. Previously, New Zealand had said it would use these remaining qualifying matches to give a taste to its fringe players and perhaps to contrive to avoid Australia in the semi-finals. Now, Crowe admitted that this line of thinking had been 'naive', that New Zealand would field its strongest team, seeking to win every match, and that it would think of a Sydney semi-final as a challenge to be relished, not an appointment to be feared.

New Zealand appeared to have shed its inferiority complex. Instead of hoping it was a team capable of performing honourably in the semi-finals, it firmly believed it could reach and win the final.

India batted first, backing its own eccentric opener, Krish Srikkanth, to break the spell Patel had cast over opening batsmen in this tournament. But Srikkanth (0) belted Patel's third ball directly to Latham at long-on. Ajay Jadeja retired hurt with a hamstring strain and not, as first suspected, frostbite.

Captain Mohammed Azharuddin and Sachin Tendulkar restored parity with a partnership of 127 in 20 overs; this was the delightful duet Antipodean fans had been awaiting all summer. Azharuddin raised 50 with a clean 6 from Patel over long-on, but was out in the same over to Greatbatch's tumbling outfield catch. This gave Patel 2/29 from his 10 overs; he was conceding less than three per over in the tournament.

Tendulkar reached 84 with six 4s, all through the off-side, but was smartly caught by wicketkeeper Ian Smith, standing up to Harris. Kapil Dev cavorted for 33 (17 balls) and India settled at 6/230.

New Zealand's innings began with the now obligatory Greatbatch whirlwind. With licence to exploit the 15-over rule, he warmed up with a couple of short irons over mid-on, then moved into his work, crashing Kapil Dev for two upwind 6s over square leg. Kapil was taken for three 6s altogether, a previously unknown indignity.

Greatbatch's third six was a curio, two with four overthrows, but his fourth was a classic, hitting Subroto Banerjee into the patched-up sightscreen. The wind was now at gale force, but Greatbatch was its equal. He reached 50 from 47 balls and New Zealand outscored India by almost 40 runs over the first 15 overs. Like Curtly Ambrose before him, Manoj Prabhakar protested Greatbatch's impudence with lame words.

Sanjay Manjrekar lost track so completely of a high catch, swirling on the wind, that he failed to get a hand on it. But so had Ken Rutherford in the morning.

Eventually, the wind and Greatbatch were spent, and it fell to Andrew Jones to guide New Zealand home with a carefully manufactured 67 not out. Crowe was dismissed for only the second time in the tournament by a stroke of genius from wicketkeeper Kiran More, who reached out with one glove and batted the ball, backhand and unsighted, into the stumps. Nevertheless, New Zealand won with 17 balls remaining.

By the day's end, India had an estimated five captains on the field, excluding Azharuddin, such was its disarray. Meanwhile, the sun was smiling weakly on Dunedin. It had been a day for New Zealand's new hard hearts and its hardy souls.

PLAYER PROFILE: Andrew Jones

Andrew Jones will never win style marks, nor does he seek them. When he first came into international cricket five years ago, his manners at the crease gained him the unflattering epithet of 'Ugly Duckling' in Australia. He forced that back down his detractors' throats with a big Test century.

Though he averages about 45 in more than 60 one-day internationals, he remains unfashionable. When he walked out on to Carisbrook that afternoon, he was introduced as Martin Crowe, which was probably wishful thinking on the announcer's part. Just so there would be no further mistakes, Jones stayed to the end, making 67 not out, his highest score of the tournament, and piloting New Zealand to victory

Jones, 32, told the *Evening Post's* Lynn McConnell that batting behind Mark Greatbatch was not the party it might have seemed. 'It makes me more nervous. It is pretty tense stuff,' he said. 'You hope he keeps going because that sort of hitting often forces errors in the field. It also has a big effect on the run-rate, so that you are not looking at such a big requirement.'

Jones met the requirement with eight cover and straight drives for boundaries. They were very nearly classical. The ugly duckling had played India's swansong.

12 March. New Zealand v India— Dunedin.
Weather: cold, windy.

INDIA

	Runs	Balls	4s/6s
A JADEJA ret hurt	13	32	1/0
K SRIKKANTH c Latham b Patel	0	3	-
M AZHARUDDIN c Greatbatch b Patel	55	99	3/1
S TENDULKAR c Smith b Harris	84	105	6/0
S MANJREKAR c and b Harris	18	25	-
KAPIL DEV c Larsen b Harris	33	17	5/0
S BANERJEE c Greatbatch b Watson	11	9	1/0
K MORE not out	2	8	-
J SRINATH not out	4	3	-
Sundries (1b 4lb 4w 1nb)	10		
TOTAL for six wickets	230		

Fall: 4, 149, 167, 201, 222, 223.

	O	M	R	W	Eco	W	NB
C Cairns	8	1	40	0	5.0	-	1
D Patel	10	0	29	2	2.9	-	-
W Watson	10	1	34	1	3.4	-	-
G Larsen	9	0	43	0	4.7	-	-
C Harris	9	0	55	3	6.1	2	-
R Latham	4	0	24	0	6.0	2	-

Overs: 50

NEW ZEALAND

	Runs	Balls	4s/6s
M GREATBATCH c Banerjee b Raju	73	76	5/4
R LATHAM b Prabhakar	8	22	1/0
A JONES not out	67	107	8/0
M CROWE run out	26	29	3/1
I SMITH c sub (Amre) b Prabhakar	9	8	1/0
K RUTHERFORD lbw b Raju	21	24	3/1
C HARRIS b Prabhakar	4	17	-
C CAIRNS not out	4	5	1/0
Sundries (4b 3lb 4w 8nb)	19		
TOTAL for six wickets for	231		

Fall: 36, 118, 162, 172, 206, 225.

	O	M	R	W	Eco	W	NB
Kapil Dev	10	0	55	0	5.5	1	1
M Prabhakar	10	0	46	3	4.6	-	2
S Banerjee	6	1	40	0	6.6	-	1
J Srinath	8	0	35	0	4.3	2	3
V Raju	10	0	38	2	3.8	1	-
S Tendulkar	1	0	2	0	2.0	-	-
K Srikkanth	1.1	0	8	0	6.4	-1.	

Overs: 46.1
Umpires: I Robinson, P McConnell
Crowd: Approx 9000
Player of the match: Mark Greatbatch (New Zealand)

NEW ZEALAND WON BY FOUR WICKETS.

The Windies apply the heat

*13 March: West Indies **v** Sri Lanka in Berri*

The West Indies chances of triumph in the World Cup were not considered great when their squad – minus the veteran core of Viv Richards, Gordon Greenidge and Jeff Dujon – was announced.

After all, the players had floundered their way around Australia in the World Series competition against Australia and India earlier in the summer. They failed to reach the finals and gave no hint – unless there was a massive transfusion of talent – that their World Cup campaign would be any more successful. However, when the West Indies returned to Australia for the World Cup, their selectors resisted the temptation to restore the old order and were roundly criticised for such an omission.

But in the horrible heat (38 degrees) of Berri, South Australia, the Windies captain Richie Richardson was confidently predicting a finals berth and a worthwhile tilt at the cup. After the West Indies defeated Sri Lanka with precision and purpose by 91 runs, they were on eight points and heading for a last-round showdown with Australia for the fourth spot in the finals. 'Bring on Australia,' Richardson said after the match. 'It is always good to beat Australia.'

His optimism appeared well-placed. Certainly the demolition of the Sri Lankan threat was as cool and calculated as the weather was hot and ennervating. Sent into bat, the West Indies set the Sri Lankans the significant task of topping 8/268 off 50 overs. Phil Simmons, a bit player in the cup campaign so far, faced 125 balls for a delightful, often brutal, 110 runs. The Sri Lankans could have had him twice on 47, but the chances were not held. Simmons prospered from their generosity, cracking nine 4s and two 6s, something that would have made Sri Lankan skipper Aravinda De Silva hot under the collar whether it had been 38 or 3.8 degrees.

The Windies total could have been far greater, but after Simmons left at 4/197 in the 40th over the innings lost direction and five wickets fell for 31 runs. Chandika Hathurusinghe, whose placid medium pacers are rarely considered a key to the Sri Lankan attack, claimed three wickets in two overs. It was left to late-order thrashings from Winston Benjamin and Curtly Ambrose to restore the balance in favour of the batting side.

The Sri Lankan batsmen wilted in the run chase after Athula Samarasekera belted a rapid 40 in even time off Benjamin and Ambrose before being trapped in front.

PLAYER PROFILE: *Phil Simmons*

Nobody need tell Phil Simmons how hard a game of cricket can be.

In 1987, when the West Indies went to the fourth World Cup on the Indian subcontinent, opener Gordon Greenidge declined the trip, and Simmons was introduced to the most powerful team in the world.

Early indications were that the Caribbean champions had discovered an opener to fill the shoes of Greenidge or Desmond Haynes when either of that illustrious pair retired.

But in England in 1988, the high hopes were put on hold. Playing in a tour game for the West Indies against Gloucestershire, Simmons was hit in the head by a delivery from David Lawrence, himself of West Indian origin. The blow fractured Simmons' skull.

Four years on, the Trinidadian was still on the long haul back. To nearly all batsmen, the effect of a blow to the head takes years to overcome, and more than one promising career has been ruined by the psychological effects. Put simply, batsmen who have been hit in the head often become tentative. Fast bowlers being uncharitable souls, they prise open these small weaknesses with little subtlety.

Simmons fought through this period, forcing out another opener, Philo Wallace, who toured Australia for the triangular World Series but was dropped for the World Cup.

Then at Berri in South Australia, Malcolm Marshall, who was troubled by an ankle injury, could not play against Sri Lanka; so Simmons played, and struck 110 in a typically free-wheeling fashion. He won the player-of-the-match as the West Indians kept alive their semi-final hopes.

Simmons was dropped three times before he was 50 – but would anyone deny him a slice of good luck?

Back in business:
West Indian
Phil Simmons crashes
a drive against
Sri Lanka in his furious
century that marked
his comeback from a
serious head injury.

13 March. West Indies v Sri Lanka — Berri
Weather: hot

WEST INDIES

	Runs	Balls	4s/6s
D HAYNES c Tillekeratne b Ranatunga	38	47	3/1
B LARA c and b Ramanayake	1	6	-
P SIMMONS c Wickremasinghe b Hathurusinghe ...	110	125	9/2
R RICHARDSON run out	8	23	-
K ARTHURTON c Tillekeratne b Hathurusinghe	40	54	1/0
G LOGIE b Anurasiri	0	2	-
C HOOPER c Gurusinha b Hathurusinghe	12	12	1/0
D WILLIAMS c Tillekeratne b Hathurusinghe	2	3	-
C AMBROSE not out	15	14	0/1
W BENJAMIN not out	24	20	1/0
Sundries (9lb 3w 6nb)	18		
TOTAL for eight wickets	268		

Fall: 6, 72, 103, 197, 199, 219, 223, 228.

	O	M	R	W	Eco	W	NB
P Wickremasinghe	7	0	30	0	4.2	2	1
C Ramanayake ..	7	1	17	1	2.4	1	1
D Anurasiri	10	0	46	1	4.6	-	-
A Gurusinha	1	0	10	0	10	-	-
A Ranatunga	7	0	35	1	5.0	-	-
R Kulpage	10	0	64	0	6.4	-	-
C Hathurusinghe .	8	0	57	4	7.1	-	4

Overs: 50

SRI LANKA

	Runs	Balls	4s/6s
R MAHANAMA c Arthurton b Cummins	11	50	-
A SAMARASEKERA lbw Hooper	40	41	4/1
C HATHURUSINGHE run out	16	25	1/0
A DE SILVA c and b Hooper	11	19	-
A RANATUNGA c Benjamin b Arthurton	24	40	1/1
A GURUSINHA c Richardson b Ambrose	10	30	-
H TILLEKERATNE b Ambrose	3	9	-
R KALPAGE not out	13	45	-
C RAMANAYAKE b Arthurton	1	6	-
D ANURASIRI b Benjamin	3	14	-
P WICKREMASINGHE not out	21	21	2/0
Sundries (8lb 14w 2nb)	24		
TOTAL for nine wickets	177		

Fall: 56, 80, 86, 99, 130, 135, 137, 139, 149.

	O	M	R	W	Eco	W	NB
C Ambrose	10	2	24	2	2.4	6	-
W Benjamin	10	0	34	1	3.4	5	-
A Cummins	9	0	49	1	4.9	3	-
C Hooper	10	1	19	2	1.9	-	-
K Arthurton	10	0	40	2	4.0	-	1
P Simmons	1	0	3	0	3.0	-	-
A Jadeja	0.3	0	5	0	10.0	-	-

Overs: 50
Umpires: D Shepherd, S Woodward
Crowd: 2650
Player of the match: Phil Simmons (West indies)

WEST INDIES WON BY 91 RUNS

Everyone's a comedian: A banner at the SCG reminds the Australian fans that their team is nowhere to be seen.

Major breakthrough: The South Africans descend on Meyrick Pringle after he bowled the dangerous Ian Botham for 21.

Winner's smile: Javed Miandad leaves the field surrounded by teammates and supporters after he helped guide Pakistan into the final with his maturely gathered 57 runs.

Sad farewell: Dejected and shell-shocked New Zealanders Mark Greatbatch and Martin Crowe farewell and thank their supporters.

The Waugh whirlwind

14 March: Australia v Zimbabwe in Hobart

If a soothsayer had told David Houghton before the World Cup that Zimbabwe would trail Australia by one place with two games remaining, his smile would have been as wide as Victoria Falls.

No one, including Houghton – whose faith in the Australians extended to a small financial outlay – expected the defending champions to be lurking at second last place on the table.

That, of course, left Zimbabwe in its familiar role as a shoe-shine boy, going about its business at the foot of the list and shining the reputations of others in the process.

Houghton was smiling anyway. At birth he was handed a liberal dose of fatalism, surely a prerequisite for the job as captain of the world's best non Test-playing nation. Which other World Cup captain had to prepare to meet the world's elite by playing Malaysia on coconut matting wickets in The Hague?

And yet, suddenly, Zimbabwe, the 1990 ICC Trophy champion, and Australia, the 1987 World Cup champion, were bottom-of-the-ladder bedfellows for their match at Bellerive Oval in Hobart.

Could Zimbabwe repeat the heroics of 9 June 1983, when, on its one-day international debut, it defeated Australia by 13 runs at Trent Bridge, a win that has never been repeated and stands out like a beacon in the history of Zimbabwean cricket?

Houghton thought probably not. He rated this Australian side as vastly superior to the 1983 misfits and said it would be intent on 'annihilating' his travel-weary men.

Houghton had his annihilation all right – 128 runs. Australia needed to lift its net run-rate if it was to have any chance of making the semi-finals and it applied the turbo-charge against Zimbabwe.

If there was a temptation for some teams earlier in the competition to toy with Zimbabwe, like an A-grade pennant tennis player making a game of it with a social hitter, then Australia resisted it. For the first time in the tournament, albeit against a less than formidable opponent, Australia batted, bowled and fielded with conviction.

The desperation of Australia's plight finally provided the team with a catalyst for getting its attitude and its batting order right. Geoff Marsh, who had made 151 runs in five innings but used up more than 60 overs – an entire innings plus 10 overs – in the process, was discarded, and David Boon and Dean Jones were restored to their rightful places as opening batsman and No. 3 respectively.

After being sent in to bat, Australia's innings followed a familiar pattern with the first wicket falling to a run-out involving Boon. This time the victim was not

Boon himself, but Moody, left stranded after Boon sent him back.

The Tasmanian quickly made amends, batting with poise and balance during a partnership of 94 (131 balls) with Dean Jones for the second wicket. Boon made 48 and Jones 54 in the first of two important Australian double acts before lunch.

The second, a fifth-wicket partnership of 113 (69 balls!) between the Waugh twins lifted Australia's tournament out of the mundane. The Waughs should have been separated almost immediately, had Zimbabwean wicketkeeper Andy Flower not dropped Steve – a diving catch off Mark Burmester that he should nevertheless have held – before he had scored.

Steve made Zimbabwe pay with a quickfire 55, gleaning runs by changing his shot midstream and sending fine leg and third man in pursuit of balls deflected just wide of the wicketkeeper while he and Mark belted between wickets. He was thunderous as well as deft, smashing one ball back so hard at Eddo Brandes that it was more a case of a lucky escape from serious injury than a dropped catch.

But, for all his energy, not even Steve could keep up with Mark, who blasted an unbeaten 66 from only 39 balls. Together they guided Australia to a formidable 6/265 from 46 overs, the match having been reduced when rain interrupted play during the Australian innings. John Traicos was the only bowler to escape serious punishment.

As was the case in several of its earlier matches, Zimbabwe set out not to make the target, but to make itself look respectable. Bowled out for 137, it was hard to say whether they achieved their aim.

Certainly the opening batsmen, left-handers Ali Shah and Andy Flower, looked all at sea during a fine opening assault from Craig McDermott and Bruce Reid. The outside edge was beaten so often it was funny, although, to give them credit, they were two of only three Zimbabweans to pass 20. The other was Brandes, whose strong-arm tactics were, perhaps, laced with retribution for Steve Waugh's widow-making drive earlier in the day.

All three threatened to frustrate Australia's aim of a quick kill, particularly Shah and Flower with an opening partnership of 47 that ended only when Shah chanced Bruce Reid's arm.

Michael Whitney, with 1/15 from 10 overs, was the stingiest of a frugal bunch of bowlers, although his generosity to the crowd knew no bounds. He not only responded to each round of applause at fine-leg, but stayed out on the ground for almost an hour after play signing several hundred autographs.

PLAYER PROFILE: *Mark Waugh*

Mark Waugh is noted, above all, for his elegance. His strokeplay and slips catching are a delight for their simplicity of movement, intrinsic balance and apparent effortlessness.

Which is why one-day cricket can be a nice leveller. For a moment at Bellerive Oval, Waugh was transformed into one of those weekend golfers who hack their way around public courses and swing lustily at everthing in the hope that, one day, they will hit the perfect ball.

That is the only way to describe Waugh's two 6s in one over off Zimbabwean medium-pacer Kevin Duers, hit straight into a stiff wind blowing off the Derwent River estuary and across Bellerive Oval.

The difference, of course, was that, despite the ungainly method, both balls were hit with the sweet timing that weekend golfers only dream about. After all, it is difficult to question the credentials of a man who needs only 39 balls to compile a small masterpiece of 66 not out.

With Australia in the middle of a run frenzy, Duers was attempting to restrict the flow by pitching as full as possible. Waugh, who wanted distance and elevation in a hurry, improvised to counter him.

'If they bowl short of a length you can hit it off the front foot in the air, but if they're bowling full you've got to try to lean back and get underneath them and hit them off the back foot,' he explained.

No one really cared. Australian audiences had waited what seemed like an eternity for the sight of Waugh at full flight – this was his first one-day international half-century in more than a year – and somehow it was appropriate that the people of Hobart, normally starved of top-level cricket, were given a treat that their mainland cousins had been denied.

Waugh zone:
Mark Waugh launches another boundary in his return-to-form against the hapless Zimbabweans in Hobart.

14 March. Australia v Zimbabwe — Hobart.
Weather: showers

AUSTRALIA

	Runs	Balls	4s/6s
T MOODY run out	6	8	1/0
D BOON b Shah	48	84	4/0
D JONES b Burmester	54	71	4/0
A BORDER st Flower b Traicos	22	29	2/0
M WAUGH not out	66	39	5/2
S WAUGH b Brandes	55	43	4/0
I HEALY lbw b Duers	0	2	-
P TAYLOR not out	1	1	-
Sundries (2b 8lb 2w 1nb)	13		
TOTAL for six wickets	265		

Fall: 8, 102, 134, 144, 257, 258.

	O	M	R	W	Eco	W	NB
E Brandes	9	0	59	1	6.5	-	1
K Duers	9	1	48	1	5.3	1	-
M Burmester	9	0	65	1	7.2	1	-
A Shah	9	0	53	1	5.8	-	-
J Traicos	10	0	30	1	3.0	-	-

Overs: 46

ZIMBABWE

	Runs	Balls	4s/6s
A SHAH run out	24	47	2/0
A FLOWER c Border b S Waugh	20	49	1/0
A CAMPBELL c M Waugh b Whitney	4	20	-
A PYCROFT c M Waugh b S Waugh	0	1	-
D HOUGHTON b McDermott	2	10	-
A WALLER c Taylor b Moody	18	39	2/0
K ARNOTT b Whitney	8	15	-
E BRANDES c McDermott b Taylor	23	28	3/0
M BURMESTER c Border b Reid	12	24	-
J TRAICOS c Border b Taylor	3	9	-
K DUERS not out	2	10	-
Sundries (11lb 8w 2nb)	21		
TOTAL	137		

Fall: 47, 51, 51, 57, 69, 88, 97, 117, 132, 137

	O	M	R	W	Eco	W	NB
C McDermott	8	0	26	1	3.2	3	1
B Reid	9	1	18	1	2.0	-	1
S Waugh	7	0	28	2	4.0	4	-
M Whitney	10	3	15	2	1.1	-	-
T Moody	4	0	25	1	6.5	1	-
P Taylor	3.4	0	14	2	3.8	-	-

Overs: 41.4
Umpires: B Aldridge, S Bucknor
Crowd: 7363
Player of the match: Steve Waugh (Australia)

AUSTRALIA WON BY 128 RUNS.

South Africa grabs semi spot

15 March: India v South Africa in Adelaide

Twenty-one years after the world wagged its finger, drew a deep breath and threw the best cricket team on the planet out of its clique, South Africa grasped a chance of climbing back to the summit when it toppled India at Adelaide Oval.

At 5.30 pm Wessel 'Hansie' Cronje scooped Manoj Prabhakar over mid-wicket, and by the time it trickled into the gutter he was engaging in an unpretentious victory jig. Even the stoic Kepler Wessels broke into a grin, and with good reason.

South Africa was into the semi-finals, joining New Zealand and England. The republic's fifth win gave it an unassailable 10 points, leaving the more highly rated Australia, Pakistan and West Indies to squabble over the fourth berth and fret about run rates, rain rules and the like.

Wessels' team had achieved its stated aim, and a celebration was in order. 'They won't be in bed by nine, that's for sure,' said the manager, Alan Jordaan.

The match was reduced to a 30-over lottery by persistent rain that delayed the start until 1.15pm. The Indians, sent in by Wessels, put together an imposing 6/180, but South Africa answered the challenge and had five balls to spare and six wickets in hand when Cronje sealed the issue.

The Indians had surrendered their chance of reaching the last four at the previous outing, but their spirit remained intact, and the batsmen cut loose on a typically benign Adelaide Oval strip. After the early departure of Krish Srikkanth (0), captain Mohammed Azharuddin conjured another astonishingly beautiful innings of 79 from only 77 balls.

The skipper's contribution, along with a brutal 42 from only 29 balls by Kapil Dev, saw India accumulate 80 runs from the final 10 overs. Azharuddin and Kapil Dev added 71 in eight overs, the latter finding his best vintage by hoisting Allan Donald over fine leg for 6 in the second-last over.

Richard Snell suffered most in the onslaught, conceding 46 runs in his six overs, but South Africa's grit was epitomised by Brian McMillan, who agreed to play despite a serious ankle injury. McMillan had pain-killers to get through the previous game; this time he knocked back the doctor's treatment and completed his six overs for only 28 runs. He had to leave the field immediately, but it was worth the effort. By day's end McMillan knew he had a valuable week to recover.

When the South Africans replied they had elevated Peter Kirsten to open instead of Wessels, who acknowledged later that the shorter games do not suit his style. The ploy worked, as Andrew Hudson (53) and Kirsten, who played superbly for 83, put together the stand that set up South Africa's win, 128 in 24 overs.

Given licence to hit over the top, Hudson struck four boundaries and impressed again, although the television replays showed he was lucky to escape a run-out decision when he was 34. Sachin Tendulkar's freakish fielding – as though the save from his own bowling was not enough, he had the cheek to throw down the stumps as Hudson retreated – surprised everyone, not least umpire Khizar Hayat.

Kirsten merely rolled on, piercing the gaps in the manner of a batsman of the highest quality along the way to 84, his fourth half-century of the tournament and clinching a second player-of-the-match award. His innings, halted when Kapil Dev yorked him in the flurry at the end, came from just 86 balls.

The drama kept coming. Jonty Rhodes strode out, smacked the second ball he faced from Manoj Prabhakar over square leg for 6, then sliced the next one into Venkatapathy Raju's safe hands at gully. So it was left to Wessels and Cronje.

South Africa had required 30 off the last five overs, and the tension did not subside until Kapil Dev delivered his last ball of the 29th over, a rare full toss. Wessels smeared it to the cover boundary; Cronje jumped and punched the air. Only two were wanted from Prabhakar's last over, and Cronje needed just one ball to seal it.

India's assignment, spanning four months and including air travel estimated by its manager, Abbas Ali Baig, at more than 100,000 kilometres, was complete, albeit unsuccessful. Luck had gone against it, and the hurt was evident in Azharuddin's voice as he told how he had genuinely believed his side could reach the semi-finals.

The South Africans had a week to prepare for either England or New Zealand, in Sydney or Auckland. Wessels would not even name a preferred opponent. 'We don't really mind, because we've got absolutely nothing to lose now.'

Scrambling Kambli: Indian youngster Vinod Kambli is short of his crease as South African's Meyrick Pringle breaks the stumps and successfully appeals for a run-out.

PLAYER PROFILE: *Mohammad Azharrudin*

Almost ritually, Indian cricket teams have been riddled with the sort of political trouble that brings down governments. Factions, infighting, and backstabbing are there for all to see. Captains are chosen and replaced in the shortest time spans, and it is nothing to see a side that includes three or four former captains.

In electing Mohammad Azharuddin as its latest leader, the Indian authorities showed a spirit of compromise. Azharuddin is Muslim, while the teams generally are dominated by Hindus and Sikhs. Moreover, he is a patently decent man, universally popular and respected for his great talent as a batsman.

But for all his efforts to galvanise India in the Australian summer of 1991-92, he could not elicit the best from his side. In the Test series against Australia, he lost 0-4, although the consensus indicated the margin flattered Allan Border's team. The Indians also were beaten in the finals of the World Series, and failed to reach the semi-finals of the World Cup.

The match against South Africa at Adelaide Oval was their last, the possibility of reaching the semi-finals already having disappeared. Azharuddin played a cameo, wristily flicking balls off his stumps to the leg-side boundary and pounding cover drives. He hit 79 from 77 balls, but India lost. And finally the frustration came out. 'The young players disappointed me,' he said. 'I thought they would have been keener, but they weren't up to the mark.'

Azharuddin's tournament tally stood at 332 runs, averaging 47. At least no one could blame the captain this time.

The master: Mohammad Azharrudin lashes a ball through the off-side in his masterly innings against South Africa.

An old hand: South Africa's veteran Peter Kirsten leaps high to his left to hold a marvellous catch and send India's Kris Srikkanth on his way.

15 March. India v South Africa — Adelaide.
Weather: cold, rain

INDIA

	Runs	Balls	4s/6s
K SRIKKANTH c Kirsten b Donald	0	5	-
S MANJREKAR b Kuiper........................	28	53	-
M AZHARUDDIN c Kuiper b Pringle	79	77	6/0
S TENDULKAR c Wessels b Kuiper	14	14	1/0
KAPIL DEV b Donald	42	29	3/1
V KAMBLI run out	1	3	-
P AMRE not out	1	1	-
J SRINATH not out	0	-	-
Sundries (7lb 6w 2nb)	15		
TOTAL for six wickets	180		

Fall: 1, 79, 103, 174, 177, 179

	O	M	R	W	Eco	W	NB
A Donald	6	0	34	2	5.6	3	-
M Pringle........	6	0	37	1	6.1	2	2
R Snell	6	1	46	0	7.6	-	-
B McMillan 6		0	28	0	4.6	-	-
A Kuiper	6	0	28	2	4.6	1	-

Overs: 30

SOUTH AFRICA

	Runs	Balls	4s/6s
A HUDSON b Srinath..........................	53	73	4/0
P KIRSTEN b Kapil Dev	84	86	7/0
A KUIPER run out	7	6	-
J RHODES c Raju b Pravhakar	7	3	0/1
K WESSELS not out	9	6	1/0
H CRONJE not out	8	6	1/0
Sundries (10lb 3nb)	13		
TOTAL for four wickets	181		

Fall: 128, 149, 157, 163

	O	M	R	W	Eco	W	NB
Kapil Dev........	6	0	36	1	6.0	-	-
M Prabhakar ...	5.1	1	33	1	6.4	-	-
S Tendulkar	6	0	20	0	3.3	-	-
J Srinath	6	0	39	1	6.5	-	3
V Raju	6	0	43	0	7.1	-	-

Overs: 29.1
Umpires: J Buultjens, K Hayat
Crowd: 6272
Player of the match: Peter Kirsten (South Africa)
SOUTH AFRICA WON BY SIX WICKETS.

Pakistan makes its move

15 March: Pakistan v Sri Lanka in Perth

Pakistan, shoddy at the start and indifferent in the middle, was suddenly looming as the team with the momentum and skill to take a strong hand in shaping the finals of the World Cup. Certainly, it looked every bit the genuine contender as it handsomely and calmly defeated Sri Lanka at the WACA ground in Perth.

And while Pakistan won with just four balls to spare, it always had control over the match, patiently pacing itself to victory and just two points short of reaching the semi-finals. Victory over New Zealand and a loss by Australia to the West Indies in the final round-robin games would cement its place in the play-offs for a trophy it had never won.

'We are very confident of victory in Christchurch (New Zealand),' Intikhab Alam told the media. 'New Zealand wickets usually don't have much pace in them and they have a low bounce which suits the players in our team. We need another match to go our way, but we just have to concentrate on what we have to do to make the finals.'

Set a task of 213 runs against Sri Lanka, experienced batsmen Salim Malik (51) and Javed Miandad (57) structured the victory after in-form openers Aamir Sohail (1) and Rameez Raja (32) failed to make a substantial start.

Captain Imran Khan was striking the ball as well as anyone in the tournament but this day he struggled to take the initiative away from the honest but humble Sri Lankan attack. He made 22, at one stage dithering over 37 balls for two runs, but it was invaluable practice for the campaign ahead.

Malik and Javed then added 101, both displaying such marvellous creativity with the bat that field placings almost became irrelevant.

In the end, the equation read two overs remaining and eight runs required, a simple task for batsmen who keep their head.

Pakistan tackles one-day cricket differently from any other nation, happily taking in leg-spinners and feeding them to the middle-order.

And it was the wrist spin of Mushtaq Ahmed, a whirling, whizzing copy of Pakistan's great but eccentric spinner Abdul Qadir, that stopped Sri Lanka in its tracks. The 21-year-old showed his potency when he grabbed three wickets at crucial times against Australia in their previous match. He did the same to Sri Lanka.

Manager Intikhab admitted he tended to be expensive. 'He may have been giving up 40 runs but he has been the one to get the wickets the pace bowlers haven't been able to dismiss.'

But Mushtaq is so aggressive and confident, bowling wrong'uns and often employing teasing flight, and his strike rate more than balances the ledger. He claimed two Sri Lankans – Chandika Hathurusinghe (five) and Athula

Samarasekera (38) – and stymied the Sri Lankan push towards a score that would daunt Pakistan's old pros.

Telling evidence: Sri Lanka's Roshan Mahanama looks back to see the damage done by Pakistan's elite fast bowler Wasim Akram.

PLAYER PROFILE: *Aravinda De Silva*

He has an uncomfortable-looking, two-eyed stance, perhaps because his right leg is two centimetres shorter than the left. He rocks and shuffles around the crease as the bowler prepares to deliver, defying the old convention that says a batsman must remain still until the ball is delivered.

But then, convention is anathema to him. In moments of frustration, he has been known to conceive shots that seem physically impossible, let alone products of the textbook – shots such as the reverse hook.

He is Aravinda De Silva, Sri Lanka's captain and premier batsman.

De Silva came to Australia for the World Cup with a reputation as being among the best batsmen in the world. He had risen to his national team while he was still at school, much to his mother's trepidation. His mother wanted him to stay at school; his father, who had ensured that the young Aravinda had cricket bats to match his (lack of) size from his childhood, smoothed things over.

He came to Australia to represent the Sri Lankans in 1984-85 as a 19-year-old, and learned the hard ways of international cricket. Four years later he was to take centuries in successive Tests from the Australians on the hard, fast wickets, thrashing their bouncers to and over the square-leg fences of the Brisbane and Bellerive grounds.

He had taken such a toll of Pakistan in a Sharjah match that Imran Khan had publicly wondered where he could bowl to such a player. He had hit a Test double-century against New Zealand in Wellington.

When people asked him whom he admired of his peers, he would reply that Viv Richards' unorthodoxy and presence inspired him. But he was also his own man.

Against Pakistan at the WACA Ground, with his team needing a win to stay in the semi-final race, De Silva gathered 43. Imran had the field set so deep that he was able to take 23 singles. But when he was out, Sri Lanka's hopes subsided. This is often the way for Sri Lanka.

Premier bat: The inventive style of Sri Lankan captain and No. 1 batsman Aravinda De Silva is perfect for the hustle of one-day cricket.

15 March. Pakistan v Sri Lanka — Perth.
Weather: fine

SRI LANKA

	Runs	Balls	4s/6s
R MAHANAMA b Akram	12	36	1/0
A SAMARASEKERA st Moin b Mushtaq	38	59	1/0
C HATHURUSINHA b Mushtaq	5	29	-
A DE SILVA c Aamir b Ijaz	43	56	2/0
A GURUSINHA c Malik b Imran	37	54	2/0
A RANATUNGA c sub (Zahid) b Aamir	7	19	-
H TILLEKERATNE not out	25	34	3/0
R KALPAGE not out	13	14	-
Sundries (15lb 6nb 11w)	32		
TOTAL for six wickets for	212		

Fall: 29, 48, 99, 132, 158, 187

	O	M	R	W	Eco	W	NB
Wasim Akram	10	0	37	1	3.7	2	4
Aaqib Javed	10	0	39	0	3.9	3	2
Imran Khan	8	1	36	1	4.5	-	-
Mushtaq Ahmed	10	0	43	2	4.3	2	-
Ijaz Ahmed	8	0	28	1	3.5	3	-
Aamir Sohail	4	0	14	1	3.5	1	-

Overs: 50.

PAKISTAN

	Runs	Balls	4s/6s
AAMIR SOHAIL c Mahanama b Ramanayake	1	10	-
RAMEEZ RAJA c Gurusinha b Wickremasinghe	32	56	3/0
IMRAN KHAN c De Silva b Hathurusinha	22	69	2/0
JAVED MIANDAD c Wickremasinghe b Gurusinha	57	84	3/0
SALIM MALIK c Kalpage b Ramanayake	51	66	2/0
INZAMAM-UL-HAQ run out	11	11	-
IJAZ AHMED not out	8	6	1/0
WASIM AKRAM not out	5	5	1/0
Sundries (12lb 9w 8nb)	29		
TOTAL for six wickets for	216		

Fall: 7, 68, 84, 185, 201, 205.

	O	M	R	W	Eco	W	NB
K Wijegunawardena	10	1	34	0	3.4	-•	7
C Ramanayake	10	1	37	2	3.7	4	-
P Wickremasinghe	9.1	0	41	1	4.4	1	-
A Gurusinha	9	0	38	1	4.2	1	-
C Hathurusinha	9	0	40	1	4.4	2	1
R Kalpage	2	0	14	0	7.0	1	-

Overs: 49.1
Umpires: K Liebenberg, P McConnell
Crowd: 3048
Player of the match: Javed Miandad (Pakistan)
PAKISTAN WON BY FOUR WICKETS.

Sweet revenge for Kiwis

*15 March: New Zealand **v** England in Wellington*

The New Zealand captain, Martin Crowe, wore the air of a man who dared not pinch himself at the end of this momentous day. Already this World Cup had been a fantasy realised, but victory over England had transported it into another realm. This was the same England which, just two months previously, had humiliated the Kiwis so thoroughly that there were calls across the nation for Crowe's head. Now, they wanted to crown him.

This was for New Zealand a record-equalling seventh consecutive victory, and denied England what would have been a world record 11th straight win. The emerging heroes of the tournament, Dipak Patel, Chris Harris and Mark Greatbatch, again blazed the trail, and Crowe and player-of-the-match Andrew Jones marched down it in splendour. This New Zealand side was changed out of all recognition from the one England last played; only the personnel were the same.

But this was a different England, too, a lame and listless residue. While its players hobbled, its selectors cobbled and eventually went with Phil DeFreitas and Dermott Reeve at less than full fitness, and Chris Lewis as batting cover for the returning Allan Lamb. Graham Gooch was still unfit and Neil Fairbrother was too indisposed by a virus to play. By day's end, there was another casualty, with Derek Pringle suffering pain under his ribs.

Crowe, relieved to learn that England had overlooked left-arm spinner Phil Tufnell, chose to bowl first. Remembering the hiding Ian Botham had dispensed to the New Zealand fast attack in an earlier international in Christchurch, Crowe pushed up Harris to open the bowling for the first time for any team.

But Patel, now entrusted with the first over, soon rid the Kiwis of the Botham menace. Botham was so undecided about where to hit a straight ball on middle-and-leg that by the time he had made up his mind, it had bowled him. Pre-match, Botham had publicly challenged Greatbatch to take him on in 6s, but for once his crude psychological warfare failed. Patel again transfixed good batsmen.

Nonetheless, England made a dashing start. The daily-more impressive Alec Stewart, a star of the earlier Test series in New Zealand, found this attack familiarly mild, and Graeme Hick settled into it as comfortably as if it were a favourite armchair. They pierced the field for regular boundaries, ran up 70 in 14 overs for the second wicket, and a score of 250 beckoned.

Harris was unsuccessful with the new ball, Willie Watson and Chris Cairns were both wayward early, and wicketkeeper Ian Smith retired with a migraine, leaving the gloves to Greatbatch.

But these Kiwi insurgents had the scent of success, and with a bit of tactical musical chairs, they struck back. Stewart (41) swept Patel to mid-wicket, where

Harris accepted a sharp catch, and Hick (56) dabbled with a ball from Harris and was caught by Greatbatch. These wickets were bought in part by Gavin Larsen, who again bowled with sparing economy of effort and result.

Meanwhile, New Zealand uncovered another bowler, the sometime off-spinner Jones, who conceded 14 from his first two overs, but returned for the wickets of Robin Smith and Pringle, both hitting ill-advisedly into the wind. In the image of Patel, Jones was so effective that Crowe was able to bowl him 'in the death', the one-day jargon for the end of the innings.

Lamb, who had not had a game for a month, played the innings of a man a month out of the game. England proceeded exclusively in singles for 11 overs, managed one solitary boundary after the 37th over, and stopped at 8/200.

New Zealand was again sent on its merry way to victory by Greatbatch, whose 35 was a tempered innings by recent, radical standards, though he did swipe Pringle behind square leg for 6. His only real sacrilege was to charge Botham's first ball. Next over, Botham had him caught at deep backward square, and did his jig.

But the next dance was from the all-New Zealand combination of Jones and Crowe, who batted the Kiwis to the threshold of victory with a 108-run partnership in 23 overs. Jones is a batting contradiction, seeming to potter for much of the time, but suddenly unfurling a glorious on, off or cover drive. Thus he made 78 before Hick ran him out.

Crowe's idiosyncrasy of hanging his head at the crease was at odds with his most obvious qualities in this tournament: pride in self and nation. Nevertheless, he made an authoritative 73 not out, without fireworks, for none were needed. New Zealand gained victory with the luxury of seven wickets and 9.1 overs unspent.

New Zealand now could boast three of the 12 highest run-makers in the tournament: Crowe, Jones and Greatbatch. It also boasted the tournament's leading wicket-taker, the seemingly guileless Harris, and the most thrifty bowler, Patel (2.9 runs conceded per over). Crowe called Patel the best spinner in the tournament, not to mention best opening bowler.

England's major concern was not the defeat, in itself unimportant, but whether it could raise a fit XI by the semi-finals. To every other question, coach, captain and acting captain replied, 'I don't know.' New Zealand was having that effect on everyone.

PLAYER PROFILE: Chris Harris

If Chris Harris were to develop any airs about his run of success in the World Cup, he would only have to return to his home club of St Albans in Christchurch to be brought back promptly to earth. There, he is regarded strictly as a second-change bowler.

Harris, 22, is the son of a former New Zealand player, Zin Harris, who died of cancer late last year and so missed Chris's glory. He takes from his father his unusual second name, Zinzan, which has been handed down through his family's generations.

Harris was blooded in the World Series in Australia in 1991, and performed with honour in a subsequent short series against England. He has not yet played a Test. His bowling action is quaint, almost wrong-footed, primarily because all his coaching was directed towards his batting. He scored two centuries for Canterbury in New Zealand's domestic competition leading up to the World Cup, but rarely bowled.

But when the Kiwis formulated their slowly-slowly policy, Harris was their man. His 15 wickets in the series to date included Desmond Haynes, Sachin Tendulkar, Kapil Dev, Graeme Hick, Gus Logie and Arjuna Ranatunga. As a further development of that policy, Harris was given the new ball against England, his first appearance as a new-ball bowler for any team. Though the ploy failed initially, Harris returned later for the important wickets of Hick and later Phil deFreitas.

Harris is also a national indoor cricket representative.

Secret weapon: Chris Harris, who rarely bowls his plain medium pacers at club level, was New Zealand's secret weapon.

15 March. New Zealand v England — Wellington.
Weather: warm, windy

ENGLAND

	Runs	Balls	4s/6s
A STEWART c Harris b Patel	41	59	7/0
I BOTHAM b Patel	8	25	1/0
G HICK c Greatbatch b Harris	56	70	6/1
R SMITH c Patel b Jones	38	72	3/0
A LAMB c Cairns b Watson	12	29	-
C LEWIS c and b Watson	0	1	-
D REEVE not out	21	27	1/0
D PRINGLE c sub (Latham) b Jones	10	17	-
P DEFREITAS c Cairns b Harris	0	1	-
R ILLINGWORTH not out	2	2	-
Sundries (1b 7lb 4w)	12		
TOTAL for eight wickets	200		

Fall: 25, 95, 135, 162, 162, 169, 185, 195.

	O	M	R	W	Eco	W	NB
D Patel	10	1	26	2	2.6	-	-
C Harris.........	8	0	39	2	4.8	1	-
W Watson	10	0	40	2	4.0	1	-
C Cairns	3	0	21	0	7.0	1	-
G Larsen	10	3	24	0	2.4	1	-
A Jones	9	0	42	2	4.6	-	-

Overs: 50

NEW ZEALAND

	Runs	Balls	4s/6s
M GREATBATCH c DeFreitas b Botham	35	37	4/1
J WRIGHT b DeFreitas	1	5	-
A JONES run out	78	113	13/0
M CROWE not out	73	81	6/0
K RUTHERFORD not out	3	12	-
Sundries (1b 8lb 1nb 1w)	11		
TOTAL for three wickets	201		

Fall: 5, 64, 172.

	O	M	R	W	Eco	W	NB
D Pringle	6.3	1	34	0	5.2	1	1
P DeFreitas	8.3	1	45	1	5.3	-	-
I Botham	4	0	19	1	4.7	-	-
R Illingworth	9	1	46	0	5.1	-	-
G Hick	6	0	26	0	4.3	-	-
D Reeve	3	0	9	0	3.0	-	-
G Small	4	0	13	0	3.2	-	-

Overs: 41
Umpires: S Randell, I Robinson
Crowd: Approx 12,500
Player of the match: Andrew Jones (New Zealand)
NEW ZEALAND WON BY SEVEN WICKETS.

Australia wins, loses

18 March: Australia **v** West Indies in Melbourne

It was a night for spoilers.

First, the news from Christchurch, that Pakistan had beaten New Zealand and put Australia out of the World Cup, was flashed across the giant electronic scoreboard at the MCG to anti-climactic groans from the crowd.

Then, almost as if out of spite, the Australians played like they had not played all tournament and dragged the West Indies down with them.

Australia won the match, but lost the trophy; the West Indies just lost.

As the night progressed, the news filtered through that President F. W. De Klerk had won his referendum on racial reform and that the South African cricket team, which had qualified for the semi-finals, would not have to do the honourable thing and quit the tournament.

The president of the United Cricket Board of South Africa, Geoff Dakin, had promised to do as much if a 'no' vote threatened to disrupt the tournament. In the end, such talk became academic, just as talk about Australia needing to win by a certain margin to qualify for the semi-finals ahead of the West Indies became academic.

By becoming the first team in the competition to defeat New Zealand, Pakistan administered the punch-drunk Australians with the inevitable and lethal blow they had been avoiding like a man putting off a visit to the dentist.

But fourth spot was still up for grabs and the West Indies needed only to defeat the demoralised Australians to pip Pakistan for a place in the semi-finals. True to the disappointing form of the three previous Cup winners – the West Indies, India and Australia, none of which qualified for the semi-finals – they failed dismally.

Perhaps, it was a direct response to having the burden of favouritism lifted, for it is easy to be brave when you have nothing to lose, but the Australians suddenly turned tenacious fighters. In their best and last display of the tournament, they won their first World Cup victory over the West Indies by 57 runs with 7.2 overs to spare. (The margin, incidentally, would have been more than enough to secure Australia a semi-final place ahead of the West Indies on run rate, had Pakistan lost).

If not for Brian Lara, the West Indies would have gone home without a fight in a match they always anticipated would decide their fate in the tournament. Lara fought like a pirate on the deck of a sinking ship, brandishing his bat like a cutlass, every elaborate flourish designed to wound mortally. That backlift is not designed for taking prisoners. In the end he was brought down not by Australia, but by some inane running, or non-running, from Winston Benjamin, who refused to budge when Lara called him through for a quick single.

Australia opted to bat first and made 6/216, almost half of which was put on in an opening stand of 107 between Tom Moody and David Boon. Moody was out for 42, trying to force the pace, to a fine catch by Benjamin diving forward at deep square-leg. Boon went on to make 100, although the batting fell away dramatically after those two, with six other players and sundries providing the balance.

Allan Border's calamitous World Cup came to an end when he missed an attempted bunt off medium pacer Phil Simmons and was lbw for 8, only slightly below his tournament average of 8.57. He fielded questions after the match about his future, but said he would like to stay on as captain if the selectors wanted him.

There were early signs that all was not well in the West Indian camp. A series of misfields included uncharacteristic errors from the captain, Richie Richardson, and the vice-captain, Gus Logie. David Williams had a poor night behind the stumps – even his stumping of Mark Waugh was on the second attempt to remove the bails – and the bowlers over-pitched to Boon, who gleefully punished anything full.

The Australians then managed what they had failed to do for most of the competition. They took early wickets. Craig McDermott struck twice in the seventh over, removing Desmond Haynes, in his 200th one-day international, and Phil Simmons with successive deliveries.

Pressure on: Australia's campaign never recovered from its disastrous start. And the pressure on Allan Border never eased.

Richardson survived the hat-trick ball, but not a devastating spell from Michael Whitney, who took the next four wickets. Richardson was ruled caught behind by Indian umpire Piloos Reporter although, with his side's World Cup campaign hanging in the balance, the West Indian skipper quickly and rather nervously indicated that the ball had hit pad, not bat. Too late, Reporter's finger was already on the way up.

Keith Arthurton hit two cracking boundaries, freeze-framing the follow through of his first one for the cameras, but played a loose drive to mid-off soon afterwards; Gus Logie fell to magnificent diving catch by Ian Healy in front of vacant first slip; and Carl Hooper glided the ball neatly to third man, forgetting that, by this stage, a first slip had been employed.

Whitney had taken 4/20 in the space of 36 balls and, once again, the West Indies' talented but brittle middle-order had been the team's weak link.

While the Australians dispersed to their home cities, the West Indies returned to their islands to prepare for the landmark Test with South Africa. They returned without the World Cup, the trophy Richardson said the people of the Caribbean still regarded as their own, even though it had not been in West Indian hands since 1979. They would have to wait another four years.

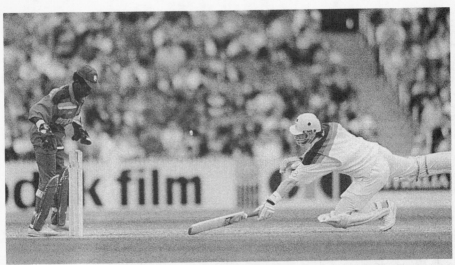

Dive in vain: Mark Waugh fails to make safe his ground and is stumped by West Indian wicketkeeper David Williams.

PLAYER PROFILE: *David Boon*

David Boon's World Cup finished the way it started, with an even century made on an uneven knee. One hundred in Auckland and 100 in Melbourne, both made as an opening batsman, provided him with an impressive set of book ends as a souvenir of the tournament.

Boon limped through the World Cup on a dicky right knee that was destined for the surgeon's knife, but that did not impede his appetite for runs. He emerged sore, but with his reputation enhanced as Australia's premier batsman of the moment.

In between the book ends, Australia got it wrong. For some inexplicable reason, Boon spent four of those matches in the m dle batting down the order at No. 3, when it was plain to see that Australia was best served with the pugnacious and in-form Tasmanian leading from the front.

Boon's two centuries were the only ones made by Australians in the tournament and continued a prolific summer in which he made a total of six international centuries (three Test and three one-day), compared with a grand total of three from the rest of his teammates combined.

While others scratched and fidgeted, Boon stood calmly at the crease and played with poise and balance. His superior form was again evident against the West Indies from the moment he leant into a straight drive in Winston Benjamin's second over and eased the ball into the boundary in front of the members' stand, a shot he repeated throughout the night.

When he reached 99, Boon became the fourth Australian to pass 4000 runs in one-day internationals, behind Allan Border, Dean Jones and Geoff Marsh. Importantly, he left Border and Marsh for dead in the World Cup, despite being run out in three of his first four innings. Even the dynamic Jones could not keep up with the one-legged wonder from Tasmania.

Best bat:
David Boon acknowledges the applause for his even 100 that was crucial in Australia's win over the West Indies.

18 March. Australia v West Indies — Melbourne.
Weather: Cool, some drizzle.

AUSTRALIA

	Runs	Balls	4s/6s
T MOODY c Benjamin b Simmons	42	70	3/0
D BOON c Williams b Cummins	100	147	8/0
D JONES c Williams b Cummins	6	14	-
A BORDER lbw b Simmons	8	10	-
M WAUGH st Williams b Hooper	21	31	-
S WAUGH b Cummins	6	14	-
I HEALY not out	11	11	-
P TAYLOR not out	10	6	1/0
Sundries (3lb 3w 6nb)	12		
TOTAL for six wickets	216		

Fall: 107, 128, 141, 185, 189, 200.

	O	M	R	W	Eco	W	NB
C Ambrose	10	0	46	0	4.6	2	6
W Benjamin	10	1	49	0	4.9	-	-
A Cummins	10	1	38	3	3.8	-	-
C Hooper	10	0	40	1	4.0	1	-
P Simmons	10	1	40	2	4.2	-	-

Overs: 50

WEST INDIES

	Runs	Balls	4s/6s
D HAYNES c Jones b McDermott	14	24	2/0
B LARA run out	70	97	3/0
P SIMMONS lbw b McDermott	0	1	-
R RICHARDSON c Healy b Whitney	10	44	-
K ARTHURTON c McDermott b Whitney	15	15	2/0
G LOGIE c Healy b Whitney	5	15	-
C HOOPER c M Waugh b Whitney	4	11	-
D WILLIAMS c Border b Reid	4	15	-
W BENJAMIN lbw b S Waugh	15	21	1/0
C AMBROSE run out	2	7	-
A CUMMINS not out	5	10	-
Sundries (3b 5lb 3w 4nb)	15		
TOTAL	159		

Fall: 27, 27, 59, 83, 99, 117, 128, 137, 150, 159.

	O	M	R	W	Eco	W	NB
C McDermott	6	1	29	2	4.8	-	3
B Reid	10	1	26	1	2.6	2	1
M Whitney	10	1	34	4	3.4	-	-
S Waugh	6.4	0	24	1	3.6	-	-
P Taylor	4	0	24	0	6.0	-	-
T Moody	6	1	14	0	2.3	1	-

Overs: 42.4
Umpires: P Reporter, D Shepherd
Crowd: 47,572

Player of the match: David Boon (Australia)
AUSTRALIA WON BY 57 RUNS

Zimbabwe turns giant killer

18 March: England **v** Zimbabwe in Albury

With its latest application for full International Cricket Council membership on the negotiating table, Zimbabwe needed at least one victory from the World Cup if it was to carry a credible dossier to the crucial ICC meeting in London in July.

That David Houghton's team achieved the win at the expense of raging tournament favourite England in the final game at Albury is testament to the theory that anything can happen in one-day cricket.

The Zimbabwe players were mobbed by excited schoolchildren as they embraced after Gladstone Small chipped a catch to Andy Pycroft at mid-wicket in the final over, England finishing 10 runs short of its target.

Houghton, a member of the Zimbabwe team that defeated Australia at Nottingham in the 1983 World Cup, was misty-eyed as he faced the press. 'It's been a long time from '83 to now. I didn't remember how good it felt until now.'

That win over Kim Hughes' Australians in 1983 was Zimbabwe's first in international cricket. This victory at the Lavington Sports Complex was the second. Such is the way of Zimbabwe cricket, where the players compete only at weekends because they have full-time jobs to attend, there is no first-class cricket, and the chance to play at official international level has been limited to the past three World Cups. Nine years after its debut this was only its 20th limited-overs international.

England's performance had to be taken into that perspective. Notwithstanding the fact that it had been hit by injuries and had already qualified for the semi-finals, it can have had few more humiliating defeats in any cricket.

Sent in by Graham Gooch, the tournament's so-called minnows could manage only 134 on a difficult wicket. Given that they were unable to defend 312 in the opener against Sri Lanka, England ought to have won easily. After all, its most in-form batsman, Alec Stewart, was listed to come in at No. 7, and Gooch was back from injury.

But England did not reckon with Eddo Brandes, Zimbabwe's boisterous fast bowler, who put a gaping tear in the top order by trapping Gooch in front with the first ball of the innings, tilted back Robin Smith's off-stump, induced a mistimed pull to mid-on from Allan Lamb, and yorked his friend and former schoolmate Graeme Hick for a duck.

England lost 5/43 inside the first 15 overs, and never fully recovered. There was only one stand of note – 52 compiled by Alec Stewart and Neil Fairbrother – but that used up 24 overs and left the lower-order batsman under immense pressure. Stewart's 29 took 95 balls to gather; Fairbrother laboured through 77 balls in reaching 20. Certainly shotmaking was made difficult by the pitch, but the indictment was that they could not even push the ball off the square for ones and twos: Zimbabwe delivered 11 maiden overs.

All the Zimbabwe bowlers extracted lateral movement from the wicket, most notably John Traicos, whose virtually unplayable spell of 10 overs conceded just 16 runs. Houghton was moved to call the 44-year-old off-spinner the best one-day slow bowler in the world, and certainly this effort completed an excellent tournament.

England's miserable batting spoiled what was an excellent effort by its bowlers, given the injury toll. Ian Botham's 3/23 brought his tally of wickets for the series to 14, and once again he had conceded fewer than three runs an over.

Only the classy Houghton (29) looked comfortable and even he succumbed to a mis-timed pull in a moment of rashness.

Gooch was admirably positive, saying that England had to look forward. Later he would learn that the team's semi-final opponent would be South Africa, and the venue Sydney. But for the moment, it was difficult to escape the inkling that the injury curse, and its resultant instability, had England wavering.

But the focus was on Zimbabwe. Gooch, for one, thought it unlikely that the ICC would admit the African country since it had no first-class system in place. Manager Don Topley said his team needed continued exposure at this level to improve. 'What's important for us is to keep our young ones,' he said. 'One or two boys in this team have got to have a goal, and playing against Malawi and Mozambique won't be a goal for them in a few years. We have to give them an incentive, otherwise we could lose them to South Africa quite easily, believe me.'

PLAYER PROFILE: Eddo Brandes

Eddo Brandes, chicken farmer and Zimbabwe's new-ball bowler, dined with an old friend in Albury on the eve of his team's final World Cup game against England. The fact that Graeme Hick would be playing with the opposition was irrelevant for a few hours.

Next day, Brandes' best yorker shattered the stumps of the same old pal before he had scored, and the red, white and blue painted-face brigade on the terraces at the Lavington Sports Complex fell silent for once. Brandes charged down the wicket waving his finger in the air, passing close to Hick. 'I told him to get off,' he was to admit later, indicating that the friendship did not necessarily extend to the field of battle.

Brandes and Hick went through Harare's Prince Edward School together before the latter emigrated to England and made his name. Brandes played Lancashire league with Haslingden in 1987, but went home and bought a chicken farm outside Harare, ensuring that he would remain a part-time player. Indeed, he had hired his next door neighbour to manage the farm for two months so that he could compete in his second World Cup.

This was to be his finest day in cricket. He took 4/21 from 10 overs, demolishing the top-order of the tournament favourite, and triggering a top-order collapse that handed Zimbabwe a famous victory – its first for the tournament, and only its second international victory in 20 matches.

In Zimbabwean cricket, the best players are tempted to leave for places where they can achieve higher honours. But thanks to Brandes, the Africans were not to be frustrated by a master innings by their former countryman.

Said David Houghton, Zimbabwe's captain: 'When you want to get the best out of Eddo, you just put Graeme Hick in the opposition.'

18 March. England v Zimbabwe — Albury.
Weather: fine.

ZIMBABWE

	Runs	Balls	4s/6s
W JAMES c and b Illingworth	13	46	1/0
A FLOWER b DeFreitas	7	14	1/0
A PYCROFT c Gooch b Botham..................	3	13	-
K ARNOTT lbw b Botham	11	33	-
D HOUGHTON c Fairbrother b Small	29	74	2/0
A WALLER b Tufnell	8	16	1/0
A SHAH c Lamb b Tufnell	3	16	-
I BUTCHART c Fairbrother b Botham	24	36	2/0
E BRANDES st Stewart b Illingworth	14	20	1/0
J TRAICOS not out	0	6	-
M JARVIS lbw b Illingworth....................	6	6	-
Sundries (8lb 8w)	16		
TOTAL	134		

Fall: 12, 19, 30, 52, 65, 77, 96, 127, 127, 134.

	O	M	R	W	Eco	W	NB
P DeFreitas	8	1	14	1	1.7	2	-
G Small	9	1	20	1	2.2	1	-
I Botham	10	2	23	3	2.3	4	-
R Illingworth ...	9.1	0	33	3	3.5	-	-
P Tufnell	10	2	36	2	3.6	1	-

Overs: 46.1

ENGLAND

	Runs	Balls	4s/6s
G GOOCH lbw b Brandes	0	1	-
I BOTHAM c Flower b Shah	18	34	4/0
A LAMB c James b Brandes	17	26	2/0
R SMITH b Brandes	2	13	-
G HICK b Brandes	0	6	-
N FAIRBROTHER c Flower b Butchart............	20	77	-
A STEWART c Waller b Shah	29	95	3/0
P DEFREITAS c Flower b Butchart	4	17	-
R ILLINGWORTH run out	11	20	-
G SMALL c Pycroft b Jarvis	5	18	-
P TUFNELL not out	0	0	-
Sundries (4b 3lb 11w 1nb)	19		
TOTAL.....................................	125		

Fall: 0, 32, 42, 42, 43, 95, 101, 108, 124, 125.

	O	M	R	W	Eco	W	NB
E Brandes	10	4	21	4	2.1	-	-
M Jarvis	9.1	0	32	1	3.5	2	-
A Shah	10	3	17	2	1.7	3	-
J Traicos	10	4	16	0	1.6	-	-
I Butchart	10	2	32	2	3.2	6	1

Overs: 49.1
Umpires: B Aldridge, K Hayat.
Crowd: approx. 6000
Player of the match: Eddo Brandes (Zimbabwe)

ZIMBABWE WON BY NINE RUNS

Double triumph for Pakistan

18 March: New Zealand **v** *Pakistan in Christchurch*

This was Pakistan's long day's journey into night. It was about 5.30 pm at Lancaster Park when it defeated New Zealand, in itself an achievement without precedent in this World Cup, and by a handsome margin.

But it was more than six hours later, when Australia had beaten the West Indies in Melbourne, that this became a victory of substance, a triumph of man's spirit over fate's caprice. Its sting drawn by the pre-tournament withdrawal of Waqar Younis and regular injuries to other leading players, and despite an unlucky defeat against South Africa, Pakistan had made the semi-finals.

New Zealand's eventual defeat was inevitable in this game of chance, but untimely now. Nevertheless, Martin Crowe remained composed. 'There's nothing wrong with losing the eighth game if you've won seven before, as long as the effort and application was put in,' he said.

The consolation prize was at least as handsome as the medallion, for New Zealand was rid, at last, of its *bete noir,* Australia – which it had feared out of proportion to its results – and had secured a semi-final at its cherished Eden Park.

On both sides of the Tasman, there had been fevered speculation that New Zealand would 'throw' this game as the means to those ends. It was all beneath contempt.

New Zealand had chased targets with gathering confidence in all except the first game against Australia and in a truncated frolic with Zimbabwe. Recognising this, Imran Khan sent the Kiwis in, sensing that to get through their first four was to win.

Briefly, New Zealand's star continued to climb, Mark Greatbatch clouting two 4s and a 6 from the last three balls of Aaqib Javed's first over. It was his twelfth 6 of the tournament. But Wasim Akram, making the ball twitch and swerve and mixing the wayward with the wicked, had Andrew Jones plainly lbw and Crowe caught behind square leg. Left cross, right hook.

Adventurously, Imran brought in leg-spinner Mushtaq Ahmed to tame Greatbatch, who was immediately deceived twice by wrong'uns and was never again at ease. Greatbatch perservered to 42 before he swept Mushtaq directly to Salim Malik, but Numbers 2 to 8 read like a telephone number: 6,2,3,8,1,7,1. The jaunty Mushtaq did not concede a boundary in his 10 overs.

Gavin Larsen (37) and Danny Morrison (12), both batting for the first time in the tournament, scratched up a ninth-wicket partnership of 44, the second-highest of the innings, enough to save face, but not Australia. Morrison tarried 40 minutes and 28 balls for his first run, which was greeted with uproar by the crowd. Morrison saluted with a flourish of his bat.

Pakistan surrendered 42 in extras, equal to top score, but Imran was long ago resigned to this prodigality, for its tournament total was now 189. 'We can't do anything about it. We've tried everything, but we have to accept we are going to give extras,' he said.

Chasing 167, Pakistan tripped over the starting blocks. Left-hander Aamir Sohail, facing Morrison around the wicket, hooked the first ball of the innings from the region of his helmet to fine leg where he was caught by Dipak Patel. It was a mode of dismissal presumed extinct, not least by Sohail, who stared in horror when he realised that neither umpire had called no-ball, then made a slow, anguished exit.

Imran later bridled at the bouncer rule. 'I think it is ridiculous,' he said. 'Either you have a bouncer rule or you don't.' Then Inzamam-Ul-Haq played on to Morrison's off-cutter and it was 2/9. But New Zealand was to wait two hours and make 11 bowling changes before the next wicket.

Rameez played a perfectly metered innings, neither rushing nor loitering, as near in quality to a Test innings as one-day cricket allows. His 119 not out (155 balls, 16 4s) was the highest score of this World Cup, and his second century.

Patel again bowled splendidly, trimming his overall economy rate to a tightwad 2.8 per over, but economy of itself was not enough in New Zealand's predicament. Javed Miandad in particular would have looked more comfortable in a hair shirt than facing Patel, who very nearly caught-and-bowled him with a sideways dive when he was three and Pakistan 2/28.

But Javed, of course, drew on his bank of experience and pulled through, eventually sharing 115 with Rameez. His contribution was 30 from 85 balls.

Crowe bowled everyone except himself and wicketkeeper Ian Smith, making 14 changes altogether, to no avail. Pakistan reached victory with seven wickets and 5.2 overs in reserve. 'The saddest aspect of this win is that we've got another match to play now, sitting in hotel room, watching television,' Imran said. At 11.50 pm, Pakistan won again.

Yorked: Gavin Larsen's first innings in the tournament comes to a comprehensive end, bowled by Wasim Akram for a gallant 37.

PLAYER PROFILE: *Mushtaq Ahmed*

In the image of Abdul Qadir, and true to his tradition, leg-spinner Mushtaq Ahmed produced one of the most captivating bowling performances of this World Cup. It looks bland enough on paper – 10 overs, 2/18 – but the player-of-the-match judges, with rare insight, saw fit to give Mushtaq their award ahead of the Rameez Raja (119 not out) or Wasim Akram (4/32).

Mushtaq, 21, was introduced after just seven overs, specifically to cast his spell over the flailing bat of Mark Greatbatch. With a great whirling of arms, Mushtaq sent down two wrong-uns in his first over, both fizzing past the outside edge. The battle was already won, though it was not until Mushtaq's ninth over that Greatbatch swept a catch to Salim Malik behind square leg that the formalities were complete.

Mushtaq's other wicket was a trivia collector's piece, unprecedented at this standard. Chris Harris, like Greatbatch a left-hander, jumped down to what again proved to be a wrong-un, missed and was stumped, the decision made easy for square leg umpire Steve Bucknor. Meanwhile, though, umpire Steve Randell had signalled wide. Both rulings stood; it was 1/1 for the delivery.

Pakistan, in variance with the practice of other countries, has never been afraid to play a leg-spinner in its one-day team, with Qadir and Wasim Raja preceeding Mushtaq. Qadir had been replaced by Mushtaq in the Pakistan team more than three years ago, and comparisons were as inevitable as they were odious. But whether nor not he follows every Qadir footstep, Mushtaq had already made his mark on this World Cup.

Rich tradition: Pakistan's long-time faith in spin was rewarded by Mushtaq Ahmed's telling contribution against New Zealand.

18 March. New Zealand v Pakistan — Christchurch.
Weather: fine.

NEW ZEALAND

	Runs	Balls	4s/6s
M GREATBATCH c Malik b Mushtaq	42	67	5/1
R LATHAM c Inzamam b Aaqib	6	9	1/0
A JONES lbw b Akram	2	3	-
M CROWE c Aamir b Akram	3	20	
K RUTHERFORD run out	8	35	-
C HARRIS st Moin b Mushtaq	1	6	-
D PATEL c Mushtaq b Aamir	7	13	1/0
I SMITH b Imran	1	2	-
G LARSEN b Akram	37	80	3/0
D MORRISON c Malik b Akram	12	45	1/0
W WATSON not out	5	13	-
Sundries (3b 23lb 12w 4nb)	42		
TOTAL	166		

Fall: 23, 26, 39, 85, 87, 93, 96, 106, 150, 166.

	O	M	R	W	Eco	W	NB
Wasim Akram	9.2	0	32	4	3.4	9	2
Aaqib Javed	10	1	34	1	3.4	2	1
Mushtaq Ahmed	10	2	18	2	1.8	1	-
Imran Khan	8	0	22	1	2.7	-	1
Aamir Sohail	10	1	29	1	2.9	-	-
Ijaz Ahmed	1	0	5	0	5.0	-	-

Overs: 48.2

PAKISTAN

	Runs	Balls	4s/6s
AAMIR SOHAIL c Patel b Morrison	0	1	-
RAMEEZ RAJA not out	119	155	16/0
INZAMAM-UL HAQ b Morrison	5	8	1/0
JAVED MIANDAD lbw b Morrison	30	85	1/0
SALIM MALIK not out	9	21	1/0
Sundries (1lb 1w 2nb)	4		
TOTAL for three wickets for	167		

Fall: 0, 9, 124.

	O	M	R	W	Eco	W	NB
D Morrison	10	0	42	3	4.2	-	2
D Patel	10	2	25	0	2.5	-	-
W Watson	10	3	26	0	2.6	-	-
C Harris	4	0	18	0	4.5	-	-
G Larsen	3	0	16	0	5.3	-	-
A Jones	3	0	10	0	3.3	-	-
R Latham	2	0	13	0	6.5	-	-
K Rutherford	1.4	0	11	0	6.6	1	-
M Greatbatch	1	0	5	0	5.0	-	-

Overs: 44.4
Umpires: S Randell, S Bucknor.

Crowd: 11,907

Player of the match: Mushtaq Ahmed (Pakistan)
PAKISTAN WON BY SEVEN WICKETS.

Heartbreak for the Cup romantics

21 March: New Zealand v Pakistan in Auckland

Rod Latham had played a lot of rugby, but had never felt pain like this, and he cried. Martin Crowe and Warren Lees blinked back tears. New Zealand's brave challenge for the World Cup was over, but only after a titanic struggle with Pakistan, and a semi-final to be hoarded in the memory. Now Eden Park said goodbye, or perhaps *au revoir*, for their Kiwis to the last had been the romantics of this tournament.

For more than a month, they had the cricket world bluffed, with a selection of feints and flourishes previously unseen. They fought heavy artillery with small arms, they were guerillas at large in a conventional battlefield, and now they came within a single over of a stunning *coup d'etat*.

Yet at 'the death', the Kiwis' weapons were exposed for what they were, pop-guns and pen-knives, too flimsy even to defend 262 from Pakistan. Opening bowlers Dipak Patel and Danny Morrison were both hit for 50. Chris Harris was hammered for 72, which was only what might have been expected of a man who bowls irregularly for his club side in Christchurch, but who until now had fooled the world well enough to be the tournament's leading wicket-taker.

Finally, though, these magnificent upstarts were crushed not by Pakistan's council of generals, but by another magnificent upstart. Uncapped in Tests and unknown before this tournament, Inzamam-Ul-Haq laid waste to New Zealand with 60 from 37 balls, leaving the road free for Javed Miandad and sidekicks to ride into town with the flag. Imran Khan said Inzamam was one of the finest strokeplayers in the world, on the same lofty plain as Sachin Tendulkar, and who could now take issue with him?

Crowe, captain of New Zealand, player of the tournament, hero of the morning, but now lame from battle, watched helplessly from the sidelines, his hairline receding a millimetre a minute. He sensed the rising panic on the field and believed to the end that it would have been different if only he could have been in the thick of battle with his men.

With six balls to spare, Moin Khan crashed Harris into the furthest bleachers of this theatrette of a ground, and Pakistan, beaten semi-finalist in the last three World Cups – most painfully by Australia at home in Lahore in 1987 – was, at last, in the final. The Pakistanis rushed as one on to the field, Moin danced like a dervish and Javed Miandad kissed the ground.

The Kiwis, meanwhile, stayed in their fielding positions, disbelieving, spent. Eventually they trudged a lap of honour – and it was honour, though it felt less noble at that moment. In the rooms, there was reverberating silence as they reflected on the World Cup final they would now only watch. Wicketkeeper Ian Smith, inconsolable, announced his retirement.

Everything had seemed in order at the start of the day. Like a good bartender, Mark Greatbatch had two of the usual waiting for the early crowd, missing his first two balls from Wasim Akram and then opening his tab by carving him over third man for 6. Another followed from Aaqib Javed, his 14th 6 of the tournament. But Aaqib, noticing Greatbatch advancing with menace outside leg stump, did him with virtually an off-break.

Crowe that morning had been crowned World Cup champion, and now played an innings worthy of his title, an innings which surpassed even his previous four masterpieces in this tournament, at once bewitching, efficient and technically perfect. He made 91 from 83 balls without anything remotely resembling a slog, but from shots played with seemingly complete understanding of the behaviour of every ball and, simultaneously, a highly developed instinct for angles and gaps in the field. Captains were fond of talking of game plans, and Imran admitted that Crowe wrecked his, which had been to get Crowe out – somehow – and then roll up the others with two leg-spinners.

For all the breathtaking effrontery of New Zealand's tactics in this tournament, it still took a player of the most pure, classic orthodoxy to lead and to command. Crowe finished with 456 runs at 114, and at a strike rate of more than 90 runs per 100 balls faced. 'Personally, it's nice to know that for a month I was possibly the best batsman in the world,' he said.

Crowe was ably assisted by Ken Rutherford, who fretted for 21 balls to break his duck, then disentangled himself from those early knots to race to 50 from his next 46 balls. He and Crowe shared 107 for the fourth wicket.

In the escalating drama, Aaqib appeared to step over the boundary line trying to save 4, prompting howls of protest from the Eden Park crowd. After a quick inquiry, Imran directed the umpires to signal 4. Rutherford reached his half-century by swishing Aaqib's once-proud slower ball away with such contempt that it had to be sent back to the workshop for repairs.

But he was out next ball, mis-pulling Akram, a setback masking a calamity. Crossing Rutherford as the catch went up, Crowe felt his hamstring tighten. 'I thought it was a bit of a turning point in that it took me out of the match,' said Crowe. 'I just wonder why these things (injuries) happen some time.'

As a hush fell over the crowd, he hobbled a few more runs, then called Greatbatch to run for him, meanwhile heaving Akram over fine leg for his third 6. Three overs later, Crowe was a helpless witness to his own run out as Greatbatch and Smith confused their signals.

Apart from losing Crowe short of his century, the immediate consequences were not severe, for New Zealand's remaining batsmen kept up the helter-skelter, and when 50 overs were bowled, it had 7/262, including 161 from its last 20 overs. 'I always thought 262 was plenty, if you did the basic job, of keeping cool and calm and just always a step ahead of the batsmen,' said Crowe.

But Crowe felt the habits and patterns of the previous month would be disrupted without him on the field, even allowing for John Wright's vast experience. So it proved. Pakistan was immediately on the offensive, Aamir Sohail (14) and Rameez Raja (44) ominously at ease.

Imran (44) batted at No 3, for stability, but also to protect the precocious Inzamam, later to be sprung on to the unsuspecting Kiwis with such devastation. 'It's very difficult to defend here once a team starts hitting out. We realised that if we had wickets in hand at the end, even seven an over was quite gettable,'

Imran said. 'But it just got a bit out of hand, it went over seven (briefly to eight-and-a-half), and we were beginning to think we wouldn't get close.'

The crisis arose at Salim Malik's dismissal, 4/140 in the 35th over, and it passed in three-quarters of an hour. With languid movements to disguise immense power and timing, and strokes as clean as a guillotine, Inzamam smashed 60, along the way equalling Crowe's World Cup record 31-ball half-century against Zimbabwe at Napier two weeks previously. Suddenly, the attack seemed too feeble and the ground only a scale model.

Crowe's heart sank. 'We were on a bit of a downer. You could just see the body language,' he said. Inzamam was run out and Akram (9) bowled, but these wickets were comfortably within Pakistan's budget. The Kiwis' fielding and catching remained unimpeachable, but the bowling loosened by a few, fatal degrees. Wright, seemingly lacking Crowe's instinct, fretted over changes and may never forgive himself for leaving the final over to Harris. 'Overall, we played out of our skins,' said Crowe. 'We'd done pretty well everything right (in the tournament) except the last hour or so.'

Javed (57 not out) saw the job through. Javed's own powers of improvisation had noticeably diminished in this tournament, but not his cunning. Javed was a travelling salesman, talking himself and his teammates into their impossible task until it all seemed as simple as Inzamam made it look.

Unforgiving: New Zealander Chris Harris and Pakistan's Wasim Akram collide heavily as Harris tries in vain to catch the Pakistan allrounder short of the ground.

Conquering heroes: The Pakistan players are escorted off the field by raptuous supporters after the triumph at Eden Park.

21 March. New Zealand v Pakistan — Auckland.
Weather: fine, windy

NEW ZEALAND

	Runs	Balls	4s/6s
M GREATBATCH b Aaqib Javed	17	22	0/2
J WRIGHT c Rameez Raja b Mushtaq Ahmed	13	44	1/0
A JONES lbw b Mushtaq Ahmed	21	53	2/0
M CROWE run out	91	83	7/3
K RUTHERFORD c Moin Khan b Wasim Akram	50	68	5/1
C HARRIS st Moin Khan b Iqbal Sikander	13	12	1/0
I SMITH not out	18	10	3/0
D PATEL lbw b Wasim Akram	8	6	1/0
G LARSEN not out	8	6	1/0
Sundries (4b 7lb 8w 4nb)	23		
TOTAL for seven wickets for	262		

Fall: 35, 39, 87, 194, 214, 221, 244.

	O	M	R	W	Eco	W	NB
Wasim Akram	10	0	40	2	4.0	2	4
Aaqib Javed	10	2	45	1	4.5	2	-
Mushtaq Ahmed	10	0	40	2	4.0	-	-
Imran Khan	10	0	59	0	5.9	3	-
Iqbal Sikander	9	0	56	1	6.2	1	-
Aamir Sohail	1	0	11	0	11.0	-	-

Overs: 50.

PAKISTAN

	Runs	Balls	4s/6s
AAMIR SOHAIL c Jones b Patel	14	20	1/0
RAMEEZ RAJA c Morrison b Watson	44	55	6/0
IMRAN KHAN c Larsen b Harris	44	93	1/2
JAVED MIANDAD not out	57	69	4/0
SALIM MALIK c (sub) Latham b Larsen	1	2	-
INZAMAM-UL-HAQ run out	60	37	7/1
WASIM AKRAM b Watson	9	8	1/0
MOIN KHAN not out	20	11	2/1
Sundries (4b 10lb 1w)	15		
TOTAL for six wickets for	264		

Fall: 30, 84, 134, 140, 227, 238.

	O	M	R	W	Eco	W	NB
D Patel	10	1	50	1	5.0	-	-
D Morrison	9	0	55	0	6.1	1	-
W Watson	10	2	39	2	3.9	-	-
G Larsen	10	1	34	1	3.4	-	-
C Harris	10	0	72	1	7.2	-	-

Overs: 50
Umpires: S Bucknor, D Shepherd.
Crowd: approx 32,000
Player of the match: Inzamam-Ul-Haq (Pakistan)

PAKISTAN WON BY 4 WICKETS.

England qualifies in high farce

22 March: England v South Africa in Sydney

The plug might as well have been pulled on the giant light towers that illuminated the SCG in the middle of the last over, such was the anti-climactic conclusion to the World Cup semi-final between England and South Africa.

It was worse than anti-climactic. It was farcical and it was wrong. And it was a low blow to the credibility of cricket's supposed showpiece.

Sydney was always going to struggle to sustain the level of drama that Auckland established in its sublime semi-final the previous day. But it went as close as could reasonably have been expected before the unavoidable intervention of rain and the unnatural intervention of the rule book reduced the game to some sort of sick joke at the expense of the game of cricket, and South Africa in particular.

When Graham Gooch pragmatically, but entirely understandably, accepted an offer to leave the field because of rain late in the evening, the scene was set for a thrilling conclusion with South Africa needing 22 runs from 13 balls to make the World Cup final.

It was an improbable target, but one for which the South Africans had developed considerable momentum. Whichever side won from that point would have richly deserved its place in the final.

Instead, the 28,410-strong crowd and millions of television viewers worldwide, not to mention the 22 players, were deprived of the right to see the match through to its proper conclusion because the playing conditions were not sufficiently flexible to allow an extension of the playing time.

A 12-minute interruption for rain does not sound much, but it was more than enough to destroy this match and produce a World Cup finalist virtually by default, reducing South Africa's target to a scandalous 21 runs from one ball.

Not even that was clear in the final chaotic minutes of this match. When umpires Steve Randell and Brian Aldridge walked out for the resumption of play, they told the competing teams that only one over had been lost and that South Africa needed 22 runs from seven balls.

A message to that effect was relayed to the crowd via the score board and greeted with a chorus of boos. Nevertheless, it was still technically possible, especially with the combative and big-hitting Brian McMillan on strike.

McMillan was angry at having to leave the field in the first place, and he returned even angrier, letting anyone within earshot know his thoughts on the charade and what he was going to do about it. Nothing, though, could have prepared him for the next development.

Reserve umpire Steve Woodward ran out on to the field and consulted with Aldridge and another over was subtracted from the equation. South Africa now had to score at the rate of England's 'best' 43 overs, which left McMillan with 21 runs to make from one ball. (Even this was not made clear to the public, the scoreboard announcing that South Africa needed 22, not 21, to more jeers from the crowd).

Instead of wrapping his bat around the nearest head – as he must have been sorely tempted – McMillan blocked the last ball with dignity and ran a single as the crowd poured forth its condemnation. Ian Botham fielded the ball and threw it into the ground in disgust, summing up the mood of just about everyone.

The South Africans, to their credit, were gracious losers, filing out from their dressing room to congratulate every England player and then becoming the weekend's second losing semi-finalist to run a lap of honour. It was sympathetically received.

England, on the other hand, was booed. The South Africans, consummate diplomats, said that was unfortunate as England could hardly be blamed for the rules. Kepler Wessels did not blame Gooch for accepting the offer to leave the field, saying that he would have had their positions been reversed. Gooch said he had second thoughts, but that his primary responsibility was to England, which was disadvantaged by a wet ball and a wet outfield.

'As a cricketer and someone who loves the game, my heart goes out to them,' said Gooch. 'We would liked to have won fair and square.'

Both sides defended the umpires who were, after all, simply enforcing inadequate rules. The crazy part about the whole affair was that there was no earthly reason, other than a clause in the playing conditions, that the full 13 balls could not have been bowled. It was not as though the electricity was about to run out.

Even before its bizarre ending, this game had a slightly curious flavour. For a start, with rain threatening – the match was actually delayed by 10 minutes because of showers – Wessels ignored the unfortunate history of rain-interrupted matches in the tournament and decided to chase a target when he won the toss.

Despite having its full allotment of time, the South Africans bowled only 45 of their 50 overs, for which they were each fined 20 per cent of their match payments. This tardiness appeared to be a cynical attempt at damage control when more conventional methods – like trying to bowl line and length – failed, although Wessels insisted it was not a deliberate ploy. Whatever, at the rate England was scoring, it could have made a score in the vicinity of 300 had it faced its full quota.

The only mitigating factor for South Africa was that it bowled an extra 16 balls for sundry indiscretions, although that, of course, was nobody's fault except its own.

Donald was the main offender in what turned out to be an unhappy farewell to the tournament in which his potent brand of fast bowling made such an impact. He bowled three wides in the first over of the innings, was hit for 18 from the last (including 17 to Dermot Reeve), and fared little better in between other than having Gooch caught behind, a decision that the English captain and the television replay disputed.

The match might have taken a vastly different course had Graeme Hick not enjoyed a generous slice of luck early in his innings. England was 2/39 when Botham played on to Meyrick Pringle, the best of the South African bowlers, and it should have been 3/40 when Hick was caught at first slip by Wessels before he had scored. Unfortunately for South Africa, it was a no-ball.

Besides the rules, the Zimbabwean-born Hick went on to be South Africa's greatest impediment, a slight irony given his southern African origins. Hick played the most important innings of his brief but largely disappointing international career, top-scoring with 83 to steer his adopted nation into its third World Cup final.

Despite the early wobbles, Alec Stewart (batting at No. 3 in place of the injured Robin Smith) maintained an admirably positive outlook and with Hick compiled 71 in 85 balls for the third wicket. It was the first of two substantial partnerships in which Hick was involved, the second being 73 from 90 balls for the fourth wicket with Neil Fairbrother.

The next three batsmen – Allan Lamb, Chris Lewis and Reeve – ensured that England's run-rate kept accelerating to the death. Lamb's 19 was special for one shot, a flat cover drive off McMillan that almost hit the fence on the full, while Lewis and Reeve each scored at better than a run a ball. Reeve signalled his intentions by calling Lewis through for a bye, even though the ball went straight through to the wicketkeeper, and he fulfilled them by taking the long handle to Donald in the final over.

South Africa's reply was handicapped by a groin injury to its best batsman, Peter Kirsten, who had to leave the field midway through England's innings. Batting with Wessels as a runner, Kirsten was clearly restricted in his movements, although, to be fair to Phil DeFreitas, his dismissal to a fast leg-break that knocked his off-stump out of the ground had little to do with his state of health.

It was a sign of South Africa's development through the tournament that it was able to cover so well for Kirsten. Andrew Hudson continued to blossom, dispatching anything on his legs, before his vulnerability to slow bowling was exposed by Richard Illingworth, who trapped him plum in front.

Even Adrian Kuiper and Jonty Rhodes, whose previous contributions with the bat had been ineffectual, lifted for the occasion, each posting his highest score for the series. Kuiper twice hit Illingworth back over his head for 4 before he was out trying to hit him out of the park, while Rhodes' gallantry set South Africa up for what would have been an improbable victory.

That was when the improbable turned to the unthinkable, the lights went out for South Africa and the World Cup lost a lot of its sparkle.

Campaign over: Coach Mike Procter and captain Kepler Wessels embrace after the semi-final — and South Africa's role in the World Cup — is over.

22 March. England v South Africa — Sydney.
Weather: Cool, showers

ENGLAND

	Runs	Balls	4s/6s
G GOOCH c Richardson b Donald	2	8	-
I BOTHAM b Pringle	21	27	3/0
A STEWART c Richardson b McMillan	33	58	4/0
G HICK c Rhodes b Snell	83	90	9/0
N FAIRBROTHER b Pringle	28	50	1/0
A LAMB c Richardson b Donald	19	22	1/0
C LEWIS not out	18	17	2/0
D REEVE not out	25	14	4/0
Sundries (1b 7lb 9w 6nb)	23		
TOTAL for six wickets for	252		

Fall: 20, 39, 110, 183, 187, 221.

	O	M	R	W	Eco	W	NB
A Donald	10	0	69	2	6.9	5	2
M Pringle	9	2	36	2	4.0	2	4
R Snell	8	0	52	1	6.5	2	-
B McMillan	9	0	47	1	5.2	-	-
A Kuiper	5	0	26	0	5.2	-	-
H Cronje	4	0	14	0	3.5	-	-

Overs: 45

SOUTH AFRICA

	Runs	Balls	4s/6s
K WESSELS c Lewis b Botham	17	23	1/0
A HUDSON lbw b Illingworth	46	53	6/0
P KIRSTEN b DeFreitas	11	26	-
H CRONJE c Hick b Small	24	46	1/0
A KUIPER b Illingworth	36	44	5/0
J RHODES c Lewis b Small	43	39	3/0
B McMILLAN not out	21	22	-
D RICHARDSON not out	13	10	1/0
Sundries (17lb 4w)	21		
TOTAL for six wickets for	232		

Fall: 26, 61, 90, 131, 176, 206.

	O	M	R	W	Eco	W	NB
I Botham	10	0	52	1	5.2	3	-
C Lewis	5	0	38	0	7.6	-	-
P DeFreitas	8	1	28	1	3.5	1	-
R Illingworth	10	1	46	2	4.6	-	-
G Small	10	1	51	2	5.1	-	-

Overs: 43
Umpires: B Aldridge, S Randell.
Crowd: 28,410
Player of the match: Graeme Hick (England)

ENGLAND WON BY 19 RUNS.

The Final

One by one, the extraneous forces in this World Cup had been eliminated. For Sri Lanka and Zimbabwe there had been supreme optimism and the joy simply of taking part. These, of course, were not enough. Nor was past success enough for the West Indies, India and Australia, the three previous World Cup winners: all perished before the semi-finals.

Then, in the semi-finals, the last strands of sentimentalism were wound up. The tension and drama that surrounded the last few balls of each match – and the heartache which followed in Auckland, and the outrage in Sydney – distracted attention from the fact that this was the death knell for New Zealand and South Africa.

The Kiwis had been the most imaginative team of the tournament, and the South Africans had generated the most profound emotions. Both had lost with honour intact, and won universal accolades. But neither imagination nor emotion, or themselves, were durable enough for this competition.

Now, just two teams still stood. England, with an even spread of talent, was the most professional and organised team, and had shown a great deal more heart than first suspected as it played through an epidemic of injuries to reach this final. Ian Botham now had the opportunity to fulfill his prediction to win the World Cup before '100,000 convicts'; regrettably for him, England had done its job too well and there were far fewer convicts in the stands and none at all on the ground.

Pakistan was, in many ways, the antithesis of England, seemingly disorganised much of the time, prone to infighting and a sartorial rabble in the nets. Yet it was also the most sublimely talented team of the tournament, capable of springing an Inzamam-Ul-Haq at short notice on to an unprepared world. And it was blessed with a captain in Imran Khan who not only performed exceptional deeds of his own, but with feats of the most delicate diplomacy, managed to make the Pakistan XI play as a team.

Pakistan had never played in a World Cup final and England had lost in 1979 and 1987. The only certainty before the match was that these teams were too proud to allow this final to be anything less than a proper finale, and that by the time the lights dimmed at the MCG, there would be a new World Cup champion.

Pakistan's triumph

25 March: England **v** *Pakistan in Melbourne*

The star and crescent of the Pakistan flag flew defiantly at the Melbourne Cricket Ground on the night of the World Cup final in celebration of a precocious team that hijacked cricket's greatest prize by daring to attack.

Imran Khan crowned his glittering career by telling his young charges to play like cornered tigers. They responded, making off with the trophy as brazenly as a boy climbing a fence to steal an apple.

In front of an official world record one-day crowd of 87,182 (although Calcutta has probably hosted bigger, but unconfirmed audiences), Pakistan shunned many of the conventions of the abbreviated form of the game to produce a nerveless display of raw cricketing talent.

So fast bowlers have to watch their ps and qs in one-day cricket? Try telling that to Wasim Akram who, with Imran's blessing, strived so hard that he bowled six wides and four no-balls, but still managed to devastate England's middle order and remove the man for big occasions, Ian Botham.

So wrist spinners have no place in one-day cricket? Try telling that to Mushtaq Ahmed, who, continuing the World Cup tradition started by Abdul Qadir in 1983, bamboozled Graeme Hick with his top spinners and googlies, eventually trapping him lbw with a wrong'un.

The performance of Mushtaq, who also picked up Graham Gooch and Dermot Reeve, did not reflect well on the selectors of United Bank, his first-class side in Pakistan, who cannot find room for him in their XI. Yet Imran persisted with his leggie and the United Bank reject became a world champion.

Akram conceded far more sundries than any other player in the tournament, yet finished the leading wickettaker. Mushtaq was equal-second. The World Cup final was a victory for genuinely attacking bowlers over the more clinical, medium pace variety preferred by England.

And yet it was not always like that. Pakistan won the toss and batted so slowly that, after 34 overs, it was 2/113. The tactics appeared potentially fatal, but Imran was simply demonstrating a profound appreciation of the strengths and weaknesses of his team.

He and Javed Miandad came together with Pakistan in a mini-crisis at 2/24, its only two century-makers in the series – Aamir Sohail and Rameez Raja – back in the dressing room. Both men having seen similar situations turn quickly into calamities for Pakistan sides, they set about sheltering their vulnerable middle order like concerned parents protecting their young.

With 10 World Cups between them, the captain and vice-captain refused to be consumed by the demons of panic, playing unflappable, if not particularly memorable innings as the crowd waited in almost eerie silence for something to happen.

Imran might not have trusted his middle order to survive a collapse, but he did trust them to score quickly at the end of the innings, which is precisely what they did. Imran and Javed made their move in the 35th over and, in the last 16 overs, Pakistan made 136, a dramatic contrast with the previous inactivity.

Inzamam-Ul-Haq, described by Imran before the match as the most talented young player since Viv Richards, did not disappoint when he made his delayed arrival. He produced close to a full manual of shots – the most majestic being a dismissive flick off his pads to dispatch Botham to the leg-side boundary – in his 35 balls, which yielded a blistering 42. Most of them were legitimate shots, and it was only when he tried to slog at the end that he slowed down, if you could call it that.

Akram scored even faster, launching into some savage drives on his way to 33 from 19 deliveries. In what seemed like no time Pakistan had recovered to the extent that England needed 250 to become the first team in five World Cup finals to successfully chase a target.

England suffered a major setback in its third over when Akram made a ball explode off the wicket and caught the outside edge – at least in the opinion of the Pakistan players and umpire Brian Aldridge – of Botham's bat. Botham disagreed, but if he was in any doubt Aamir Sohail let him know where the dressing room was.

Botham, who with Graham Gooch walked out of the World Cup banquet on the eve of the final in protest at a comedy act satirising the Queen, again found himself making a premature departure, this time to a chorus of booing.

He was followed by Alec Stewart who, batting at No. 3 in the place of the injured Robin Smith, was lured by one of a succession of nagging outswingers from Aaqib Javed, the most economical of Pakistan's bowlers. Then came the joy of watching Mushtaq make a mess of Hick, and of Akram bowling two virtually unplayable balls to remove Allan Lamb and Chris Lewis in successive deliveries. Coming from around the wicket, the left-armer hit Lamb's off-stump with a ball that straightened off the pitch and cut Lewis in two with a vicious in-cutter.

That left England 6/141, with only Neil Fairbrother providing any serious hope. The perky left-hander moved rapidly but unobtrusively to 62 but, with the required run-rate climbing as quickly as he was losing partners, he skied an attempted pull.

The final act in Pakistan's greatest sporting achievement was executed, appropriately enough, by Imran, who removed Richard Illingworth at 10.18 pm to give Pakistan victory by 22 runs in its first World Cup final.

A core of Pakistan players immediately fell to their knees and kissed the sacred MCG turf in praise of Allah. The battle-weary Javed, suffering from stomach cramps, stormed out of the dressing room with a Pakistan flag to embrace his excited teammates. Imran, 39, climbed the podium and accepted the trophy to the cheers of a Melbourne crowd that, for once, supported rather than decried Pakistan.

The great allrounder later described it as 'the most fulfilling, satisfying cricketing moment of my life'. It was also a fine moment for Javed, 34, the other half of a leadership team that has dragged Pakistan cricket through some trying times on the path to the summit.

In truth, it was a young man's World Cup. Imran and Javed might have provided a steadying influence with their 139-run partnership, but after that the match was dominated by Akram (25 years), Inzamam (22), Mushtaq (21) and Aaqib (19).

The Pakistanis did not jog their victory lap around the MCG, they ran it.

In dispute: Alec Stewart stands his ground amongst puzzled Pakistan players after their appeal for caught behind was turned down.

The end: Javed Miandad's patient and vital innings ends when this reverse sweep lands in the hands of Ian Botham at point.

The tyros: Three of Pakistan's young players — wicketkeeper Moin Kahn, spinner Mushtaq Ahmen and fast bowler Aaquib Javed — cannot restrain their joy at becoming world champions.

On his way: Wasim Akram enjoys his dismissal of Ian Botham, caught behind for a duck.

Golden run: Inzamam-Ul-Haq beats Ian Botham home during his brilliant 42 in the final, an innings that confirmed his potential.

Spoils of victory: The exultant Pakistanis celebrate with the World Cup trophy. From left, they are Salim Malik, Inzamam-Ul-Haq, Rameez Raja (partly obscured) and Moin Khan.

Cometh the hour, cometh the man: Imran Khan waited 20 years and five World Cup tournaments to get his hands on the trophy. This is the moment.

25 March. England v Pakistan in Melbourne.
Weather: hot.

PAKISTAN

	Runs	Balls	4s/6s
AAMIR SOHAIL c Stewart b Pringle	4	19	-
RAMEEZ RAJA lbw b Pringle	8	26	1/0
IMRAN KHAN c Illingworth b Botham	72	110	5/1
JAVED MIANDAD c Botham b Illingworth	58	98	4/0
INZAMAM-UL-HAQ b Pringle	42	35	4/0
WASIM AKRAM run out	33	19	4/0
SALIM MALIK not out	0	1	-
Sundries (19lb 6w 7nb)	32		
TOTAL for six wickets	249		

Fall: 20, 24, 163, 197, 249, 249.

	O	M	R	W	Eco	W	NB
D Pringle	10	2	22	3	2.2	3	5
C Lewis	10	2	52	0	5.2	1	2
P DeFreitas	10	1	42	0	4.2	-	-
I Botham	7	0	42	1	6.0	1	-
R Illingworth	10	0	50	1	5.0	-	-
D Reeve	3	0	22	0	7.3	1	-

Overs: 50

ENGLAND

	Runs	Balls	4s/6s
I BOTHAM c Moin b Akram	0	6	-
G GOOCH c Aaqib b Ahmed	29	66	1/0
A STEWART c Moin b Aaqib	7	16	1/0
G HICK lbw b Mushtaq	17	36	1/0
N FAIRBROTHER c Moin b Aaqib	62	70	3/0
A LAMB b Akram	31	41	2/0
C LEWIS b Akram	0	1	-
D REEVE c Rameez b Mushtaq	15	32	-
D PRINGLE not out	18	16	1/0
P DEFREITAS run out	10	8	-
R ILLINGWORTH c Rameez b Imran	14	11	2/0
Sundries (5lb, 13w, 6nb)	24		
TOTAL	227		

Fall: 6, 21, 59, 69, 141, 141, 180, 183, 208, 227.

	O	M	R	W	Eco	W	NB
Wasim Akram	10	0	49	3	4.9	6	4
Aaqib Javed	10	2	27	2	2.7	3	1
Mushtaq Ahmed	10	1	41	3	4.1	1	-
Ijaz Ahmed	3	0	13	0	4.3	2	-
Imran Khan	6.2	0	43	1	6.8	-	1
Aamir Sohail	10	0	49	0	4.9	1	-

Overs: 49.2
Umpires: S Bucknor, B Aldridge.
Crowd: 87,182.
Player of the match: Wasim Akram (Pakistan)

PAKISTAN WON BY 22 RUNS

STATISTICS

LEADING WICKETKEEPERS

Keeper	Cntry	M	Ct	St	Total
D Williams	WI	8	11	3	14
DJ Richardson	SAF	9	13	1	14
Moin Khan	PAK	10	11	3	14
IA Healy	AUS	7	9	-	9
AJ Stewart	ENG	10	8	1	9
KS More	IND	8	6	1	7
HP Tillekeratne	SL	8	6	1	7
A Flower	ZIM	8	6	1	7
IDS Smith	NZ	9	5	-	5

LEADING FIELDSMEN

Fieldsman	Cntry	M	Ct
KC Wessels	SAF	9	7
NH Fairbrother	ENG	8	6
DA Reeve	ENG	8	5
CL Cairns	NZ	5	5
PAJ DeFreitas	ENG	8	5
AR Border	AUS	8	5
GR Larsen	NZ	9	5
GA Hick	ENG	10	5

LEADING WICKETTAKERS

Bowler	Cntry	M	Overs	Mdn	Runs	Wkts	Avrge	Best	Eco/Rt
Wasim Akram	PAK	10	89.4	2	338	18	18.78	4/32	3.77
CZ Harris	NZ	9	72.1	4	342	16	21.38	3/15	4.74
IT Botham	ENG	10	89.0	8	306	16	19.13	4/31	3.44
Mushtaq Ahmed	PAK	9	68.0	3	311	16	19.44	3/41	4.57
EA Brandes	ZIM	8	70.1	7	355	14	25.36	4/21	5.06
AA Donald	SAF	9	78.0	5	329	13	25.31	3/34	4.22
AC Cummins	WI	6	59.0	1	246	12	20.50	4/33	4.17
M Prabhakar	IND	8	56.1	5	245	12	20.42	3/41	4.36
W Watson	NZ	8	79.0	11	301	12	25.08	3/37	3.81
BM McMillan	SAF	9	73.0	7	306	11	27.82	3/30	4.19
PAJ DeFreitas	ENG	10	85.3	12	319	11	29.00	3/34	3.73
Aaqib Javed	PAK	10	74.5	11	328	11	29.82	3/21	4.38
WKM Benjamin	WI	8	79.0	8	297	10	29.70	3/27	3.76

LEADING ECONOMY RATES (MINIMUM 30 OVERS)

Bowler	Cntry	M	Overs	Runs	Eco/Rt
DN Patel	NZ	9	79.0	245	3.10
MR Whitney	AUS	7	66.0	215	3.26
DR Pringle	ENG	8	66.4	218	3.27
IT Botham	ENG	10	89.0	306	3.36
CJ McDermott	AUS	8	73.0	246	3.37
GR Larsen	NZ	9	76.0	262	3.45
CEL Ambrose	WI	7	68.0	235	3.46
GC Small	ENG	5	35.0	127	3.63
DA Reeve	ENG	9	34.4	126	3.63

MOST FOURS STRUCK BY BATSMEN

Batsman	Cntry	4s
MD Crowe	NZ	47
AH Jones	NZ	41
DC Boon	AUS	35
BC Lara	WI	35
Rameez Raja	PAK	35
MJ Greatbatch	NZ	34
AC Hudson	SAF	32
Aamir Sohail	PAK	32

MOST SIXES STRUCK BY BATSMEN

Batsman	Cntry	6s
MJ Greatbatch	NZ	14
MD Crowe	NZ	6
AC Waller	ZIM	5
KLT Arthurton	WI	4
ME Waugh	AUS	4
Imran Khan	PAK	4

LEADING STRIKE RATES (MINIMUM 150 RUNS)

Batsman	Cntry	Runs	Balls	Stk/rt
Kapil Dev	IND	161	129	124.81
AC Waller	ZIM	192	191	100.52
Inzamam-Ul-Haq	PAK	225	242	92.98
MD Crowe	NZ	456	503	90.66
MJ Greatbatch	NZ	313	356	87.92
SR Tendulkar	IND	283	337	83.98
BC Lara	WI	333	408	81.62
A Ranatunga	SL	262	322	81.37
MAR Samarasekera	SL	219	273	80.22
GA Hick	ENG	264	334	79.04

LEADING RUN SCORERS

Batsman	Cntry	M	Inn	NO	Runs	H.S	50	100	Avrge	Stk/rt
MD Crowe	NZ	9	9	5	456	100*	4	1	114.00	90.66
Javed Miandad	PAK	9	9	2	437	89	5	-	62.43	62.34
PN Kirsten	SAF	8	8	2	410	90	4	-	68.33	66.56
DC Boon	AUS	8	8	1	368	100	-	2	52.57	68.91
Rameez Raja	PAK	8	8	2	349	119*	-	2	58.17	64.99
BC Lara	WI	8	8	1	333	88	4	-	47.57	81.62
M Azharuddin	IND	8	7	-	332	93	4	-	47.43	77.39
Aamir Sohail	PAK	10	10	-	326	114	2	1	32.60	61.39
AH Jones	NZ	9	9	2	322	78	3	-	46.00	61.57
MJ Greatbatch	NZ	7	7	-	313	73	3	-	44.71	87.92
KC Wessels	SAF	9	9	2	313	85	3	-	44.71	53.32
AC Hudson	SAF	8	8	-	296	79	3	-	37.00	62.71
NH Fairbrother	ENG	9	7	2	285	75*	3	-	57.00	69.17
SR Tendulkar	IND	8	7	1	283	84	3	-	47.17	83.98
DM Jones	AUS	8	8	1	276	90	2	-	39.43	67.48
GA Hick	ENG	10	9	1	264	83	3	-	33.00	79.04
A Ranatunga	SL	8	7	2	262	88*	2	-	52.40	81.37
AJ Stewart	ENG	10	8	1	259	77	2	-	37.00	70.19
DL Haynes	WI	7	7	1	251	93*	1	-	41.83	56.66

FINAL POINTS TABLE

Team	P	W	L	NR	Pts	N/R/R	Runs	BATTING Ovrs	BATTING Rate	BOWLING Runs	BOWLING Ovrs	BOWLING Rate
New Zealand	8	7	1	-	14	0.59	1606	337.2	4.761	1512	362.4	4.1
England	8	5	2	1	11	0.47	1400	321.3	4.355	1289	331.5	3.8
South Africa	8	5	3	-	10	0.13	1519	348.1	4.363	1437	340.1	4.2
Pakistan	8	4	3	1	9	0.16	1423	328.5	4.327	1381	331.5	4.1
Australia	8	4	4	-	8	0.20	1630	386.0	4.223	1531	380.4	4.0
West Indies	8	4	4	-	8	0.07	1603	387.1	4.140	1562	384.2	4.0
India	8	2	5	1	5	0.14	1440	291.0	4.948	1355	281.5	4.8
Sri Lanka	8	2	5	1	5	-0.68	1469	349.1	4.207	1671	341.3	4.8
Zimbabwe	8	1	7	-	2	-1.14	1345	333.1	4.037	1697	327.3	5.1

WORLD CUP MATCH BY MATCH

Date	Venue	Batted First	Batted Second	Result	Crowd
22 Feb	Auckland	*NZ 6/248 (50.0)	Aus 211 (48.1)	NZ by 37 runs	27,000
22 Feb	Perth	*Eng 9/236 (50.0)	Ind 227 (49.2)	Eng by 9 runs	12,902
23 Feb	N.Plymouth	Zim 4/312 (50.0)	*SL 7/313 (49.2)	SL by 3 wkts	3500
23 Feb	Melbourne	Pak 2/220 (50.0)	*WI 0/221 (46.5)	WI by 10 wkts	14,161
25 Feb	Hamilton	SL 9/206 (50.0)	*NZ 4/210 (48.2)	NZ by 6 wkts	9000
26 Feb	Sydney	*Aus 9/170 (49.0)	SAf 1/171 (46.5)	SAf by 9 wkts	39,789
27 Feb	Hobart	Pak 4/254 (50.0)	*Zim 7/201 (50.0)	Pak by 53 runs	1101
27 Feb	Melbourne	WI 157 (49.2)	*Eng 4/160 (39.5)	Eng by 6 wkts	18,521
28 Feb	Mackay	Ind 0/1 (0.2)	*SL	No result	4300
29 Feb	Auckland	*SAf 7/190 (50.0)	NZ 3/191 (34.3)	NZ by 7 wkts	30,000
29 Feb	Brisbane	WI 8/264 (50.0)	*ZIM 7/189 (50.0)	WI by 75 runs	2190
1 Mar	Brisbane	*Aus 9/237 (50.0)	Ind 234 (47.0)	Aus on run rate	11,721
1 Mar	Adelaide	Pak 74 (40.2)	*Eng 1/24 (8.0)	No result	7537
2 Mar	Wellington	SAf 195 (50.0)	*SL 7/198 (49.5)	SL by 3 wkts	4500
3 Mar	Napier	NZ 3/162 (20.5)	*Zim 7/105 (18.0)	NZ on run rate	6500
4 Mar	Sydney	*Ind 7/216 (49.0)	Pak 173 (48.1)	Ind by 43 runs	10,330
5 Mar	Christchurch	SAf 8/200 (50.0)	*WI 136 (38.4)	SAf by 64 runs	14,000
5 Mar	Sydney	*Aus 171 (49.0)	Eng 2/173 (40.5)	Eng by 8 wkts	38,951
7 Mar	Hamilton	*Ind 7/203 (32.0)	Zim 1/104 (19.1)	Ind on run rate	1000
7 Mar	Adelaide	SL 9/189 (50.0)	*Aus 3/190 (44.0)	Aus by 7 wkts	11,663
8 Mar	Auckland	WI 7/203 (50.0)	*NZ 5/206 (48.3)	NZ by 5 wkts	25,000
8 Mar	Brisbane	SAf 7/211 (50.0)	*Pak 8/173 (36.0)	SAf on run rate	8108
9 Mar	Ballarat	*Eng 6/280 (50.0)	SL 174 (44.0)	Eng by 106 runs	13,000
10 Mar	Wellington	*Ind 197 (49.4)	WI 5/195 (40.2)	WI by 5 wkts	4500
10 Mar	Canberra	Zim 163 (48.3)	SAf 3/164 (45.1)	SAf by 7 wkts	2500
11 Mar	Perth	*Pak 9/220 (50.0)	Aus 172 (45.2)	Pak by 48 runs	22,500
12 Mar	Dunedin	*Ind 6/230 (50.0)	NZ 6/231 (47.1)	NZ by 4 wkts	9000
12 Mar	Melbourne	SAf 4/236 (50.0)	*Eng 7/226 (40.5)	Eng on run rate	25,248
13 Mar	Berri	WI 8/268 (50.0)	*SL 9/176 (50.0)	WI by 91 runs	2650
14 Mar	Hobart	Aus 6/265 (46.0)	*Zim 137 (41.4)	Aus by 128 runs	7363
15 Mar	Wellington	Eng 8/200 (50.0)	*NZ 3/201 (40.5)	NZ by 7 wkts	12,500
15 Mar	Adelaide	*Ind 6/180 (30.0)	SAf 4/181 (29.1)	SAf by 6 wkts	6272
15 Mar	Perth	*SL 6/212 (50.0)	Pak 6/216 (49.1)	Pak by 4 wkts	3048
18 Mar	Melbourne	*Aus 6-216 (50.0)	WI 159 (42.4)	Aus by 57 runs	47,572
18 Mar	Albury	Zim 134 (46.1)	*Eng 125 (49.1)	Zim by 9 runs	6000
18 Mar	Christchurch	*NZ 166 (48.2)	Pak 3/167 (44.4)	Pak by 7 wkts	11,907
21 Mar	Auckland	*NZ 7-262 (50.0)	Pak 6/264 (49.0)	Pak by 4 wkts	32,000
22 Mar	Sydney	Eng 6/252 (45.0)	*SAf 6/232 (43.0)	Eng by 19 runs	28,410
25 Mar	Melbourne	*Pak 6/249 (50.0)	Eng 227 (49.2)	Pak by 22 runs	87,182

* won toss.